HIGHLIGHTS

The MIT Press Writing Art series, edited by Roger Conover

Art after Philosophy and After: Collected Writings, 1966–1990, by Joseph Kosuth [out of print]

Rock My Religion: Writings and Projects 1965–1990, by Dan Graham [out of print]

Continuous Project Altered Daily: The Writings of Robert Morris (October Books), by Robert Morris [out of print]

Remote Control: Power, Cultures, and the World of Appearances, by Barbara Kruger

The Daily Practice of Painting: Writings 1960–1993, by Gerhard Richter

Reasons for Knocking at an Empty House: Writings 1973–1994, by Bill Viola

Out of Order, Out of Sight. Volume I: Selected Writings in Meta-Art 1968–1992, by Adrian Piper

Out of Order, Out of Sight. Volume II: Selected Writings in Art Criticism 1967–1992, by Adrian Piper

Imaging Desire, by Mary Kelly

Destruction of the Father/Reconstruction of the Father: Writings and Interviews, 1923–1997, by Louise Bourgeois

Critical Vehicles: Writings, Projects, Interviews, by Krzysztof Wodiczko

Two-Way Mirror Power: Selected Writings by Dan Graham on His Art, by Dan Graham

Imaging Her Erotics: Essays, Interviews, Projects, by Carolee Schneemann

Essays on Art and Language, by Charles Harrison

Conceptual Art and Painting: Further Essays on Art and Language, by Charles Harrison

Leave Any Information at the Signal: Writings, Interviews, Bits, Pages (October Books), by Ed Ruscha

MUSEUM

Foul Perfection: Essays and Criticism, by Mike Kelley

Please Pay Attention Please: Bruce Nauman's Words: Writings and Interviews, by Bruce Nauman

Decoys and Disruptions: Selected Writings, 1975–2001 (October Books), by Martha Rosler

Minor Histories: Statements, Conversations, Proposals, by Mike Kelley

The AIDS Crisis Is Ridiculous and Other Writings, 1986–2003, by Gregg Bordowitz

Cuts: Texts 1959–2004, by Carl Andre

Museum Highlights: The Writings of Andrea Fraser, by Andrea Fraser

MUSEUM

Andrea Fraser Edited by Alexander Alberro

WRITING **ART** SERIES

HIGHLIGHTS

The Writings of Andrea Fraser

THE MIT PRESS · CAMBRIDGE, MASSACHUSETTS · LONDON, ENGLAND

MIT Press books may be purchased at special quantity discounts for business or sales promotional use. For information, please email special_sales@mitpress.mit.edu or write to Special Sales Department, The MIT Press, 55 Hayward Street, Cambridge, MA 02142.
Printed and bound in Canada
This book was set in FF Scala and FF ScalaSans by Graphic Composition Inc.

Library of Congress Cataloging-in-Publication Data

Fraser, Andrea
Museum highlights : the writings of Andrea Fraser / Andrea Fraser ; edited by Alexander Alberro.
p. cm.
Includes bibliographical references and index.
ISBN 978-0-262-06244-2 (hardcover: alk. paper), ISBN 978-0-262-56230-0 (paperback).
1. Fraser, Andrea—Written works. 2. Fraser, Andrea—Aesthetics. 3. Performance art—United States. 4. Art—Social aspects—United States. I. Alberro, Alexander. II. Title.
NX512.F73A35 2005
700—dc22

2004058756

10 9 8 7 6 5 4 3 2

CONTENTS

PROFESSIONAL INTERESTS

IN CONCLUSION? ONWARD TO THE PAST, OR, ART AT THE FOREFRONT OF REGRESSION

LIST OF ILLUSTRATIONS

FOREWORD: REVOLUTION AND REVELATION

Pierre Bourdieu

Imagine a cleric, of no matter what creed, who discovered that "religion is the opium of the people" and that "the agents of religion struggle for the exclusive right to control the benefits of salvation." Would such a cleric be able to continue priestly work? If so, how? This is precisely the position in which Andrea Fraser has quite consciously and deliberately placed herself. As an artist perfectly well acquainted with the logic and functions of the artistic field, she mounts *analytical interventions* meant not just to interpret the artistic world but also to transform it. Unlike the analyst, who remains detached, remains a spectator, she puts herself personally into play and joins the action. This presupposes the talent, but also the courage, to go to the furthest limits of one's convictions, after the fashion of an exemplary prophet who acts as much through the expressive virtue of actions as through words. By doing so, Fraser creates a genuine *experimental situation:* a provocation that challenges the existent itself, as when a museum's security apparatus is parodically described in the language of aesthetic analysis, or when the celebratory discourse surrounding the artwork is ironically evoked during a fake guided visit to a gallery exhibiting interchangeable black canvases. As she puts it herself, she makes the socially unsayable "actual and manifest." Being convinced that, "like symptoms," museums "cover over conflicts with displaced representations," she is able, like a sorcerer's apprentice, to trigger a social mechanism, a sort of *machine infernale* whose operation causes the hidden truth of social reality to reveal itself, exposing or calling up underlying power relationships and confronting human agents with an unblinking view of what they are doing. This is what happens when, invited by an insurance company to address an issue anticipated in her offer of "artistic services"—namely the analysis of the conflicts that arise when a business installs works of art in its offices—she plays midwife to the various parties involved by bringing to light for some their contradictions and bad faith, and for others their discomfort or rebelliousness. Thus she demonstrates—*pace* Hans Haacke and his vision of the sponsor as censor—that sponsors do not in fact threaten the autonomy of artistic production but rather demand it, to the detriment of the reassuring atmosphere of a business held together by "corporate culture," because they have grasped that it is essential to the image of philanthropists—at once disinterested and avant-gardist—that they want to construct for themselves.

The properly artistic mise-en-scène of analysis and of the analyst-artist makes an artistic performance into a specific political act capable, by way of avenues appropriated and altered for its own purposes, of having an effective impact on the artistic field and eventually sparking a full-blown revolution in the power relationships that define that field. This revolution through revelation confronts cultural production, as Andrea Fraser says so clearly, "not only substantively, as a symbolic system, but on the level of the social relations and social structures of which this system is the site"; and since it deploys the means proper to art (and hence the specific artistic culture that those means bespeak), as well as the artist's own authority in the artistic performance, it works and convinces far more effectively than any abstract analysis as it exposes the unseeable and unsayable in that social universe, so highly armored against ordinary forms of objectification, which we call the field of art.

What we have here is thus a perfectly exemplary intellectual act, lucid and courageous, which breaks with all the complicities and complacencies of the ordinary routine of artistic life and casts a brutal, cold, and sometimes blinding light on the sacrosanct mysteries of the cult of the artwork.

translated by Donald Nicholson-Smith

ACKNOWLEDGMENTS

Acknowledgments, as I said of introductions when I performed *Official Welcome* at the opening of my retrospective at the Kunstverein in Hamburg, are among the rituals of recognition and incorporation that so much of my work has been about. There are times when I wish I could perform such rituals without distance and without reflection. This, again, is one of those times.

With the MIT Press Writing Art series, Roger Conover has maintained a space for artists' voices in a field where we are increasingly restricted to being mute objects of academic art history, on the one hand, and coffee-table catalogues on the other. This series has been a vitally important resource for me. It has also been an inspiration to continue writing when such activities are more and more considered an inefficient investment of artistic capital within market-driven divisions of art world labor. A poet and boxer as well as an editor, Roger is the perfect guardian of this place of transgressed borders. I am privileged to be part of his series. I also want to thank Erin Hasley at the MIT Press for her beautiful design, Paula Woolley for her meticulous copyediting, and Matthew Abbate for following the manuscript through production and for his generous help with the index.

This book would not have found its way to print without the support and editorial guidance of Alexander Alberro. Alex's scholarship on conceptual art and commitment to contemporary artists inspired by conceptualism have helped to preserve a place for critical practice in today's art world, even as studio production returns as the dominant model. I am proud to share in that commitment and grateful for his support, encouragement, and, of course, for his hard work on this book. Readers will share my gratitude to Alex for untangling my practice in his lucid and illuminating introduction. Alex's work was aided by financial assistance from the University of Florida Scholarship Enhancement Fund, and by the careful commentary of Nora M. Alter.

I am especially honored to follow Gregg Bordowitz in the Writing Art series. Gregg has challenged and inspired me ever since we met in the early 1980s as students of Craig Owens. In the course of many long discussions and as the first reader of many of my early texts, he helped to shape my work as an artist and writer. I continue to cherish his friendship.

It was in Craig Owens that I found my first model for political and ethical commitment to a critically reflexive use of academic and cultural competence. In a sense, all of the texts collected in this volume owe their existence both to his early intellectual example and to the encouragement he gave an anxious 19-year-old to write a feature essay about Louise Lawler's work. In the process of editing "In and Out of Place" for *Art in America,* he also taught me how to write. I still mourn his death to AIDS.

Many of the texts in this volume were developed thanks to the intellectual context provided by critical journals and encouragement by their editors. "Museum Highlights: A Gallery Talk," "What's Intangible, Transitory, Mediating, Participatory, and Rendered in the Public Sphere," and my tribute to Bourdieu were all generated for publication in the journal *October* and completed under the generous editorial care of Douglas Crimp, Silvia Kolbowski, and George Baker. "It's Art When I Say It's Art, or . . ." and "A Speech on Documenta" first appeared in *Texte zur Kunst* and owe their existence to the early and ongoing support of its founder and editor, Isabelle Graw, who also published my tribute to Bourdieu in German translation. "A 'Sensation' Chronicle" was first published in *Social Text,* with many thanks to Toby Miller.

"A 'Sensation' Chronicle" developed out of a presentation I made at the Privatization of Culture Project seminar, convened by George Yúdice and held at the New School University, in 1999. "Slashing the *American Canvas*" is one of a number of short papers I prepared for symposia organized by George, Toby, and other seminar participants, who created a vital forum for cultural policy debates and who were generous in their openness to contributions by nonacademics like myself. "Isn't This a Wonderful Place?" was also first conceived as a conference paper. I was unable to attend the conference, however, and it was completed thanks only to many months of patient and persistent encouragement by Corinne Kratz.

Many of the texts in this volume also have their origins in the contexts and support provided by curators. Brian Wallis, who as the curator of the exhibition "Damaged Goods" gave me the opportunity to create my first gallery talk performance in 1986, provided indispensable advice as an editorial consultant in early stages of the project that became this book. "Welcome to the Wadsworth" was born of an invitation from Andrea Miller-Keller, who offered me, as she did so many other women artists since the 1970s, my first solo museum project. "A Letter to the Wadsworth Atheneum" was originally addressed to her. Larry Rinder made what may be the ultimate curatorial sacrifice on my behalf when he stepped aside and let me take over his curatorial role in creating "Aren't They Lovely?" for Berkeley's University Art Museum. *A Project in Two Phases,* the occasion for my short speech "What Do I, as an Artist, Provide?," is only the first example of the ongoing support of Sabine Breitwieser, the director of the Generali Foundation. I have deep respect for the risks that these and other curators have taken in collaborating with me on a process of critical reflection on their institutions—risks I fear that fewer and fewer curators are willing or able to take.

The three texts in this volume on the theme of services all have their origins in the project *Services. Services* was a thoroughly collaborative endeavor, and my thinking about art and service provision developed in the context of discussions in which many people participated. The project itself was coorganized by Helmut Draxler, whose friendship as well as professional and intellectual support as a curator and critic were crucial to much of my work in the mid-1990s. The project's original "working group" included my friends and peers Judith Barry, Clegg & Guttmann, Stephan Dillemuth, Renée Green, Christian Philipp Müller, and Fred Wilson, who were all central to the formation of "project work." At the Kunstraum der Universität Lüneburg where *Services* originated, Beatrice von Bismarck, Diethelm Stoller, and Ulf Wuggenig created a vital context for debates at the intersection of contemporary art and social and cultural theory. These debates continued to develop thanks to the curators of the five other institutions through which the project circulated in 1994, most notably Stella Rollig of the Depot in Vienna where I delivered "How to Provide an Artistic Service: An Introduction."

"In and Out of Place" and "'Creativity = Capital'?," the two earliest texts in this volume, deal with the work of my friends, mentors, and collaborators Louise

Lawler and Allan McCollum. These essays bear witness to my enormous debt to these artists. It was the example of Louise's work that first convinced me that one cannot simply be an artist, accepting invitations, producing shows, putting one's name on objects and labels; one cannot simply execute the functions of an artist without attempting to reflect, in every instance, on the relations one reproduces in performing that role. It was from Allan that I first learned to think about the relationship between culture and class and to consider the conditions of artistic production as the central object of artistic practice itself. All this should be evident from the essays. What I want to thank Allan and Louise for here, above all, is their friendship.

The work of a number of other artists who have influenced and inspired me is touched upon in "What's Intangible, Transitory, Mediating, Participatory, and Rendered in the Public Sphere, Part II." I am afraid, however, that my treatment of Hans Haacke and Michael Asher, in particular, in the context of this essay is woefully inadequate to the importance of their work, without which my practice would hardly be possible. I may sometimes assume that my debt to Hans is so obvious that it needn't be noted. The critique of the political conditions of art and art institutions, the artistic engagement with social systems, and the use of sociological methods and research are among his many innovations that have defined the work of younger project artists like myself.

Reviewing this volume, I am reminded that I have only written about a few of the artists whose work was crucial to my formation. Yvonne Rainer's films, with their engagement of the relationship between the subjective and social and their extensive use of quoted text, were a central inspiration for my approach to performance. Martha Rosler's critical writings, videos, performances, and her early work on the ethics of representation were also a central influence. Adrian Piper's work offered a rigorous model of critique in the indexical present. While I have written about Mary Kelly's work, my early essay on her *Post-Partum Document* regrettably could not be included in this volume.

What all of these artists have in common is their reflexive performance of critique in ways that defy divisions of artistic and intellectual production, personal experience and political engagement. What they also have in common is that they are all women working in a feminist tradition. I hope that my own commitment to feminism has not been lost in this collection. That commitment may be most evident in my early and very recent work, and in my ten-year collaboration with Martha Baer, Jessica Chalmers, Erin Cramer, and Marianne Weems of the V-Girls—all of which have fallen mostly outside of this book's purview. My project as an artist was largely defined in the mid-1980s at the juncture of feminism and conceptual art. I saw my task as being to integrate the site-specific institutional critique that emerged in conceptual and post-studio art with the examination of the production and positioning of subjects in feminist theory, film, and performance. While I never ceased to see this as my task, my concern with what is gendered in that subject production became increasingly subsumed under the tremendous weight of the classism of the artistic field. However, gender does reemerge full-force in the script of *Official Welcome,* which seeks to perform how very gendered the positions available to artists remain.

The inclusion of my tribute to Pierre Bourdieu in this collection relieves me of the impossible task of summarizing his importance for me here. His influence is evident on almost every page. I am extraordinarily privileged to be the object of his regard in a foreword that was written in the spring of 1998, when this book had a somewhat different form and long before it had a publisher. I have no doubt that he wrote the foreword when he did thanks largely to the gentle encouragement of my dear friend Inès Champey. It is with Inès, above all, that I share my sadness that he did not live to see it in print.

When it came to reviewing the proofs of this book, many months past the point when major changes could be made, one regret formed in my stomach: that my performance script for *May I Help You?* could not be included. Staged at American Fine Arts, Co. in 1991, *May I Help You?* is probably my most precise indictment of how art functions to legitimize social hierarchies. It was also my first collaboration with Colin de Land, who created, in American Fine Arts, Co., a context that sustained me in the art world for over a decade until its closure in 2004 following his tragic death. Colin was my coconspirator against the art market even through my many years of attempting to leave it. This book is missing a tribute to Colin, which I hope someday I will manage to write.

Toward the end of *Official Welcome* I finally say that it just helps, it helps, to know that there are people who are following what you are doing and who think it's important enough to try to understand. The most sustaining form of that understanding may be its first appearance in the love of our families, love that we preserve inside ourselves and that becomes a source of strength. My family has remained a source of strength as well as inspiration. I went out into the world with an inheritance: internalized dispositions acquired in a familial culture of transgressive play, committed belief, invested argument, questioning, seeking, and struggle. My work represents what I have done with that inheritance. My brothers and sisters Robert, Philip, and especially Harbour, a writer, and Maria, my first and most brilliant collaborator, taught me how to play and how to fight. Esther, Zachary, Charles, and Luis are now carrying on those traditions. My father, Robert B. Fraser, Jr., gave me a love of books and intellectual debates. His sermons as a Unitarian minister were my first lessons in rhetoric and oratory. My mother, Carmen de Monteflores, continues to inspire me with her struggles as a feminist, a lesbian, a woman of color, and a writer. As a painter and later as a psychologist, she taught me how to look at the relations between things.

I am my parents' child and this book is dedicated to them.

Andrea Fraser

INTRODUCTION: MIMICRY, EXCESS, CRITIQUE

Alexander Alberro

> You could say that all my work is about the fantasies of our field and about the desires and interests reproduced and revealed in those fantasies. It's about what we want from art.
> —Andrea Fraser, 2003

Artists' writings, whether in the form of essays, tracts, statements, or interviews, are usually considered to be supplementary to artistic production. This is not the case with the writings of Andrea Fraser, which are an inherent part of her art practice. As she explains in a recent interview, "I think of writing and research as part of artistic work. Unfortunately, I think the growing professionalization of both the artist and the intellectual (which has become almost synonymous with 'academic') have created a division between 'writing' or 'thinking' and 'making' that may be quite new."[1] The present volume, which consists of a representative selection of Fraser's writings from 1985 to 2003, attempts to bridge this division. Although the following texts are self-standing and can be read on their own, they are also intricately interwoven with Fraser's installations, videotapes, and performances, and construct a rich intertextual dialogue.

The collection is organized into three sections, "Critical Practices," "Public Institutions, Private Objects" and "Professional Interests." The texts are not ordered chronologically; rather, they are clustered around separate problematics of Fraser's intellectual history. Thus the sections should be viewed as constellations, each setting forth a facet of the artist's practice. The writings draw from several genres, including art criticism, critical analyses of the conditions of contemporary culture, essays that examine public and private institutions, performance scripts, and more wide-ranging theoretical investigations. As such, they destabilize the increasingly rigid parameters of institutional discourse by calling into question the classification of writing into "creative writing," "journalism," "art criticism," and "cultural theory."

For almost two decades Fraser has been part of a loose group of artists that has also included Gregg Bordowitz, Tom Burr, Clegg & Guttmann, Stephan Dillemuth, Mark Dion, Renée Green, Christian Philipp Müller, Nils Norman, and others. Sometimes referred to as "Kontext Kunst" (context art) or as third-generation practitioners of institutional critique, these artists often work collaboratively and produce artworks that take the form of discursive projects. "Project art," as defined by Fraser, refers not simply to art "undertaken on a 'project-by-project basis,'" but to "site-specific art that seeks to critique and analyze aspects of culture that have largely been naturalized."[2] The aims of this relatively new artistic genre are motivated by a set of concerns that exceed the parameters of medium specificity as much as those of singular object production. Project art is also characterized by its ephemeral nature; the artistic element usually consists of an activity or installation that lasts only for the duration of the show. Moreover, the planning and development phase of these projects, which often involve vast amounts of research and analysis of data, is deemed integral to the work as a whole. Thus the art produced by those who work in this mode spurns the traditional art market as much as it opposes the manifold mechanisms of institutional incorporation.

Fraser began her career in the 1980s. A self-described autodidact and high-school dropout, she completed the Whitney Independent Studies Program in 1985 and has had a long-standing (informal) relationship with a number of art critics and intellectuals affiliated with the New York-based journal *October*.[3] Her move toward non-object-based art coincided with the publication of Peter Bürger's *Theory of the Avant-Garde* in English translation.[4] Many artists in the early years of postmodernism fused notions advanced by Bürger's reading of Frankfurt School aesthetics—e.g., that radical form is just as important as subject matter to an engaged work of art—with critiques of uniqueness, originality, and commodification. This intellectual context prompted Fraser to question the formal components of her own work, culminating in the verdict that traditional art objects were no longer tenable.[5] At the same time, she began to consider "analytical and interventionary practices" developed in disciplines such as psychoanalysis, feminism, critical pedagogy, and Pierre Bourdieu's reflexive sociology. For Fraser, these practices provided models for engaging culture—not "substantively, as a symbolic system," but systemically, "on the level of social relations and social structure"—and formed the basis, alongside specific postwar artistic traditions, for the project of developing a critical practice capable of intervening in the very structure of the artistic field and its institutions.[6]

In one of the first essays in this volume, "It's Art When I Say It's Art, or . . ." (1995), Fraser opposes "artistic practice" to "cultural production." Most of what exists as art, she argues, can be better understood as "cultural production." If culture is defined as "first, the symbolic systems that provide for the integration and reproduction of social groups and, secondly, the process of acquiring the competencies and dispositions that compose those symbolic systems," then cultural production—"whether legitimate or popular, generated for restricted or mass audiences"—should be defined as "the specialized production of the objects, representations, narratives, discourses, and practices in which these competencies and dispositions are objectified and reproduced." By contrast, "artistic practice resists, or aims to resist, functioning as the representative culture of a particular group. . . . It functions, instead, or aims to function, as analytic and interventionary." In other words, whereas cultural production is inherently affirmative, upholding established conventions and conforming to (and reproducing) the status quo, artistic practice, by definition, challenges, reflects upon, and attempts to transform the structure of the artistic field.

In "It's Art When I Say It's Art, or . . ." Fraser identifies three of the postwar artistic movements that make her own interventionary project possible: minimalism, because it rethought the relationship between the viewer and the art object; institutional critique, because it complicated the manner in which the museum/gallery nexus defines bodies in terms of gender, class, and race; and the post-studio practice of site specificity, because it called into question the conventions of artistic production, exhibition, and dissemination. For an artistic practice that wants to remain vital, she deems it crucial to produce work that does not serve to legitimate cultural institutions. Fraser also insists that in order to remain relevant artists must constantly seek new strategies and transform their work in a manner that parallels the shifting cultural, economic, and political conditions. Thus it is not surprising that she is continually in pursuit of new forms of artistic production and critique that are relevant for the contemporary context.

From an early date, Fraser's interventionary practice included live performances documented on videotape and accompanied by texts that elucidated the works' practical and theoretical dimensions. Most of the videotapes are produced in unlimited editions. As such, they function to short-circuit characteristics of uniqueness and preciousness—elements that conventionally determine an artwork's exchange value. The texts, on the other hand, could be said to exist as linguistic "performances," not only because they are performative but, as Fraser puts it, "because I feel as self-conscious about my language as an essayist as I do as a scriptwriter."[7]

By the mid 1980s, Fraser had developed museum-tour performances and adopted the functional persona of a docent as part of her work. These projects were largely prompted by her reflections on the artistic practice of the New York-based artist Louise Lawler, which culminated in Fraser's essay "In and Out of Place" (1985). Lawler's strategy of artistic production would have a profound impact on Fraser. In particular, as Fraser emphasizes in "In and Out of Place," Lawler's ability to "escape both marginalization and incorporation" encouraged the younger artist to conceptualize art as a practice of resistance. Further, Lawler's stress on art production as a collective endeavor involving not just artists "but collectors, viewers, museum and gallery workers" introduced to Fraser the importance of the often invisible and incommunicable status of labor within the cultural apparatus. The manner in which Lawler fulfilled several different functions at once—artist, publicist, museum worker, art consultant, curator—encouraged Fraser to theorize and develop a practice with multiple roles. In fact, *The Public Life of Art: The Museum* (1988), one of Fraser's early museum-tour performances produced specifically for videotape, was made in collaboration with Lawler.

Fraser begins "In and Out of Place" with a description of a project by Lawler that was ultimately unrealized. Lawler had asked three contemporary art critics to submit short texts to be printed on the covers of matchbooks. Although all of the critics refused the invitation, Fraser was significantly influenced by Lawler's attempt to work collaboratively with critics in the production of an artwork that would also self-reflexively function as criticism. The younger artist's attempt to intervene in both fields—art production and art criticism—and to subject them equally to critique follows directly from Lawler's practice. By assuming the role of a museum docent, traditionally a volunteer with a dilettante's knowledge of art, Fraser at once comments directly on the museum as an institution, on its support system, and on its viewing public. But whereas Lawler usually makes herself invisible as an artist, Fraser's performances characteristically place her in a position of excess.[8] Replicating the discourse of the museum, Fraser incorporates and inhabits the institutional role that she sets out to critique. Yet the intensity of her identification with the role produces a surplus of elements that in their extravagance dissolve the underlying ideological structure of that role and especially its function within the institution. The result is not unlike what Slavoj Žižek refers to in another context as a "radical deidentification," as the ideological elements that usually combine to constitute a reality proliferate so excessively that they fail to be articulated and find themselves instead in an empty space, floating as an unconnected series of gestures and phrases.[9]

The performance *Museum Highlights: A Gallery Talk* today exists as a videotape and as a script, complete with stage directions and discursive academic footnotes, of Fraser's tour of the Philadelphia Museum of Art during the winter of 1989. The videotape follows Fraser through the museum as she carefully creates the persona of a docent named Jane Castleton in mannerisms and appearance (she wears a houndstooth, double-breasted suit). By contrast, the script provides a displaced version of the performance. In fact, the academic commentary appended to the script in the form of preamble or footnotes adds an additional critical dimension to the performance piece. Thus, for example, footnote 3 informs the reader that "a volunteer docent is not just someone who gives tours for a small percentage of the museum's visitors; she is the museum's representative. . . . [She] is a figure of identification for the primarily white, middle-class audience."[10] This identification is precisely what Fraser sets out to perform in a radical way. With a script constructed almost entirely of quotations from museum documents committed to memory, she enacts the internalization of discourse that defines entering an institutional sphere. The gallery tour begins at the western entrance of the museum, where Fraser quotes jargon from museum brochures that urge museum membership. She also offers a brief history of the founding of the magnificent institution and plugs the greatness of the city of Philadelphia, quoting from an advertisement in *Business Week:* "'You can choose from 5 professional sports teams, a world class symphony, 100 Museums, the largest municipal park system in the country, and a restaurant renaissance the whole world is talking about.'" The tour then winds through the European art galleries, pausing frequently to examine specific details of period rooms. But rather than cementing the narrative of high art and taste that the institution seeks to advance, the stream of details presented by the "docent" serves to unravel that narrative. For example, the docent elegantly moves from a fastidious description of a seventeenth-century English paneled room complete with Dutch oil paintings to a fussy summary of the men's room located on the other side of the wall. She then neatly turns back to a discussion of the conventional objets d'art featured by the museum. In another instance, she describes a guard's stool in a jargon normally reserved for priceless antiques: "In scale and complexity . . . the most ambitious undertaking . . . in the great European tradition . . . abundance and grace . . . free from time and change. . . ." Mobilizing a highly classed mode of speaking, Fraser (in the guise of the docent) exposes the degree to which distinction is culturally created and language is mobilized to function like legerdemain to deceive.

Museum Highlights: A Gallery Talk thus demonstrates the act of cultural deception common to the self-presentation of museums of fine art. The gestures and phrases of culture-speak have the power to alienate those who are not familiar with this language; indeed, in many ways that is their central function. Yet cultural capital is also shown to open doors. Adopting "a manner of being in relation to art objects," as well as the appropriate "postures," "expressions," and "patterns of looking" and the proper "accents" in the pronouncement of names of artists and works, allows one to move gracefully through the culture of fine art museums. Fraser shows how this process legitimizes not only bourgeois subjecthood, but the ideological role of the museum as well.[11] Drawing on Pierre Bourdieu's *Distinction: A Social Critique of the Judgment of Taste* (1984) for support, she demonstrates, not without irony, the extent to which museums help to teach the public the importance of discrimination: "the ability to distinguish between a coat room and a rest room, between a painting and a telephone, a guard and a guide; the ability to distinguish between yourself and a drinking fountain, between what is different and what is better."[12] In sum, *Museum Highlights: A Gallery Talk* is as much an essay that critiques the ideological function of taste and the production of value as it is a performance script. Fraser does not critique just the institution of the museum; by extension, she also analyzes the type of viewer the museum produces and the process of identification that artists embody.

Fraser abandoned the persona of Jane Castleton in 1990. She had, apparently, come to believe that her guise as a museum docent was in effect "a misidentification, and a displacement of my status within art institutions." The problem was that her appropriation of the "dominated" position of the docent served to obscure the authority of her own position as an artist and, in so doing, functioned "to obscure the relations of domination of which museums are the sites and which its recognized agents produce and reproduce."[13] This realization led to a series of works in which Fraser no longer played a fictional role, but instead self-consciously performed under her own name and in the role of an artist. And insofar as an artist is a professional whose identity is socially constructed and validated, Fraser also identifies herself as a representative of a "class."[14]

The second script included in this volume, for the performance *Welcome to the Wadsworth* (1991), includes as a preamble a letter by Fraser to the Wadsworth Atheneum's curator of contemporary art explaining the artwork she plans to exhibit/perform. "A Letter to the Wadsworth Atheneum" (1991) also lays out Fraser's working methodology, which entails both rigorous research of particular institutions and the search for "seams in the discourse," or what Fredric Jameson refers to in *The Political Unconscious* (1981) as "flaws" in the narrative that indicate social conflict.[15] Through her research, Fraser develops the analysis that the Wadsworth Atheneum was founded to memorialize an elite "Yankee" culture. Unlike other museums, the Atheneum never pretended to serve a public other than the patrician class; it continued to resist recognizing social contradiction despite industrialization and successive waves of immigration. One conflict Fraser did find, however, occurred when a new director, A. Everett Austin Jr., set out to build a collection of contemporary art in the late 1920s. By 1945, the Atheneum's trustees had had enough, and Austin was forced to leave his job. Fraser identifies the "problem with Austin" as an intraclass one; he belonged to "the same affluent New England stock as the Atheneum's trustees [and] married into their families." The quandary arose from the fact that "he did not share their values." This leads Fraser to conclude that Austin's intervention had been so powerful and disturbing to the status quo because he had intervened from a position of belonging, as an insider. Hence, she set out to replicate this strategy in her project for the Wadsworth. From the outset she recognized that her greatest challenge would be to construct herself "as a figure of identification, rather than an object of interest and an outsider." In order to meet this challenge and present herself as an insider, she highlighted her (paternal) lineage as a Daughter of the American Revolution.

"A Letter to the Wadsworth Atheneum" prepares the reader for the ensuing performance script. The monologue that constitutes the *Welcome* begins with

Fraser introducing herself by her own name and as an artist who lives in New York City. What follows is a complexly woven text of condensed and displaced facts that, like *Museum Highlights*, is constructed largely of quotations from archival material. The facts presented pertain to the history of the Atheneum and of the city of Hartford. The fictions include personal myths about growing up in Hartford, seeing "dignified high-hatted gentlemen go in and out of the lofty pillared verandah," being raised by a widowed mother devoted to "the love of beautiful furniture and art" and the social myths about the good old days in this part of the world. The last third of the speech consists of a sequence of clichéd yet politically charged phrases from the late 1980s and 1990s—statements representative of the way the white, upper middle class explains their flight into the suburbs, their fear of the other, of desegregation, urban decay, crime, and the poor. Fraser emphasizes how such sentiments are reinforced by positions of privilege: "Homeowners should have the right to determine who lives in their neighborhoods and goes to their schools." Or: "The city is dirty and crowded and full of crime and I'm glad I'm isolated from it." And if one suspects that her vitriolic statements are exaggerated, the text is replete with meticulous footnotes identifying the original source of each phrase, most of which lead directly to the citizens of contemporary Hartford. Thus *Welcome to the Wadsworth* is as much a salutation to the upper middle class of the city of Hartford as it is an introduction to the plight of the U.S. city at the end of the twentieth century. For, as Fraser makes clear, the proliferation of urban blight that today characterizes many U.S. cities is just as much part of the heritage of the bourgeoisie as are institutions such as the Wadsworth Atheneum.

After *Welcome to the Wadsworth*, Fraser took a five-year break from scripted public performances in order to focus on what she considered another kind of performance, taking up the role of curator or consultant in projects that resulted primarily in installations. In 1997, however, she returned to scripted performance, pushing her practice to another level. Beginning in 2001, Fraser developed a series of events in which she assumed the persona of actual artists, art critics, and museum personnel. For instance, the performance *Art Must Hang* (2001), a tribute to the late German artist Martin Kippenberger, meticulously reproduces (in German) an extemporaneous dinner speech Kippenberger gave at the Club an der Grenze in Austria in 1995. Likewise, Fraser's *Official Welcome* (2001) takes the form of oratory composed largely of quotations from relatively well-known figures in the art world such as Benjamin Buchloh, Gabriel Orozco,

Kirk Varnedoe, Vanessa Beecroft, Michael Kimmelman, Larry Gagosian, Charles Saatchi, and Kara Walker. Fraser structures *Official Welcome* to oscillate between the voices of two camps: artists and their supporters. As the *Welcome* progresses, the artist strips away her clothes, gradually revealing more and more of her body to the audience. Thus, in a manner that recalls much performance art of the 1970s—and here not only the work of Carolee Schneeman and Gina Pane but also that of Valie Export and especially Hannah Wilke comes to mind—Fraser transforms her body into a vehicle for her artistic production. As such, *Official Welcome* comes close to achieving the grotesque desire articulated by the Jane Castleton character nearly two decades earlier: "I'd like to live like an art object." An art object, of course, that is exchanged for the pleasure and profit of others.[16]

At the basis of this strategy is fantasy. Fraser acknowledges as much when she writes that it is "fantasy that drives me to try to make my arguments ever more complex."[17] Fantasy allows a significant degree of projection, and enables the subject to assume and act out roles that would otherwise be inaccessible. As with fantasy, too, Fraser's performances, which strive toward a perfect mimesis, render unclear the separation between illusion and actuality. A case in point is her *A Project in Two Phases* for the EA-Generali Foundation in Vienna, a year-long undertaking represented in this collection with her brief opening speech "What Do I, as an Artist, Provide?" (1995). Initial research revealed to Fraser the large degree to which the Generali Foundation's cultural program, which successfully folded art collecting into a public sign of social benevolence, entailed granting substantial autonomy to art professionals. This led her to conceive of her project for the Generali Foundation "as a 'performance' of an extreme self-instrumentalization." The most effective way to resist the Generali Foundation's complex mechanism of appropriation, she concluded, was by seamlessly fusing with it, withholding and denying her autonomy. Once again, then, it is through an *over*identification—an identification that is excessive in its completeness—that Fraser performs her critique.[18] More than just confronting the field of art and its network of exhibitions, museums, galleries, and private foundations, she enters into and appropriates its logic to subvert it from within. This form of critique uses the field's internal contradictions to scrutinize and excoriate it in its own terms. Yet, as with all successful exercises in verisimilitude, Fraser's "performances" risk being confused with reality and being received as affirmative rather than critical. These circumstances place even more pressure on the artist's writings, for it is in these multilayered texts that the critical dimension of her position is fully articulated.

As with that of Louise Lawler, the work of the New York-based artist Allan McCollum has served as a touchstone for Fraser over the years.[19] In her essay "'Creativity = Capital'?" (1986), first published as a brochure for an exhibition of works by McCollum at the Institute for Contemporary Art in Philadelphia, Fraser begins an examination of artistic labor that she later develops in her formulation of art as "service provision." Fraser picks up on McCollum's characterization of his artistic activity as a kind of "working to rule," a job action in which workers reduce their effort to the bare minimum required by contract. Rather than their labor per se, what wage earners who work to rule withhold is "the gift of their surplus labor." In a similar fashion, Fraser proposes, McCollum offers only "the bare minimum of what still constitutes artistic labor"—even within a "maximal" production of huge quantities of objects. In so doing, he unsettles a basic tenet on which Western art is based—namely, that artists, above all others, are free in their work. For artists are compensated for their surplus labor, work that is in excess of their own necessity and for which most workers are not paid. According to Fraser, McCollum is a "worker who, posing as an artist, recalls the condition of artistic production as labor." And just as the worker labors for another's profit, so too, Fraser suggests, "the professional artist . . . works not for his or her own satisfaction, but for the enrichment of others." McCollum's resistance is thus located in his refusal to deliver surplus labor that, in Marx's analysis, is what the capitalist appropriates as surplus value, or profit. This leads Fraser to conclude: "If working to rule is a withdrawal of identification with managerial authority, when transposed to artistic practice it can be understood as a withdrawal of identification with the power and prestige that high art traditionally has represented." However, Fraser's artistic practice, which as we have seen develops a mode of negation through hyperidentification, tackles the issue of the role of labor in the production of art from an angle opposite to that of McCollum. Whereas the latter's practice explores this withdrawal of identification in the context of an intensified material production of art commodities, Fraser's mobilizes an excess of identification within a largely *im*material production of ephemeral performances and projects. This she theorizes as "artistic service" provision.

Fraser first publicly articulated the concept of artistic service in *Services* (1994), a collaborative project with the Austrian curator and art historian Helmut Draxler.[20] As Draxler and Fraser wrote in their proposal for the project, the aim of *Services* was to bring to light artistic "labor which is either in excess of, or independent of, any specific material production and which cannot be transacted as or along with a product." In economic terms, they argued, such labor could be understood only as service provision, as opposed to goods production. They saw this mode of labor as encompassing the entire range of "project work" emerging in the 1990s, from traditionally intangible forms like performance, to the research and interpretation of sites, the presentation and installation of art objects, and community-based activities directly involving artists with audiences.[21] In her two-part essay from 1996, "What's Intangible, Transitory, Mediating, Participatory, and Rendered in the Public Sphere?," Fraser draws on economic theory to develop her understanding of what constitutes an artistic service, including "the intangible as opposed to the tangible product . . . ; the execution of functions which cannot appear as values independently of their use; . . . work undertaken in an immediate relation to a client, consumer, or user."[22] However, most important for Fraser is not how the emergence of artistic service redefines the artwork, but how it redefines the "social conditions and relations" of the work, or labor, of artists, particularly in the context of the broader transformations in what social theorists have variously termed our postindustrial, post-Fordist, or service society.

Fraser provides a genealogy of artistic practice as service provision within the field of art in the second half of her 1996 essay on service. She argues that four different strategies of resistance developed in the late 1960s that culminated in what today can be considered critical "project art." These include the attempts by groups such as the Art Workers Coalition (AWC) to develop contractual controls over the circulation of artworks, the dematerialization and ephemeralization of art into language and actions by conceptual art, the temporalization of artworks in specific times and spaces and within specific relations by site-specific and post-studio art practices, and finally the emergence of new social functions for art in the context of cultural activist and community-based practices. Fraser delineates how the activities and demands of the AWC and the resulting "Artists' Reserved Rights Transfer and Sale Agreement" drafted by Seth Siegelaub and Robert Projansky were crucial to the development of institutional critique. Above all, she argues, the AWC uncovered "a radical splitting of [the] artwork into tangible and intangible value . . . , [and] this in turn implied a redefinition of artwork from a commercial product or good to a service product—in this case intellectual property." Her research suggests that the struggles of the AWC may have eventually contributed to the unionization of the employees of New York City's Museum of Modern Art (MoMA), a development that in turn transformed the overall structural operation not only of MoMA but of other museums across the United States.[23] In addition, she shows how the activities of the AWC related to contemporary protest movements, and how these developments led to the initiation of a new form of community-based artistic activity.

Along with the AWC, conceptual art's problematization of the art object also contributed significantly to the development of a critical art practice. In particular, Fraser singles out the important way that the work of Carl Andre, Dan Flavin, Douglas Huebler, and Lawrence Weiner contributed to the transformation of the conditions of artistic value.[24] Fraser locates one of the first important articulations of art as service in Robert Smithson's text "Towards the Development of An Air Terminal Site" (1966–67), in which the artist describes himself as an "art consultant" "rendering consultation and advice" to specific individuals. The conceptual artist Daniel Buren is affirmed as an equally significant figure in the elaboration of post-studio art production, especially insofar as he "recognized that the instrumentalization of art for economic and symbolic profit" is an ideological maneuver dependent "not only on the autonomy of the artworks, but on the autonomy of the aesthetic itself."[25] In addition to Smithson and Buren, Fraser singles out the important roles played by Michael Asher, Marcel Broodthaers, and Hans Haacke in the development of institutional critique. What all of these artists had in common, she concludes, was that "what they constituted as the fundamental practice of art was nothing less than work on the conditions and the relations of artistic practice itself: not only the symbolic transformation of artistic positions . . . but their material transformation as well." The legacy of their efforts, according to Fraser, can be found in contemporary artistic practices such as her own that seek to fundamentally change the system of values and beliefs upon which the art world is based. A critical artistic practice, she concludes, must aim to go beyond mere interpretation in order to actively intervene in, and indeed transform, the existent realm of cultural, social, and economic relations.

The final section of this volume includes two essays by Fraser that were initially presented as public lectures. The first, "Slashing the *American Canvas,* or, Why I Would Rather Have a Day Job" (1998), presents a trenchant critique of the National Endowment for the Arts (NEA), and the second, "A 'Sensation' Chronicle" (2001), consists of an in-depth analysis of the public controversy that arose when the former mayor of New York City, Rudolph Giuliani, tried to censor the Brooklyn Museum of Art. In both of these texts, Fraser homes in on cultural policy and the issue of public funds devoted to the support of artists and their work. She examines both the explicit and the tacit expectations that guide public funding agencies when allocating their resources, and the effects of these unwritten "social contracts" on the concept of artistic autonomy. "Slashing the *American Canvas*" traces the subtle changes in NEA policy during the 1990s as a result of right-wing attacks, and the new emphasis the agency has come to place on art's utilitarian value. This official instrumentalization of artistic practice in the name of public service leads Fraser to emphasize the regressive potential of the phenomenon she uncovered in her work on "services." Her analysis of the "Sensation" controversy is equally pessimistic about the present condition of the field of art. Here it is not so much the predictable response of Giuliani and other right-wing administrators that she singles out, as that of art professionals representing institutions such as New York's Metropolitan Museum of Art and MoMA. Public arts funding, she argues, must be disentangled and distanced from "institutionalized forms of a disinterested aesthetic." Only then can it avoid the dangers of corporate populism and state-sponsored elitism and serve a true cultural democratization that is able to expand on the autonomy enjoyed by artists, rather than reducing artistic freedom to a form of privilege.

Both "Slashing the *American Canvas*" and "A 'Sensation' Chronicle" were written during a brief spell in the late 1990s when Fraser produced and exhibited little artwork. Yet, as with all of her writing, these essays constitute an integral part of her artistic practice. Although they were both produced for a scholarly audience (one was published in the journal *Social Text* and the other delivered as a public lecture at a cultural policy conference), they still retain an element of performance. As Fraser recently stated, referring to her dance piece *Exhibition* (2002), which was enacted and videotaped at a carnival parade in Rio de Janeiro: "Being able to 'pass' as an academic in a lecture hall is not so different for me than being able to 'pass' as a samba dancer in Rio. In both cases it's about performance."[26] But with essays such as "Slashing the *American Canvas*" and "A 'Sensation' Chronicle," as indeed with most of her projects, Fraser does more than merely pass. Painstakingly imitating the signs and rigorously following the proper codes, her work at once mimics and is in excess of what it represents. Whether in the form of a live performance, a videotape, or written text, Fraser's artistic practice unrelentingly explores the ideological foundations of art and critiques the privilege upon which those foundations are built.

Notes

1. Yilmaz Dziewior, "Interview with Andrea Fraser," in Dziewior, ed., *Andrea Fraser: Works 1984–2003* (Cologne: DuMont Literatur und Kunst Verlag, 2003), 93.

2. Dziewior, "Interview with Andrea Fraser," 95.

3. "The 1980s, the theorists of postmodernism, the Whitney Program, the journal *October,* were all very very good to me. I am their product." Fraser, in Dziewior, "Interview with Andrea Fraser," 93.

4. Peter Bürger, *Theory of the Avant-Garde,* trans. Michael Shaw (1974; Minneapolis: University of Minnesota Press, 1985). I do not mean to imply a direct causal relationship between Bürger's text and Fraser's shift toward the production of non-object-based art. Indeed, two works Fraser completed in 1984, one year before the publication of Bürger's book in English translation, already represent important steps in this direction. These include her artist book, *Woman 1/Madonna and Child 1506–1967,* which problematizes art-historical constructions of the artist and the conventional representation of women by high art, as well as her *Four Posters* project, which investigates four publicity posters from the Metropolitan Museum of Art, comparing them to the legitimizing and promotional character of the wall texts that supplement the paintings on the posters.

5. "It seemed to me that such critique [as proposed by Bürger] could not be accomplished through paintings and framed photographs et cetera, no matter how appropriated their imagery or how allegorical their procedures." Fraser, in Dziewior, "Interview with Andrea Fraser," 96.

6. Andrea Fraser, "It's Art When I Say It's Art, or . . ." (1995), in this volume.

7. Dziewior, "Interview with Andrea Fraser," 92.

8. In this regard, Fraser's work reveals its affinities to the "museum fictions" performed by the Belgian artist Marcel Broodthaers in the late 1960s and early 1970s.

9. Slavoj Žižek, "The Enlightenment in Laibach" (1994), in Inke Arns, ed., *Irwinretroprincip: 1983–2003* (Frankfurt: Revolver, 2003).

10. To that extent, the "spell" of the videotape leaves open the question of whether or not the tour is genuine. A later footnote in the script to *Museum Highlights* reports that "Jane" not only constitutes the museum's ideal viewer but also gives "her body in the absence of art objects."

11. As Fraser puts it in "An Artist's Statement" (1992), museums are "gatekeepers of a culture they legitimate"; the museum decides what constitutes legitimate culture, who is to produce it, and how it is to be consumed. In her introduction to *Aren't They Lovely?* (also 1992; reprinted in this volume), she goes on to describe the transformation of "bourgeois domestic culture into legitimate public culture" as the art museum's "primary operation."

12. Here it is important to emphasize the influence of the work of Pierre Bourdieu on Fraser's intellectual formation. "'To Quote,' Say the Kabyles, 'Is to Bring Back to Life'" (2002; reprinted in this volume) was written as a tribute to the sociologist, a memorial essay for a thinker whose writings Fraser has carefully studied and whose ideas her practice has absorbed. Indeed, one might extend Fraser's tribute to this entire volume, for Bourdieu's theories of cultural legitimacy, distinction, value, reflexive analysis, heteronomy, and habitus permeate its pages.

13. Fraser, "An Artist's Statement," in this volume.

14. In "It's Art When I Say It's Art, or . . . ," in this volume, Fraser stresses that "art professionals [constitute] a class."

15. Fredric Jameson, *The Political Unconscious: Narrative as a Socially Symbolic Act* (Ithaca: Cornell University Press, 1981).

16. The recent *Untitled* (2003) takes this reification one step further. The sixty-minute videotape loop records a man and a woman engaged in a sexual encounter in real time. The central playing area of the action, depicted from an elevated point of view suggestive of a surveillance camera, is a hotel room. The videotape emanates from a relatively small monitor. Although its visual track is unedited, the soundtrack has been completely muted. The man is credited as "anonymous" and is difficult to identify. The woman is recognizable as the artist, Andrea Fraser. The piece was "pre-bought" by a private collector (the man in the video), and the transaction followed the basic structure of most art sales. The gallerist, Friedrich Petzel, who represents the artist in the United States, earned 50 percent of the agreed-upon sale price. The remaining 50 percent went to Fraser, and the buyer received a copy of the videotape (a limited edition of five) as well as the encounter in the hotel room.

17. Fraser, "An Artist's Statement."

18. "The self-instrumentalization was never intended to function as a critique but rather as a form of resistance: an attempt to withhold my autonomy from appropriation as 'profit.'" Fraser, in Dziewior, "Interview with Andrea Fraser," 97.

19. In 1991, she wrote and directed a piece, *May I Help You,* that involved three hired actors performing a fifteen-minute monologue in a gallery featuring an installation of McCollum's *Plaster Surrogates.*

20. *Services* involved not just Draxler but a number of others, including Judith Barry, Ute Meta Bauer, Ulrich Bischoff, Iwona Blazwick, Jochen Becker, Renate Lorenz, Susan Cahan, Clegg & Guttmann, Stephan Dillemuth, Renée Green, Christian Philipp Müller, Fritz Raumann, and Fred Wilson. As should be apparent by now, much of Fraser's work is collaborative in nature—a methodology that is consistent with her critique of the concept of the artist. As she indicated as early as 1985, "The conventional organization of art practices around a signature—everything that allows a work of art to be identified as a 'Pollock' or a 'Warhol'—institutes the proper name as interior to the art object; thus, artists are locked in a structure of institutionalized subjectivity. And the institutional exhibition of proper names, designating the authors and owners of objects, defines that subjectivity in terms of consumption and ownership" ("In and Out of Place"; in this volume). A collaborative work disturbs this structure and makes the owning of a discrete "Fraser" problematic.

21. Here it is important to emphasize that by clearly identifying and defining artistic service, Fraser helped to standardize the payment of a fee or honorarium as compensation for project-based work.

22. Andrea Fraser, "What's Intangible, Transitory, Mediating, Participatory, and Rendered in the Public Sphere?" (1996), reprinted in this volume.

23. According to Fraser, the MoMA unionization drive represented a conclusive moment in the transformation of curators from personal art advisors to professionals, which in turn fundamentally altered relations between artists and museums.

24. Particular emphasis is placed on the transformation of the role of the collector into that of a patron who subsidizes the artist, paying now for an artistic activity rather than for a product. Thus Fraser questions how conceptual art could "revolutionize the political economy of art, returning collectors to the more altruistic motives of patronage projected onto art's premarket past." Andrea Fraser, "What's Intangible, Transitory, Mediating, Participatory, and Rendered in the Public Sphere? Part II," reprinted in this volume.

25. For Fraser, the implications of Buren's work are vast. She concludes that "while the autonomy of artworks as commodities may allow them to produce economic profit, the autonomy of art as aesthetic construct [is what] allows it to produce the symbolic profit of social and cultural legitimacy." See Fraser, "What's Intangible. . . ? Part II."

26. Dziewior, "Interview with Andrea Fraser," 92.

CRITICAL

PRACTICES

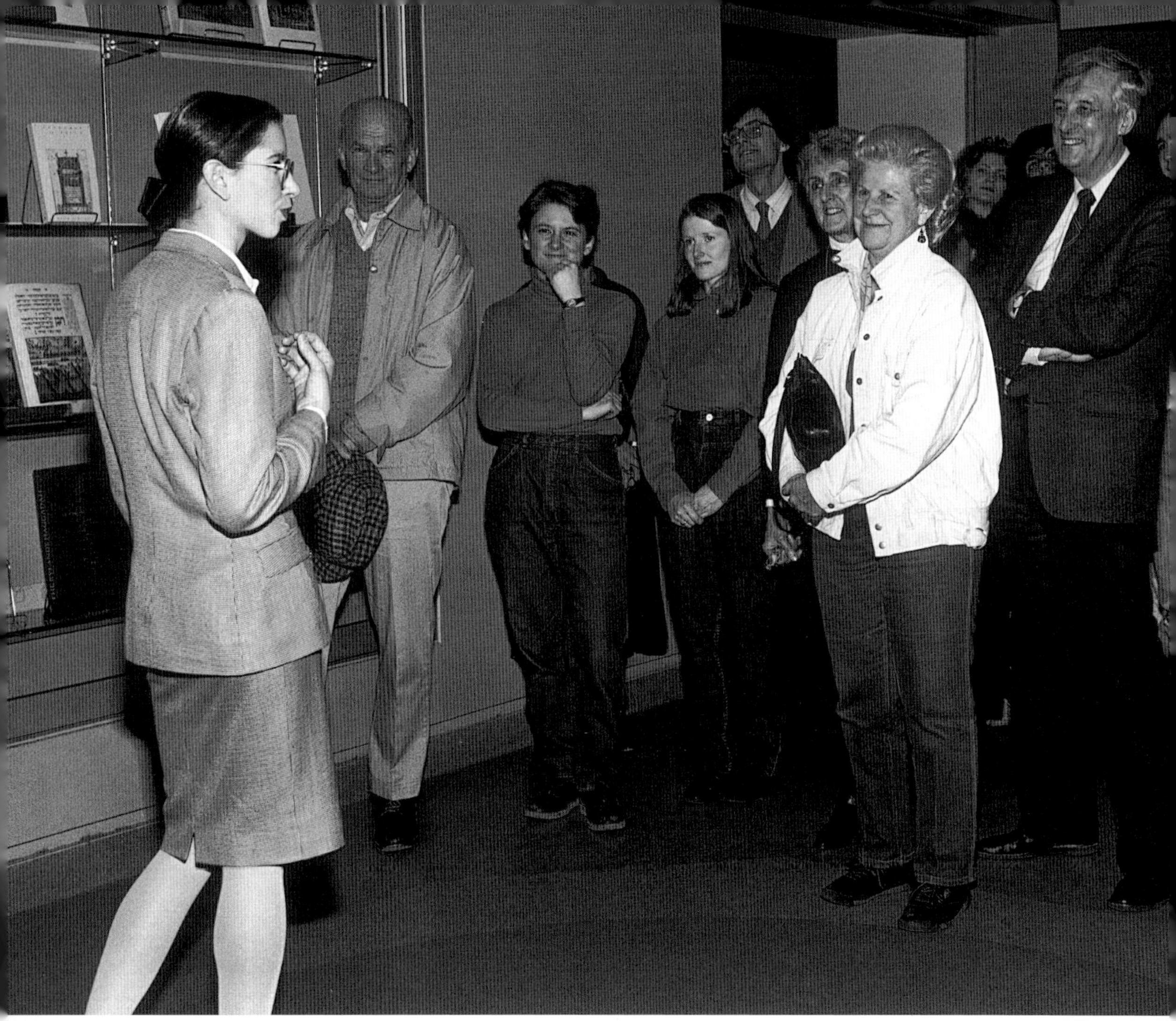

1.1 Andrea Fraser, *Museum Highlights: A Gallery Talk*, 1989. Live performance at the Philadelphia Museum of Art, Philadelphia. Courtesy the artist. Photo: Kelly & Massa Photography.

1

AN ARTIST S STATEMENT

"An Artist's Statement" was written to combine the academic performance of the conference lecture and the artistic performance of self-presentation in "artist's talks." It was first presented at the symposium "Place Position Presentation Public" at the Jan van Eyck Akademie, Maastricht, in April 1992.

Freud ended a paper called "The Dynamics of the Transference" with this statement: "in the last resort no one can be slain *in absentia* or *in effigie*."[1]

My investment in site specificity is motivated by this idea. My engagement in institutional critique follows from the fact that as an artist and as a writer, to the extent that I write, art and academic institutions are the sites where my activity is located. Psychoanalysis largely determines my conception of those sites as sets of relations, although I think of those relations as social and economic as well as subjective. And psychoanalysis also defines, largely, what is for me both a practical and an ethical imperative to work site-specifically.

The practical imperative is well represented by Freud's statement. If one considers practice—that is, critical practice, counterpractice—as the transformation of social, subjective, or economic relations, then the best, and perhaps only, point of engagement is with those relations in their enactment. The point is not to interpret those relations, as they exist elsewhere; the point is to change them.

Freud might say, the point is *not* to repeat or reproduce those relations, but to try to free oneself and others from them, with an intervention—an intervention which may include an interpretation, but the effectivity of which is limited to the things made "actual and manifest" in the particular site of its operation.

This limit also defines the ethical dimension of site specificity. It marks the boundary, not only between the effective and the ineffective, but between repetition and intervention; between the reproduction of relations and their possible transformation.

"No one can be slain *in absentia* or *in effigie*."

Freud is certainly writing of himself in this statement, or rather, of the position of the analyst, who is authorized by the institutions of psychoanalysis and of medicine to be called upon to execute the functions of authority from which his or her patients suffer: the authority to represent them, to represent their histories, their future, their wants, their appropriate demands, the criteria according to which they might be able to see themselves as acceptable.

Jacques Lacan wrote that Freud "recognized at once that the principle of his power lay there . . . but also that this power gave him a way out of the problem only on the condition that he did not use it."[2]

Any intervention or interpretation, to the extent that it depends on this power, will reproduce it.

The limit imposed by the ethics of psychoanalysis on the things made "actual and manifest" in the site of its operation is thus, first, a limit on the uses to which this power can be put—as any appeal to an outside would not only reproduce it, but extend its field of authority—and, secondly, a limit imposed on the analyst to the position determined for her within that site, as any attempt at displacement would only obscure it.

This is how I would like to understand artistic practice, that is, as a form of counterpractice within the field of cultural production.

The relations I might want to transform may be relations in which I feel myself to be dominated, or they may be relations in which I feel myself to be dominant. The ethical dimension of the imperative of site specificity, however, pertains entirely to my status as dominant: that is, to the agency and authority accorded to me as a producer and as the subject of discourse, by the institutions in which I function and of whose authority I become the representative. It doesn't really matter whether I'm an author or not, whether my status as an agent is actual or ideological. The position that I occupy in the execution of the functions of my profession is that of a producer, an author, an agent. And this position is one of privilege. I am the institution's representative and the agent of its reproduction.

So, when it comes to institutional critique, I am the institution. And I cannot be slain in absentia, in effigy.

I am an artist. As an artist I have the double role of engaging in the specialized production of bourgeois domestic culture on one hand and, on the other, the relatively autonomous reproduction of my own professional subculture.

To say that this activity is relatively autonomous is to say that it exists within a field "capable of imposing its own norms on both the production and the consumption of its products."[3] These norms are determined by the history of that field and express, above all, the primacy of the particular capacities that define the specialization of my activity; that is, the manipulation of the form of, or the formal relations in and between, objects, representations, and discourse.

Although the fact that the culture I produce functions as bourgeois domestic culture is a historical fact of economic patronage, it does not depend on this patronage. To the extent that the knowledge, propensity, and capacities that it demands constitute a "specific cultural competence" acquired largely by the "implicit learning" of prolonged contact, the culture I produce is inseparable from the economic and educational capital required to consume it.

Museums abstract this culture from its social location. The primary operation of art museums is the turning of bourgeois domestic culture into public culture. The induction of those not already disposed to this culture into the habits and manners of its appropriation is what constitutes the public education that defines museums, at least in the United States, as educational institutions. This displacement is the mechanism through which the cultural dispositions acquired in economic privilege are imposed in the public sphere and thus across the social field, as exclusively legitimate cultural competencies.

However, the displacement that museums effect is not really an abstraction. The autonomy of my field of activity and its specialization within divisions of cultural labor—that is, my distance from the class whose culture I produce—are the conditions of its possibility.

Museums realize this possibility by authorizing my activity within the public sphere. Museums define legitimate culture and legitimate cultural discourse and accord me, and other authorized individuals, an exclusive prerogative to produce legitimate culture and to possess legitimate opinion. They divide the field of material culture into legitimate culture and illegitimate culture—or rather, non-culture, to the extent that the illegitimate is denied a representative function in the public sphere framed by these institutions. And they divide the public created by this sphere into producers and nonproducers of culture.

While museums in some cases appropriate objects, I produce objects for them. They privilege this latter group—those works produced within their privileged discourse and which directly accord that discourse its authority to describe them. These are the objects produced as the common culture of the subjects of that discourse—the domestic culture of the patrons who appropriate them materially and the more or less professional culture of the class, defined by educational capital, that appropriates them symbolically. Some museums privilege the mode of appropriation defined by economic class, the domestic learning systematized as connoisseurship, offering up for emulation a manner of *being* in relation to art objects: how and how long one looks, the accents in which one pronounces the names of artists and works, posture and expression. Some museums privilege the scholastic learning defined by educational capital: ways of *knowing* about art objects which may change according to developments in contemporary art and art history as well as other academic disciplines. The relationship between these two modes of appropriation is always antagonistic.

The struggle between domestic and scholastic relations to culture and the modes of appropriation they privilege is continuously waged in art museums in the United States. It's played out between the voluntary sector of a museum (its patrons and board of trustees) and its professional staff. Although the former group is clearly the locus of economic power in museums, I would say that it is the struggle between these two sectors that constitutes the museum's discourse, the conditions of its reproduction, and the mechanism of its power. This is not only because professionals, in a competition to impose their mode of appropriation, take bourgeois domestic culture as their stake, investing in this "privileged cultural capital," and thereby increase its value. It is because this competition constitutes the discourse of museums as a discourse of affirmation and negation, putting the culture it presents into play within a system of differentiated consumption that represents and objectifies the class hierarchies on which it's based.

Tastes, Pierre Bourdieu writes, "are the practical affirmation of an inevitable difference . . . when they have to be justified, they are asserted purely negatively, by the refusal of other tastes. In manners of taste, more than anywhere else, all determination is negation."[4]

In a videotape called *Masterpieces of the Met,* Philippe de Montebello, the director of the Metropolitan Museum of Art, guides us through an encounter with art.

> We tend to enter a gallery like this and exclaim, "Here are the Rembrandts," as the mindset of admiration clicks on. But are we really liking what we see? Sure, the pictures have a Rembrandtesque look. They are dark and brownish and the faces are dramatically lit. So we exclaim, "Here are the Rembrandts." But we must go beyond this factor of recognition to really savor them.
>
> [This] self-portrait . . . is a picture that for a long time I only glanced at in passing. After all, it's not a curtain raiser. One day, I don't remember when, I sat in the gallery bench in this room and absently let my eyes rest on this particular portrait. I think I must have sat here for a full ten or fifteen minutes, which is a long time, you know. I couldn't leave.
>
> Please look straight into his eyes. Don't waver, if you please. I was hypnotized. This is a picture that compels us to attend to its silence and since I am now speaking to you I recognize that I may well be breaking its spell. But try to experience it on your own. You may find, as I did, that for a brief moment, Rembrandt intrudes into your life. . . . Out of oil on canvas he proclaims . . . "You, whoever you are, look into my eyes." And what causes our chest to constrict is that we are acutely aware that our reality, our existence will pass while his will survive for as long as the picture is preserved. It's hard to pinpoint to what all of this is due, but it has much to do with the fact that Rembrandt was not an ordinary man. . . . It is a lifetime of experience and changing expressions that have shaped and molded that . . . face. . . . Although comparatively speaking, one could show all the ties that this picture has to the northern baroque, it is hard to speak of style here. Perhaps Rembrandt's ultimate triumph of style is that he seems to have none.[5]

It's relatively easy to interpret this description as a manifestation of a struggle between "domestic" and "scholastic" relations to culture. Philippe de Montebello exemplifies an effortlessly elegant relationship to cultural objects; those capacities produced of longer and more sustained looking that transcend superficial attribution of "style," much less the vulgar recognition of "a curtain raiser."

But it's not these capacities that he is teaching. Because these capacities are the status-derived product of a "lifetime of experience" of "familiar family property," as Bourdieu has written, of "the precocious acquisition of legitimate culture . . . acquired in the course of time, by means of time, against time, that is, by inheritance," they are, strictly speaking, not transferable.[6] Even by speaking of it, he "may be breaking its spell."

What he is teaching is something else. He is guiding us, through the discourse of museums, to the individuals to whom we should apply to represent the museum's objects: those who are represented by them, as their exclusively legitimate spokesmen, who will call on us, as they call, "You, whoever you are, look into my eyes."

The imperative of identification with *these* spokesmen is established in the foreclosure of other identifications. De Montebello's rejection of the legitimacy of those other spokesmen—the representatives of the scholastic relation to culture—is purely rhetorical. His speech, after all, is not addressed to them. If it were, they could easily respond. His speech, rather, is addressed to the museum's public. And in it, it is they who must stand as the potential proxies for the phantom others of dismissed dispositions.

The stakes in the struggle between domestic and scholastic relations to culture as it's played out in art institutions are not really art objects or even the dispositions they objectify, but are, rather, the museum's public. It's the recognition by this public that will establish the primacy of those dispositions, and their subjects, as that to which this public should aspire.

As an artist I may be situated on one side or the other of this struggle, depending on the mode of appropriation demanded by the objects and discourse I produce, and according to where I position myself within an institution.

My rejection of the museum's patron class and the familiar, familial relation to culture that it privileges is expressed in my use of Philippe de Montebello's speech. Providing interpretations of such speech is what I do as a practitioner of institutional critique. In the past, when I conducted gallery-talk performances based on such interpretations, the museum's professional staff tended to identify with me in this rejection, against the museum's voluntary sector—its patrons and trustees, but also the volunteer museum guides whose function I took up. It was really this latter group that they tended to see as the object of my rejection, and rightly so, as that was the position that I put to use.

What was being rejected in this constellation, however, was actually the museum's public. Museum guides represent the most extreme form of an attempt to satisfy the contradictory and impossible demands the museum addresses to that public. In the United States, museum guides usually have no formal art-historical training. They are trained only by the museum's professional staff and thus acquire a certain quantity of knowledge about art objects. But this knowledge, as it's usually limited to the particular museum's collection, leaves the museum guide entirely dependent on its particular source and without the means to generate a legitimate opinion independently of the institution. In the United States, museum guides are almost always volunteers. As such, their position is defined by an identification with the philanthropy of the board of trustees. They invest their bodies and time in an identification with the status of the high-level patron, but for lack of economic and familial cultural capital, they continuously and necessarily fall short.

Museum guides are the embodiment of the domination museums effect. Again, to quote Bourdieu, "the imposition of legitimacy which occurs through competitive struggle and is enhanced by the gentle violence of cultural missionary work tends to produce pretension, in the sense of a need which pre-exists the means of adequately satisfying."[7] It leaves the museum guide victim to what Bourdieu calls "cultural allodoxia, that is, all the mistaken identifications and false recognitions which betray the gap between acknowledgment and knowledge . . . the heterodoxy experienced as if it were orthodoxy . . . engendered by . . . undifferentiated reverence, in which avidity combines with anxiety."[8]

This is why I stopped conducting gallery-talk performances—or at least posing as a museum guide in doing so. While I have the basis for identifying with museum guides—being a woman, an autodidact, and someone short on economic and objectified familial cultural capital—such an identification remains a misidentification, and a displacement of my status within art institutions. And, like all such displacements, its function is to obscure the relations of domination of which museums are the sites and which its recognized agents produce and reproduce.

Now I perform as an artist.

As an artist, I may try to situate myself outside of the struggle between domestic and scholastic relations to culture, rejecting both rejections that constitute the dynamics of art institutions, perhaps refusing, as I refuse, to produce objects for them; perhaps attempting to position myself more directly in relation to their real stake: the museum's public, or at least those not already disposed to the culture that I produce and that museums present.

I may try to produce other forms of culture: popular culture (as it's usually understood as the products of mass-culture industries), or the domestic culture of individuals within other communities, or the common culture of those communities.

In the United States, the first art museums were founded quite explicitly within a struggle to establish a cultural orthodoxy against developing forms of mass popular culture and against the reproduction of the domestic and common culture of immigrant communities. In the early publications of the Philadelphia Museum of Art, for example, jazz, burlesque, comic books, and pulp fiction are identified as the threats against which the museum must protect the city's citizens. The Philadelphia Museum of Art held classes and exhibitions on "Americanization through art" while the founders of the Metropolitan Museum of Art were engaged in direct confrontation with New York's Tammany Hall, whose power was based in immigrant constituencies.

Museums and the mass popular culture industry developed contemporaneously as two spheres of specialized culture to be offered up for appropriation as domestic and common culture. In the competition between them, museums, by and large, lost out.

For the most part, museums and their patrons are no longer in an antagonistic relationship to mass popular culture. They now exist alongside it, dividing it up into new hierarchies capable of creating and representing new as well as old privileges, introducing into it exclusive modes of appropriation, and taking from it new material to be put into play in struggles for distinction.

The power of the economic and cultural capital embodied in museums is represented, above all, by its ability to appropriate objects produced outside its sphere. There it gains autonomy, universalizes itself, asserts its authority beyond itself across the cultural field much more effectively than in competitive struggles over cultural orthodoxy in which the subjects of that power must recognize a stake in common with their adversary. In such appropriation its subjects become the agents and masters of culture as such and not just the new owners of a particular, if privileged, cultural production.

My power, as an artist or would-be intellectual, to appropriate objects, texts, representations, and practices symbolically—conferring value and interest where before there was none—is always linked to the economic power to appropriate them materially. I am the intermediary. The link between these forms of power does not depend on whether or not I offer my products up for material appropriation. It derives rather from homologies between monopolies of economic capital and those of cultural capital, which accords me the exclusive prerogative of a producer of culture by defining those outside my field as nonproducers.

The appropriation of mass popular culture has become less profitable, in symbolic terms, in the past few years as the increasing incorporation of its forms within art and academic discourse has led to an individualization of its authors and the recognition that they, too, are Cultural Producers. Appropriation becomes competition, and now, like Jeff Koons, I am liable to be sued.

Abandoning popular culture I may, instead, like some of my other colleagues, offer up for bourgeois consumption forms derived from domestic and common culture of nonspecialized production—my own from an earlier age or that of others, defined by ethnicity and geographical location as well as economic class.

If this apparent affirmation of the culture of others and the fact that high culture, too, is the material culture of everyday lives is turned into dispossession as it's returned back to those others, professionalized and rarefied in museums, I may again attempt to situate myself outside. I may exit those institutions and produce public art, that is, art presented in public space other than that of public art institutions.

Most public art carries with it, outside of art institutions, a demand for an aesthetic disposition and aesthetic competence that has been defined within them; demands, for example, for an attention to form—when there is nothing else, or when the formal organization of the work takes precedence over, or is autonomous from, the themes it apparently seeks to engage; or demands for familiarity with a field of artistic or academic reference that constitutes the condition of the work's legibility as a text or as an object of value justifying the prestige of its placement.

I refer my viewers back to the museum.

Public art imposes itself on a public to a greater extent than art presented in public institutions. Whereas museum visitors enter the institution voluntarily—if seduced by the promise of beauty and betterment—the audience of public art is a captive audience. To the extent that the spaces in which works are situated must be used, their audience cannot choose to enter into a relationship with them. Public art thus imposes aesthetic competencies as a condition, not just for self-education or social advancement, but of living in a city, of using its parks and streets.

Beyond these demands there may be other demands. I may, for example, identify with this public. I may attempt to articulate the interests of the pedestrians in the plazas or the workers in the buildings that surround them, for them, to them, in a critical engagement with the social as well as aesthetic conditions of the organization of public space.

In public space, the social character of the negations and rejections implicit in the autonomy of artistic forms of critical engagement may be remembered by its public when they have been forgotten by the artist. As with Richard Serra's *Tilted Arc,* behind the avowed critique of the rhetoric of monuments and the organization of public space deployed in the name of its users is an implicit critique of those users, *as users,* in the formal autonomy of the work, which developed historically as a rejection of the heteronomous function of popular as well as bourgeois realism. While that rejection has lost its force within the discourse of art over the developments of a hundred years, displaced onto public space it retains its power still. The work's public may recognize itself as the real object of a critical discourse that radically excludes it.

To the extent that art situated in public space continues to function in an art context as well, where it is described and documented, the evocation of an other audience within it may be appropriated, just as other cultural objects, representations, and practices may be appropriated in a work. "They"—the other public, the noninterested, the nonprofessional—become an object and a stake in a struggle among professionals.

Finally, with all these displacements closed to me, instead of producing bourgeois domestic culture I may opt to produce intellectual culture.

Incorporating academic discourse with an aim to produce an artwork as a theoretical text, whether this text is purely linguistic or presented in the form of a rebus to be decoded (I won't say, as I don't believe, "produced") by the viewer, I produce a work that demands a double competence in the perception of aesthetic form and a knowledge of, or mastery of, the field of discourse out of which the text is constituted. The work is thus doubly alienating, doubly exclusive.

This, again, can only be situated within a struggle for legitimacy within the artistic field in which an appropriation of academic expertise functions to produce an additional distinction. Such appropriation must be seen as the result of a partial rejection of specifically aesthetic criteria and the institutions that privilege them, without recognizing that, in social terms, these institutions are strictly homologous to those of academia.

Every demand for a particular competence addressed to a viewer, reader, or listener is also a more or less displaced demand that the addressee recognize the producer as being in possession of precisely that competence. In my attempts at intellectual production, this demand for recognition is addressed to the holders of academic titles.

This addressee is immanent in what I present, offer up, for recognition, and constitutes the real, present viewer, listener, reader as such. The difference between the real, present addressee and the addressee contained in the statement is more or less alienating depending on the social conditions of legitimacy of the latter.

What makes you the other to whom I would address a demand for recognition?

If you don't experience yourself as being in possession of the particular authority for which I ask, then my demand for recognition turns into a demand simply that you have it, or rather, have the competence that defines it.

Here in this context, as in any other context, I make certain assumptions about who you are, but those assumptions will only ever be my fantasy.

To say that they are a fantasy is not to say that I only imagine them. Because they are determined by the professional and institutional norms of the context that constitutes their *scene,* I don't have to imagine them at all. They are articulated for me—here for example, in the statements of the organizers or in the list of the other participants. To say that they are a fantasy is rather to say that in them—in you—I have invested my aspirations. And this context becomes the potential scene of their accomplishment.

It's a fantasy that drives me to try to make my arguments ever more complex, as what I have to say is certainly too simplistic. Too simplistic for whom? Not for myself, as is evident in my difficulty in thinking these things through, but for whomever I suppose you to be.

The text I am presently reading demands knowledge of my field of intellectual and artistic reference. In presenting it, I ask for recognition of my intellectual competence. As it is written in the first person, it contains a partial rejection of academic speech. But as a theoretical text, it also contains a much more complete rejection of my prerogative as an artist to simply present my work.

I ask for these things. Perhaps I cannot do otherwise if, as Lacan would have it, such demands are a condition of speech, and the aspirations produced within them are a condition of subjectivity. But those demands are historically determined and institutionally organized to particular social use. They reproduce themselves in aspirations that one is always already failing.

No one asks according to their interests.

What I want are other things. Their object is elsewhere: in my history, in the material conditions that determine my social experience. But those objects are foreclosed in the competitive, symbolic struggles that constitute the cultural field.

The stakes of those struggles are not what I want. But I invest in them anyway because, in the absence of another object, they are offered to me by the institutions I accept as the sphere of my activity.

And I ask you for these things. In so doing I become the agent of the reproduction of this institution—and the negations and exclusions through which it imposes relations of domination—by forcing you to aspire to the competencies it/I demand(s). Adequacy becomes the condition of listening. There are no other positions provided for.

Yet other positions are possible. There are other struggles not subsumed in such individualized and individualizing symbolic struggles for legitimacy. There are collective symbolic struggles, and there are collective and perhaps individual material struggles.

Arguments that there is no outside of institutions are often alibis for cynicism. However, the topography of inside and outside very often also functions as an alibi for not recognizing one's position within the extended cultural field in which those institutions are situated and the relations of power and privilege by which that field is constructed. Those relations traverse the topography of inside and outside and put it to precise use, the boundaries of the field and its institutions being one of the primary objects of struggles within them.

The transformation of those relations will not be accomplished by displacement. The mis- and dis-identifications of partial exits and entrances, the appropriation of objects, texts, practices constructed as other or outside, the changing of location, or the exchanging of criteria of one institution for another; such strategies may transform the "nature" of conditions, but they will only reproduce the structure of positions.

Notes

1. Sigmund Freud, "The Dynamics of the Transference," in *Therapy and Technique,* ed. Philip Rieff (New York: Collier Books, 1963), 115.

2. Jaques Lacan, "The Direction of the Treatment and the Principles of Its Power," in *Écrits,* trans. Alan Sheridan (New York: Norton, 1977), 236.

3. Pierre Bourdieu, *Distinction: A Social Critique of the Judgment of Taste,* trans. Richard Nice (Cambridge: Harvard University Press, 1984), 3.

4. Ibid., 56.

5. The Metropolitan Museum of Art, *Masterpieces of the Met,* hosted by Philippe de Montebello, directed by John Goberman and Marc Bauman (New York: Office of Film and Television at the Metropolitan Museum of Art, 1988).

6. Bourdieu, *Distinction,* 70–71.

7. Ibid., 163.

8. Ibid., 323.

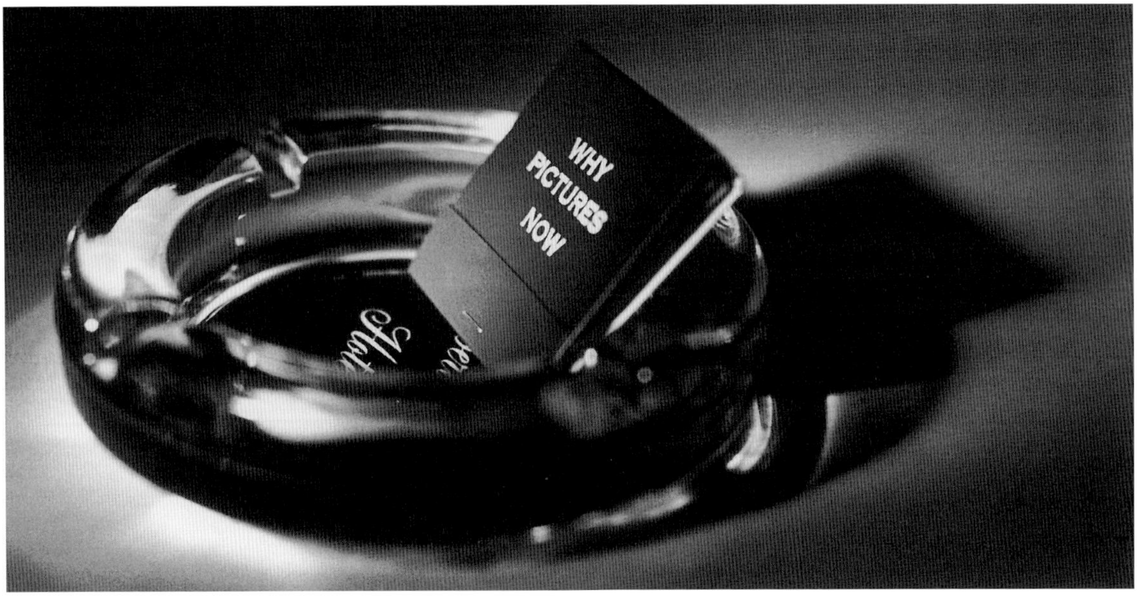

2.1 Louise Lawler, *Why Pictures Now?*, 1981. Black-and-white photograph, 3 × 6 in. Courtesy the artist and Metro Pictures Gallery.

2

IN AND OUT OF PLACE

"In and Out of Place" was first published in the June 1985 issue of Art in America.

In 1980 Louise Lawler asked three art critics to collaborate with her on the production of a matchbook by submitting short texts to be printed on its cover. The critics—all of whom are involved in critical analysis not simply of works of art, but of the institutional apparatus in which they circulate—apparently thought matchbooks too vulgar a format for their texts. Perhaps resisting the impropriety of being presented by rather than presenting the artist, they opted to preserve their proper place of publication, their proper function. Consequently, this particular matchbook was never realized.

Produced for specific contexts, distributed in galleries and at cultural events, Lawler's matchbooks do not remain in their place of origin but are continually placed, replaced, displaced. While only one aspect of her practice, they are characteristic of much of her work. For Lawler consistently challenges the proprieties both of place (the divisions of art world labor that assign artists, dealers, and critics proper places and functions) and of objects (the ideological mechanisms which establish the authorship and ownership of art). Although she frequently collaborates with other artists, for Lawler, artistic production is always a collective endeavor. It isn't simply artists who produce aesthetic signification and value, but an often anonymous contingent of collectors, viewers, museum and gallery workers—and ultimately the cultural apparatus in which these positions are delineated.

I will generalize and say that Lawler operates primarily from three different yet interdependent positions within this apparatus: that of an artist who exhibits in galleries and museums; that of a publicist/museum-worker who produces the kind of material that usually supplements cultural objects and events; and that of an art consultant/curator who arranges works by other artists (for example, her 1984 show at the Wadsworth Atheneum's Matrix Gallery in Hartford, "A Selection of Objects from the Collections of the Wadsworth Atheneum, Sol LeWitt and Louise Lawler").

For an artist to write reviews, curate exhibitions, or run a gallery is a contemporary art-world commonplace. But these occupations are usually regarded as secondary; the artist is identified primarily as a producer of a body of works, which other activities only supplement. By abdicating this privileged place of artistic identity, Lawler manages to escape institutional definitions of artistic activity as an autonomous aesthetic exploration. Her objective is not so much to uncover hidden ideological agendas, but to disrupt the institutional boundaries that determine and separate the discrete identities of artist and artwork from an apparatus that supposedly merely supplements them.

Lawler transforms the seemingly irrelevant plethora of supplements—captions that name, proper names that identify, invitations that advertise (to a select community), installation photos that document, catalogues that historicize, "arrangements" that position, critical texts that function in most of these capacities—into the objects of an art practice. Her use of these formats constitutes a double displacement: she brings the often invisible, marginal supports of art into the gallery and situates her own practice at the margins, in the production, elaboration, and critique of the frame.

Engagement with the institutional determination and acculturation of art can be traced back to the historical avant-gardes—Duchamp, Dada, and surrealism on one hand, the Soviet avant-garde on the other. Lawler's work has a more immediate relationship, however, with the post-studio practices of the 1970s, particularly the work of Michael Asher, Marcel Broodthaers, Daniel Buren, and Hans Haacke. While their work differs greatly, all these artists engage(d) in institutional critique, ranging from Asher's and Buren's situational constructions (or deconstructions) of architectural frameworks in galleries and museums, to Broodthaers's directorship of a fictional museum, to Haacke's documentation of high art's corporate affiliations.

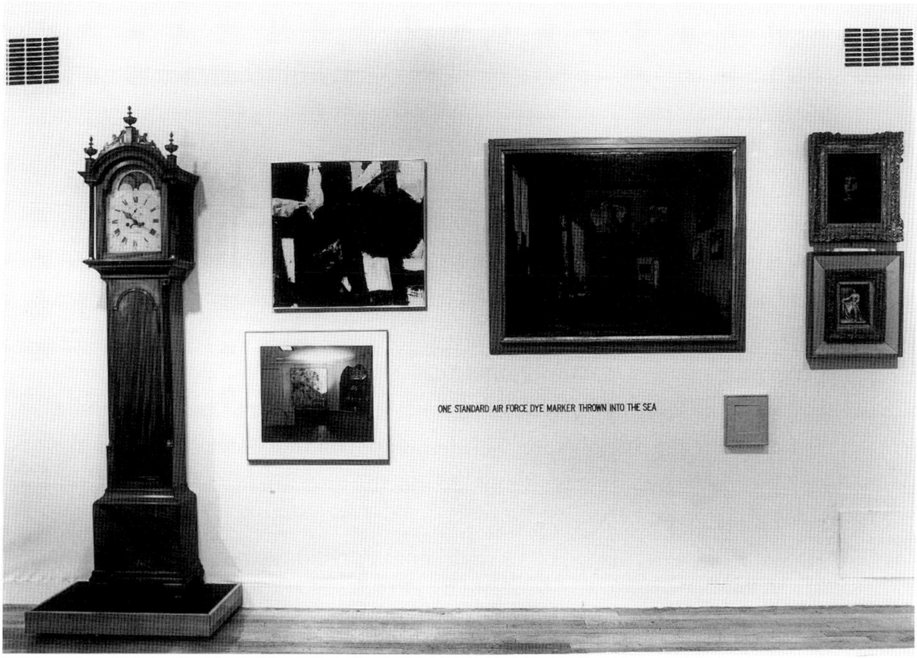

2.2 Louise Lawler, *From the Collections of the Wadsworth Atheneum, Sol LeWitt and Louise Lawler, Arranged by Louise Lawler,* 1984. Installation at the Wadsworth Atheneum. Photo: Louise Lawler. The wall label that accompanying Lawler's installation included the following text in red type:

From the Collections of the Wadsworth Atheneum, Sol LeWitt and Louise Lawler, Arranged by Louise Lawler, 1984

The museum encloses objects selected by a cumulative culture for presentation and display. They are acquired by purchases made by curators and committees or as accepted donations of single objects or collections.

This arrangement of works from the collections of the Wadsworth Atheneum, Sol LeWitt, and Louise Lawler disregards many of the conventions of museum exhibition. It is not restricted to like categories such as material, era, geographical origin, or the work of a single artist.

These objects have been arranged with considerations that might be used in a home, with special attention to the outside dimensions and aesthetic effect of the work as well as the content. Little effort has been made to make their original meaning accessible. There are no identifying labels except this one. This installation does not foster connoisseurship or the kind of understanding a more homogeneous exhibition would have provided. Also, these idiosyncratic choices were made to represent the museum and its diverse holdings. They have been extracted from their locations in the museum (as they had been previously dislocated from the original contexts for which they had been made), in order to be relocated in this matrix.

The collection of Sol LeWitt is a unique assemblage of the work of his contemporaries. The Atheneum was fortunate to receive this donation of art works that often denied or questioned the notion of art as commodity and therefore is not well represented in most museum collections. Work from the collection of Louise Lawler may or may not have entered a museum, but is here because this presentation is the work of the artist.

But Lawler can also be differentiated from these artists, for rather than situating institutional power in a centralized building (such as a museum) or in a powerful elite that can be named, she locates it instead in a systematized set of presentational procedures that name, situate, centralize. Unlike Asher's constructions of exhibition spaces within exhibition spaces, which critically contemplate the frame but continue to function within it as sculpture, Lawler's work is often conceived as a functional insert into a network of supports that is exterior to the gallery.[1] Unlike Broodthaers, Lawler doesn't occupy even fictional positions of institutional authority, but works instead to dissipate all such concentrations of power. Unlike Haacke's, Lawler's relationship with corporate and market structures is one of ironic collaboration, simultaneously revealing the place of high art in a market economy *and* moving toward a repositioning of the artist within it.

In both her early installations and her later "arrangements" of pictures, Lawler selects and presents work by other artists as well as her own. Her main contribution to a 1978 group show at Artists Space was the installation of a painting of a racehorse borrowed from the New York Racing Association. Placed high on windows in a wall dividing two galleries, the painting was flanked by two theatrical spotlights directed not at the painting but at the viewer, thereby interfering with the painting's visibility and, at night, projecting viewers' shadows onto the facade of the Citibank across the street (a Buren-like strategy of connecting the inside and outside of an exhibition space).

While her Artists Space installation is in many ways reminiscent of post-studio meditations on institutional context, on this occasion Lawler also dealt more productively with the frame, presenting the gallery rather than being passively presented by it. Instead of supplying the catalogue with the customary reproductions of her work, she designed an Artists Space logo, which was printed on the catalogue's cover and also distributed as a poster around lower Manhattan.

Two subsequent shows in Los Angeles accomplished a similar reversal of presentational positions. For a 1979 nine-person show in a loft in an abandoned department store, Lawler did another installation employing theatrical lights, again not directed at a picture—in this case, one she had painted of the exhibition's invitation, a gray, hard-edge Roman numeral nine in the New York School masking-tape tradition. Blue and pink gels and a tree-branch silhouette template on the lights emphasized the theatricality of the presentation. (Lawler used a similar lighting scheme in a 1984 show at the Diane Brown Gallery in New York,

"For Presentation and Display: Ideal Settings," done in collaboration with Allan McCollum. Bathing one hundred Hydrocal sculpture-bases in the idyllic atmosphere of corporate never-never land, the subdued but dramatic lighting indexed the commodity showcase.)

In her 1981 one-woman, one-evening show in Los Angeles, "Louise Lawler—Jancar/Kuhlenschmit, Jancar Kuhlenschmit Gallery," Lawler presented the gallery more explicitly, spelling out its name on the wall in individual postcard-size photographs of dramatically lit three-dimensional letters. She also directed the dealers to stand behind the reception desk (since they could not sit down in the tiny office) and show interested visitors other Lawler photographs contained in a small black box.

Lawler's literalization and reversal of presentational positions was also apparent in the first room of her 1982 exhibition at Metro Pictures in New York, where she presented an "arrangement" of works by gallery artists (Sherman, Simmons, Welling, Goldstein, Longo). (See figure 6.3, page 72.) Despite its somewhat unconventional hanging, Lawler's "arrangement" might have been mistaken for another anonymous group show of the Metro stable. But upon realizing (or remembering) that this was a "one-woman" show, viewers were confronted with an ambiguity of occupation, a shift in position that illuminated the role of the often unnamed "arrangers" in the exhibition and exchange of art. (Photographs documenting the "arrangement" of art in museums, homes, and offices were exhibited in the gallery's main space.) Lawler's "arrangement" also ironically revealed the economic subtext of the Metro artists' aesthetic of appropriation: her "arrangement" was for sale at the combined price of all the individual works plus 10 percent for Lawler (the fee customarily charged by art consultants).

Because it continues to function within a traditional gallery context, the reversal Lawler's installations enact is primarily symbolic: the artist-institution relationship is contemplated and questioned, but remains intact. However, her matchbooks and invitations (like her Artists Space poster and catalogue cover) come closer to subverting mechanisms of institutional presentation and to constituting a counterpractice. Inasmuch as they do not depend upon an exhibition for distribution and do not even claim the status of art objects, in these works Lawler manages to resist the tendency of many contemporary artists to parody or criticize but nevertheless conform to the traditional position of artists in exchange relations.

One of Lawler's matchbooks was inspired by the media hype surrounding a 1982 lecture by Julian Schnabel in Los Angeles. Taking the position of "publicist," unbeknownst to the lecture's sponsors, Lawler printed matchbooks with the event's title and distributed them at the auditorium. Using a publicity tool against itself, she encapsulated the exaggerated spectacle of "An Evening with Julian Schnabel" in a disposable souvenir.

For the 1983 "Borrowed Time" exhibition, a group show at Baskerville + Watson in New York, Lawler produced a matchbook advertising the show with a quotation that emphasizes the relation of aesthetic to economic value: "Every time I hear the word culture I take out my checkbook.—Jack Palance."[2] The immediate effect of such matchbooks is one of vulgarization: by employing a format usually used to promote restaurants and driving schools, Lawler amplifies polite art-market mechanisms into travesties of consumer culture.

Unlike matchbooks, which Lawler makes available to a general audience, invitations are distributed on the basis of mailing lists that consolidate a small art audience into an even smaller circle of cultural initiates for whose patronage a specific desire is expressed. The series of invitations to private, "salon-type" exhibitions that Lawler organized with Sherrie Levine under the title *A Picture Is No Substitute for Anything* (1981–82) called attention to this function, as did the 1981 event *Louise Lawler and Sherrie Levine Invite You to the Studio of Dimitri Merinoff . . .*" (a Russian émigré figurative expressionist whose New York studio had been kept intact since his death). At times, however, Lawler displaces the kind of privileged reception that such private events imply; for example, in her invitation to a performance of *Swan Lake* by the New York City Ballet, the "readymade" spectacle Lawler appropriated remained a thoroughly public event. (In the lower right-hand corner, where one would expect to read "RSVP," Lawler specified instead "Tickets to be purchased at the box office.")

Excerpts from a Letter to the Participating Artists by the Director of Documenta 7, R. H. Fuchs, Edited and Published by Louise Lawler (1982) situated the artist as invitee rather than inviter. Not invited to participate in Documenta VII, Lawler reprinted the inflated, romantic, heroicizing rhetoric of the curator's letter to invited artists as tiny raised green type at the top of two sheets of stationery and an envelope, sold at Fashion Moda's art stand outside the galleries at Kassel. In Lawler's ironic commodification, the curatorial address was displaced (literally) to the margins, where it became little more than an institutional letterhead, an authorizing corporate-like logo disguised as aesthetic rhetoric.

If Lawler's Documenta stationery reduces high-art discourse to a supplement of institutions and the market, her gift certificate for the Leo Castelli Gallery, "authorized" and exhibited there in a 1983 group show, reduces the artwork itself to a similar status. Although it was printed in a limited edition (of 500), the certificate's value isn't contingent upon its singularity (or lack thereof) or the presence of the artist's signature, but on the amount for which it is purchased and for which it could be used toward the purchase of a Warhol or a Rauschenberg. As Jean Baudrillard formulates in "The Art Auction," the value of an art object is produced not by the artist but by the collector in his or her "sumptuary expenditure" or "economic sacrifice" for art. "Good investment" and "love of art" engage in mutual rationalization: wealth is legitimized in its dissipation for the sake of aesthetic quality, while economic sacrifice pays homage to the transcendental value of high art.[3]

The collection and presentation of art has always been a display of social and economic standing before being an exhibition of aesthetic value. Lawler's photographs documenting "arrangements of pictures" in private, corporate, and museum collections demonstrate the social uses to which art is put after it leaves the artist's studio. These "installation" photographs have been exhibited in galleries and museums, where the documentation of art objects is substituted for the objects themselves; they have also been published, both as independent photo-features and as subtly sardonic illustrations for critical texts.[4]

In Lawler's photographs of private collections, art is represented as simply one object among many in a chaos of accumulation; in the domestic interior, art—whether "tastefully" arranged or indifferently juxtaposed—is assimilated into a backdrop of decorative commodities. *Arranged by Mr. and Mrs. Burton Tremaine, New York, 1984* is more than a picture of a picture hanging over the couch: Lawler includes the television set in front of a Robert Delaunay, next to a Lichtenstein sculpture head looking like a lamp base on the coffee table. And in *Pollock and Tureen,* also 1984, the artist's last painting (or at least its bottom edge—which is all Lawler photographed) is little more than apocalyptic wallpaper behind an antique china dish.

Lawler's photographs of corporate collections document how art is used to express relative position in the corporate hierarchy: if large paintings and sculpture in the reception area establish a corporation's desired public image, in *Arranged by Donald Marron, Susan Brundage, Cheryl Bishop at Paine Webber, Inc.,* two Lichtenstein silk-screens establish the position of office workers (who are quite oblivious to the presence of "art"). As the black uniformed guard in *Longo, Stella, Hunt at Paine Webber Mitchell Hutchins* somehow seems part of the corporate collection, so the artists' names in the title mimic the name of the Wall Street brokerage firm.

Even after art objects are withdrawn from exchange, the legacy of privileged expenditure is never severed from their pedigree.[5] In museums, the labels that supplement every object always begin with the artist's name and end by citing its previous owner; in establishing art's value, these two genealogies are inseparable. Such informational labels are often the subject of Lawler's "Arrangements of Pictures" in museum collections, raising the question of whether institutional authority and an exclusive caste of collectors aren't actually the primary exhibits.

Establishing authorship, ownership, pedigree, and, ultimately, value, such museum labels are the most conspicuous instance of the institutional exhibition of proper names. Yet even in these titles there is an ambiguity: Is the object "proper" to the artist or the collector? In the captions for her own photographs, Lawler extends this ambiguous poly-ownership to include an indefinite list of curators, art consultants, museum and office workers, etc. At the same time, she often withdraws or displaces her own name: for example, in a 1980 group show at Castelli Graphics, in which, as usual, artists' names were Lettraset on the wall next to their works, Lawler's own photograph of a text by another author was accompanied by the attribution "anonymous."

Lawler's work often involves an interference with the proper name. In her *Patriarchal Roll Call,* for example, she plays with artists' names, turning them into birdcalls. Recorded in 1983, Lawler's birdcalls are based only on *male* artists' names, calling attention to the fact that the proper name is always a patronymic (the name of the father); they also parody the viewer's desire to recognize, in a work of art, not a gesture or a style but the name "itself," here disguised as a call of the wild.

Signifying the essential yet imaginary identity of a unified ego, the proper name establishes the subject as such, in language, under the law. Through the proper name, individuals are inscribed within power relations and come to identify with and be identified by positions therein. The conventional organization of art practices around a signature—everything that allows a work of art to be identified as a "Pollock" or a "Warhol"—institutes the proper name as interior to the art object; thus, artists are locked in a structure of institutionalized subjectivity. And the institutional exhibition of proper names, designating the authors and owners of objects, defines that subjectivity in terms of consumption and ownership.

Because Lawler's work isn't reducible to a single theme, mode of production, or place of functioning, it often seems anonymous, or at least difficult to identify without a caption. Her January 1985 slide show at Metro Pictures—*Slides by Night: Now That We Have Your Attention What Are We Going to Say?*—confronted the institutionally organized desire to recognize a unified subject in an artist's work. It also addressed the demands placed on production by the gallery's new space. Rather than exhibiting prints of her "Arrangements of Pictures" (as in her previous show at Metro), Lawler supplied the walls with the enormous images the gallery's vast space seems to require—but immaterial ones: slides projected on the gallery's back wall and visible only after gallery hours from the street.

The program began with slot-machine signs—plums, oranges, cherries, apples, baseballs, and bells—in random combinations of three until . . . jackpot! The "payoffs" were pictures from a plaster-cast museum, copies of classical sculpture in various states of storage, decomposition, restoration (*Augustus of Prima Porta* in a plastic bag). These images faded into one another in slow dissolves, finally giving way to another random exchange of one-arm-bandit signs and another jackpot—this time Lawler's own images of "Arrangements of Pictures" in homes, museums, and corporate offices.

Thus, Lawler included her own production within the same structure of indifferent accumulation that her "Arrangements of Pictures" document, perhaps in order to refuse the audience what it is looking for in an artist's work: a lasting identity which seems to transcend (but which is actually constructed by) the arbitrary exchange and circulation of aesthetic signs. The fact that Lawler included her own work does not mean that she has finally acquiesced to the market or passively accepted its mechanisms (and her own place within them). By representing her own photographs in slide form, she symbolically withdraws them from market exchange. Once again, her position is double: that of a producer of images, and that of one who actively organizes not simply their presentation, but perhaps a new chain, a counterdiscourse in which they are only elements.

I began this essay with Lawler's unrealized "critical" matchbook in order to introduce, at the start, a certain self-consciousness about my own critical project of presenting the work of an artist who engages in a critique of institutional presentation. Lawler's practice implicates art criticism as well, especially monographic art criticism, which often functions retroactively to inscribe unruly

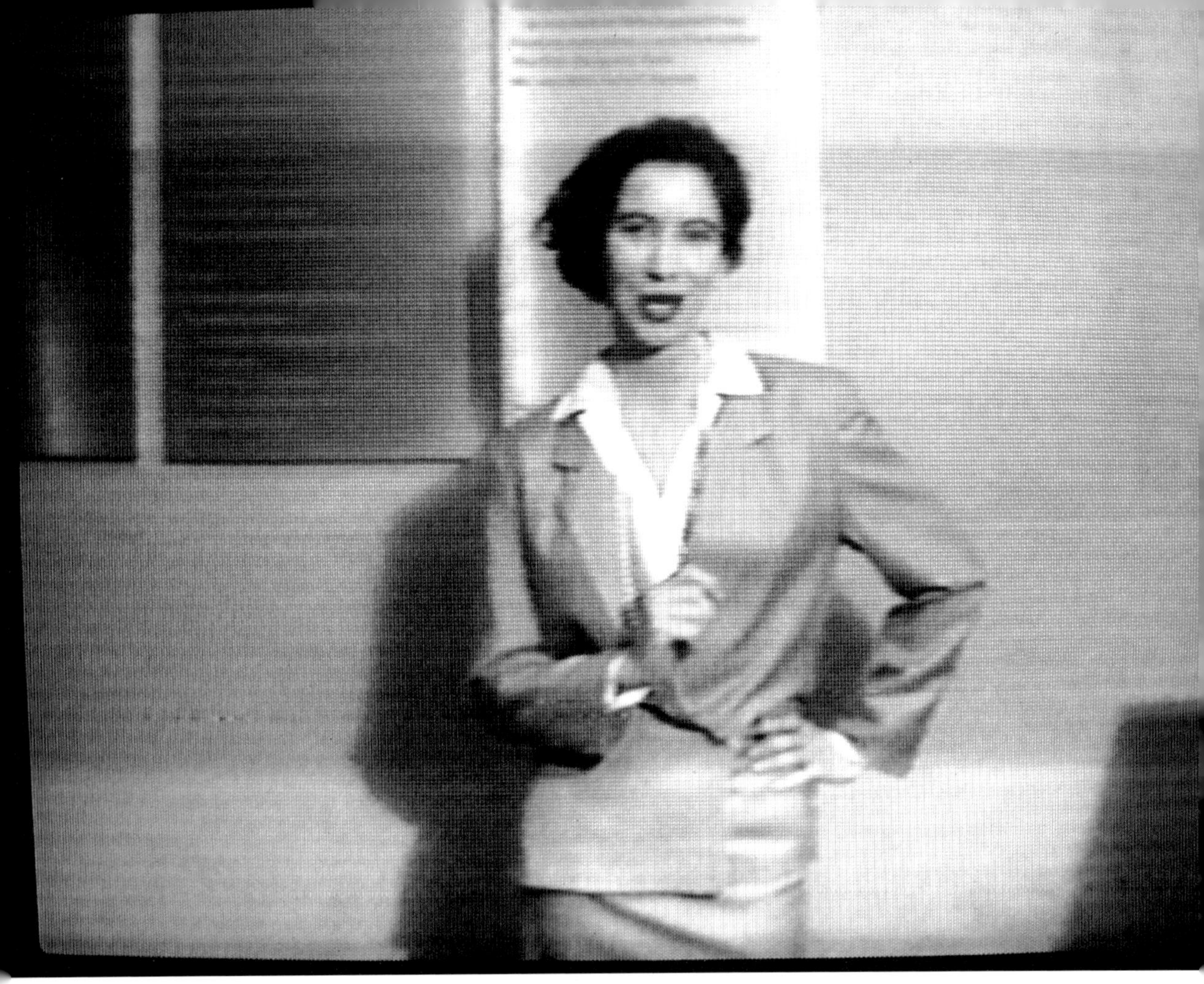

2.3 Andrea Fraser and Louise Lawler, still from *The Public Life of Art: The Museum*, 1988. Videotape recorded at the Museum of Modern Art and the Metropolitan Museum of Art, New York. Written and performed by Andrea Fraser, production design by Louise Lawler, produced by Terry McCoy. Photo: Andrea Fraser.

objects within an institutionally acceptable position, to recover from a heterogeneous practice a unified ego: the subject of a signature.

However, Lawler's work suggests a strategy of resistance, of functioning differently within an institution that reduces difference to a sign, ripe for consumption. As long as artists continue to subscribe to traditional modes of production and places of functioning—whether or not they engage in critique, appropriation, or the uncovering of hidden agendas—aesthetic signification will continue to be locked in an order of institutionalized subjectivity and legitimizing consumption. If Lawler manages to escape both marginalization and incorporation, it is because, whatever position she may happen to occupy, she is always also somewhere/something else.

Notes

1. This remark applies primarily to Asher's work of the 1970s, documented in *Michael Asher, Writings, 1973–1983 on Works 1969–1979* (Halifax: Press of the Nova Scotia College of Art and Design, 1983). His more recent production, like Lawler's, treats the institution as a set of social relations (a notion that is only implicit in his earlier work) rather than as architecture. This shift may be a response to the expansion of the information industry and the service sector of the economy, which has resulted in a further ideological effacement of productive labor. If symbolic intervention in the conditions of material production is characteristic of modernist art, Lawler and Asher engage with the institutional services and informational mechanisms which position and define cultural production.

2. This statement originates with Nazi propagandist Joseph Goebbels, who said, "Every time I hear the word 'culture' I reach for my revolver." Palance read the line, rewritten by Jean Godard, in the film *Contempt.*

3. Jean Baudrillard, "The Art Auction," in *For a Critique of the Political Economy of the Sign,* trans. Charles Levin (St. Louis: Telos, 1981).

4. Lawler's photographs of Mondrians were juxtaposed with photographs by Sherrie Levine and published in *Wedge,* no. 1 (1981), under the title "A Picture Is No Substitute for Anything." A series of the "Arrangements of Pictures" appeared in *October* 26 (1983). Lawler's photographs were also used to illustrate Douglas Crimp's "The Art of Exhibition" in *October* 30 (1984). Most recently, Lawler acted as photo editor for the New Museum's anthology *Art after Modernism: Rethinking Representation* (New York: New Museum of Contemporary Art, 1984), a position which offered yet another format for her "work."

5. As Baudrillard writes, "We have seen that the true value of the painting is its genealogical value (its 'birth': the signature and the aura of its successive transaction: its pedigree). Just as the cycle of successive gifts in primitive societies charges the object with more and more value, so the painting circulates from inheritor to inheritor as a title of nobility, being charged with prestige throughout its history" ("The Art Auction," 120–121).

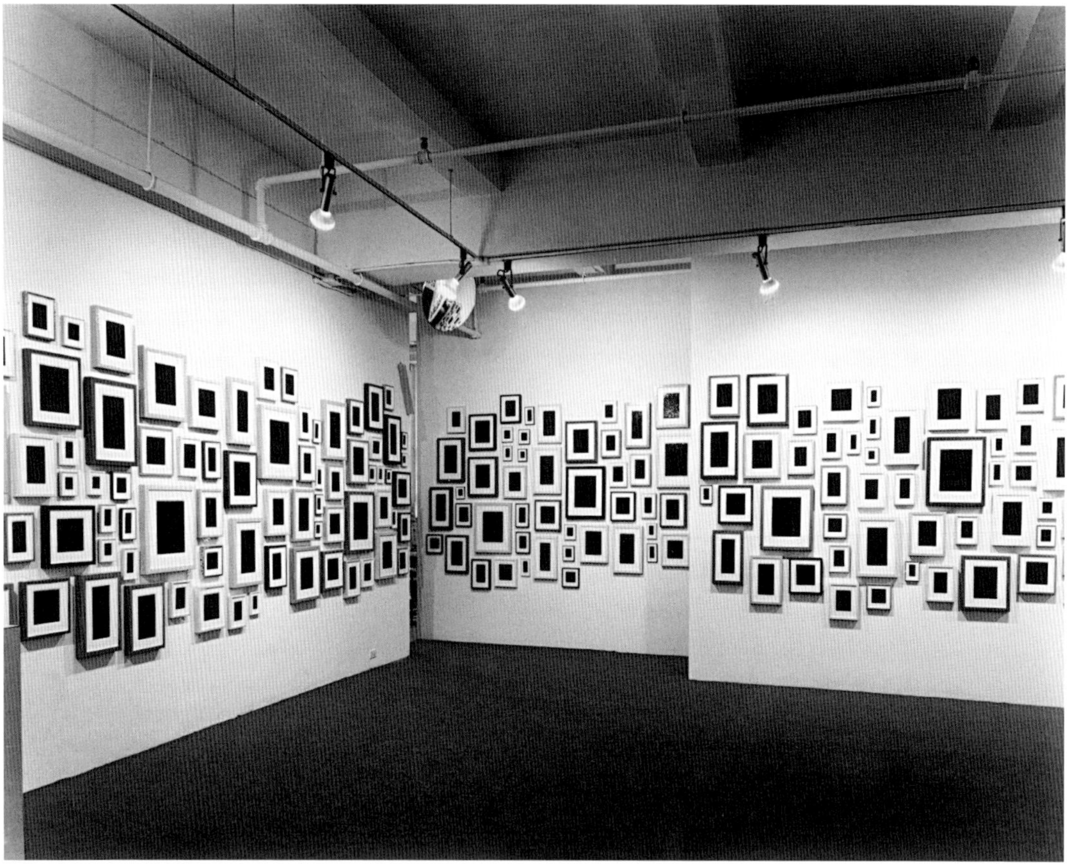

3.1 Allan McCollum, *Plaster Surrogates,* 1982–83. Enamel on Hydrostone. Installation view, Marian Goodman Gallery, New York, 1983.

3

CREATIVITY = CAPITAL ?[1]

"'Creativity = Capital'?" was first published in the brochure for an exhibition of works by Allan McCollum at the Institute of Contemporary Art, Philadelphia, in June 1986.

> Props. Decoys. Small, blank, solid stand-ins for framed images. Solid-state simulacra of paintings. Fools-gold versions of painting. Plaster surrogates. Surrogate paintings. Surrogates of surrogates. Signifiers of signifiers. Pseudoartifacts. Archetypally cultural objects. Little nonimages. Little model paintings. Generic paintings. Vacant paintings. Empty cases of paintings. False pictures . . .[2]

The terms of deception that have surrounded Allan McCollum's *Plaster Surrogates*—the work for which he is best known—can themselves be deceptive. There is, of course, nothing false about the objects themselves. (How can objects be false? Only subjects are deceptive and deceived.) McCollum doesn't employ illusionism or trompe l'oeil. His surrogates aren't forgeries of paintings. They're not even paintings—only plaster objects, which may, at a distance, resemble framed images.

Similarly, the terms of reduction that have surrounded McCollum's work can themselves be reductive. There is, of course, nothing missing, nothing lacking, in the objects themselves. (Only subjects experience lack, not objects.) The surfaces of the *Plaster Surrogates* are no less varied than those of much of the art of the past twenty years. Nor should the absence of an image in their monochrome centers be surprising. McCollum, like most contemporary artists, is not a frescoist—nor is he, like many, a figurative painter.

One may, of course, speak figuratively—even about nonfigurative art objects. But, in McCollum's case, to do so has often been to indulge in fetishization, attributing to objects what is rather a product of the conditions of their production. Might the deceptive disingenuousness attributed to McCollum's *Plaster Surrogates* be the effect not of some discrete characteristic of the objects themselves but rather of the fact that their numbers (McCollum produced over five thousand by 1982) defy our expectation of the artist's investment in each individual work? And might the reductiveness attributed to the objects be an effect not of the reduced form of individual *Plaster Surrogates,* but rather of their differences from each other—a reduction of qualities proportionate to the production of quantities and of the labor required to produce each one? McCollum's reduction of the art object to minimal signs for painting, or, with the *Perfect Vehicles,* for the culturally symbolic object in general (the vase), is not an artistic end-in-itself. It is, rather, a function of his reduction of artistic production to only that labor necessary to define it as such.

In a 1985 interview, McCollum described his practice as "a sort of 'working to rule'": a job action in which workers do precisely and only what is required contractually, both refusing excess work and excessively observing rules and regulations. "In a sense, I'm doing just the minimum that is required of an artist and no more."[3] Each of the plaster objects McCollum has produced is signed and dated. Although McCollum works with assistants, he insists on painting the outer edge of every black center and the inner edge of every frame. No two objects are identical: each member of each group is systematically distinguished from the others by color, shape, or both. McCollum thus reduces his activities to the production of unique objects and the act of signing them: the bare minimum of what still constitutes artistic labor.

The idea of an artist working to rule may seem contradictory, inasmuch as modernism is conventionally understood to have dispensed with the aesthetic codes and conventions that once determined what could be considered art. The individualization of artistic production in the twentieth century has rendered obsolete the contracts of patronage under which art was once produced, as well as the traditional technical skills required. Today, it would seem that nothing is required of artists. Yet it is precisely this "nothing," this apparent lack of requirement, that McCollum problematizes. He does so not to take up the avant-garde project of exposing and transgressing the rules that artists work to, but rather to question and refuse the apparent privilege of freedom that artists enjoy with respect to their labor.

> Qualities of thought and spirit in an economy can overshadow all the quantities of capital and contracts of labor. Indeed, so much of what is important is absent from a typical labor contract that industry can be brought to a halt, airports paralyzed, and traffic stalled merely by a decision of workers to observe exactly the written rules of work. Work, under free enterprise, depends, like investment, on "animal spirits," because work freely rendered, beyond the specifications of contract, is indeed an investment. It is made in the hope of a return.
> —George Gilder, *Wealth and Poverty*, 1981

What working to rule both violates and exposes are not the terms of factory regimen but those of an ideological pact with managerial authority, according to which workers must mistake the necessity of selling their labor for a freely chosen commitment to work. Unable to refuse work, by working to rule they refuse instead to give the gift of their surplus labor (labor expended without compensation) with which, according to Marx, this freedom is purchased.[4] Working to rule is thus a retraction of effort, cooperation, and judgment based on experience—all the "creative" aspects of work disavowed in its reduction to the commodity labor but nevertheless necessary for the efficient and profitable functioning of a capitalist economy. Thus, instead of accepting the superficial freedom and petty transgression of rules allowed by management, by working to rule workers transform a strict adherence to factory discipline into a much more radical transgression: that of collectively refusing to freely, willingly, invest their labor in work to the profit of their employers.

Engaging in the production of art is the profession of choice par excellence, motivated, by most accounts, not by material need but by desire. Artists are, above all others, those members of society who are supposed to find pleasure and satisfaction in their work. Artistic practice then, one might say, is entirely surplus labor: there is no necessity about it. And it is precisely for this excess, which wage-earning members of society expend without compensation, that artists are paid. Art can thus serve as a monument to the maxim that work is the way to freedom, but only if it is transformed into *art* work, the *work* of production being effaced in the process.

McCollum neither superimposes the conditions of industrial production on artistic practice nor attempts to raise them, in a heroic gesture, to the status of high art—as modernist sculptors, from David Smith to Richard Serra, have attempted. McCollum is not an artist posing as a worker. Nor is he—like some

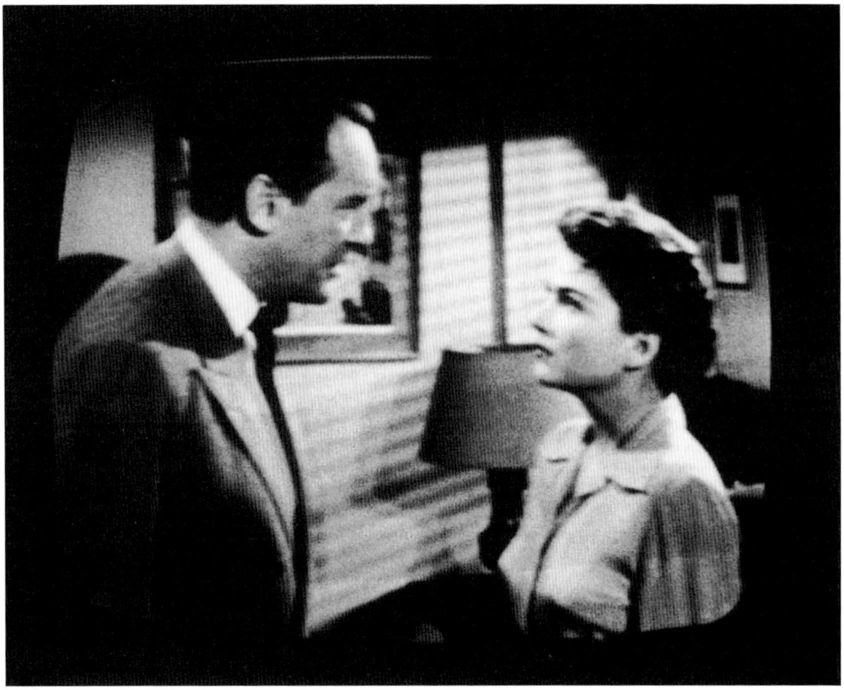

3.2 Allan McCollum, *Surrogates on Location*, 1982. Photo from TV.

of the "postmodern" sculptors with whom he had been associated—a consumer posing as an artist. Rather, he is a worker who, posing as an artist, recalls the condition of artistic production as labor. The *Plaster Surrogates* and *Perfect Vehicles* don't constitute McCollum's *work* in the usual art usage of the term. They are, rather, only the products of his work, i.e., his labor.

What defines labor as such is not the production of a commodity or even a "useful effect," much less particular materials or processes, but rather the production of value that is appropriated by another as profit. What our modern myths of artistic production have effaced is this latter fact: that the professional artist, like other laborers, works not for his or her own satisfaction, but for the enrichment of others. If one of the operations of ideology is to identify objectively opposed interests, such as those of labor with those of capital, then ideology has succeeded in the visual arts as it has in no other sphere. If artists are, above all others, those members of society who are supposed to find pleasure and satisfaction in their work, is it not because, being free from necessary labor, they can identify with the leisure class?

If working to rule is a withdrawal of identification with managerial authority, when transposed to artistic practice it can be understood as a withdrawal of identification with the power and prestige that high art traditionally has represented. The objects that McCollum produces are nothing but emblems, insignia, trophies instilled with pure prestige, installed in the places of power. For *Perpetual Photographs* and *Surrogates on Location—Incidental to the Action,* he looks for objects like those he produces, photographing them "on location" in newspapers and on television behind presidents and movie stars from news broadcasts, soap operas, reruns, late-night movies—leisure-time melodrama: an after-hours search for a specter of satisfaction. He finds them doubly alienated: first as the products of his labor, secondly as elements in narratives of which he is not a part. The imagined satisfaction to be found in artistic recognition is travestied in these photographs, appearing instead as the universal recognizability of insidious, ever-present objects-in-the-background.

Refusing the aesthetic prerogative of recognizing oneself in the products of one's labor (rather than confronting the conditions of that labor itself), McCollum's work is emptied not simply of images but of the satisfaction of the subject who produced them. He is not in them. Instead, one finds the desire, or lack, of a subject who refuses to mistake the compulsion to surplus labor for a chosen commitment to work, and who refuses to identify the emblems of another's prestige as the objects in which his or her own desire may be recognized.

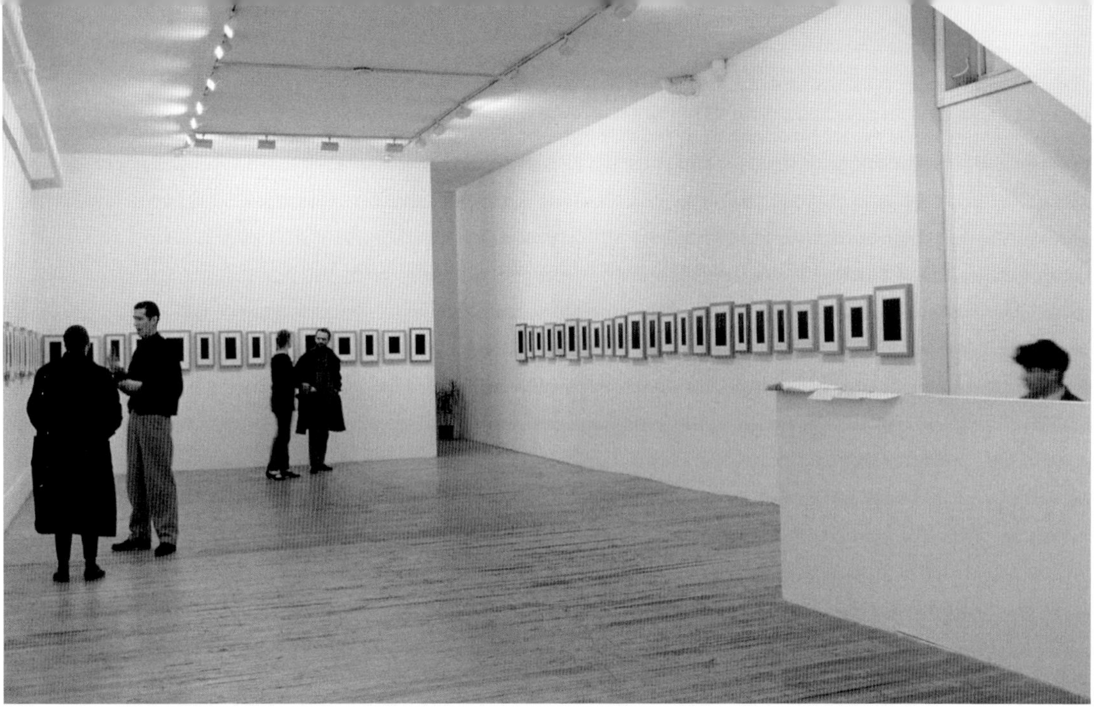

3.3 Andrea Fraser in cooperation with Allan McCollum, *May I Help You?,* 1991. Installation and live performance at American Fine Arts, Co., New York; videotape. Courtesy the artist and American Fine Arts, Co. Photo: Colin de Land.

Developed in cooperation with Allan McCollum, who produced and installed a set of *Plaster Surrogates* for the exhibition, *May I Help You?* set out to examine the ways in which art functions to legitimize social differences. The three gallery staff members overseeing the exhibition were actually performers directed to deliver a fifteen-minute monologue to everyone who came in to see the show. The script, based on interviews with artists, collectors, and dealers as well as people not involved with art, moves through six voices representing six different social positions—from a connoisseur to a person who feels herself to be excluded by museums and galleries. With each voice, the speaker articulates her particular relationship to the almost identical artworks, affirming her own position while implicitly or explicitly negating the voices preceding and following her own. With this structure, *May I Help You?* aimed not only to map a particular set of social positions, but also to perform the relations between them.

Notes

1. "Creativity = Capital" is a formulation of Joseph Beuys.

2. This list of words and phrases used to describe McCollum's *Plaster Surrogates* (by the artist as well as by critics) was gathered from various articles and interviews.

3. Allan McCollum, "Allan McCollum, interviewed by Gray Watson," *Artscribe International,* no. 55 (December/January 1985–86), 67.

4. "The laborer purchases the right to work for his own livelihood only by paying for it in surplus-labor." Karl Marx, *Capital,* vol. 1 (New York: International Publishers, 1967), 515. Surplus labor is, according to Marx, labor expended in excess of necessary labor. Necessary labor is only that labor time that produces the equivalent of the value of the worker's labor power and is necessary for the reproduction of that labor power. Surplus labor is thus that labor that produces surplus value or profit for employers, because it is given gratis.

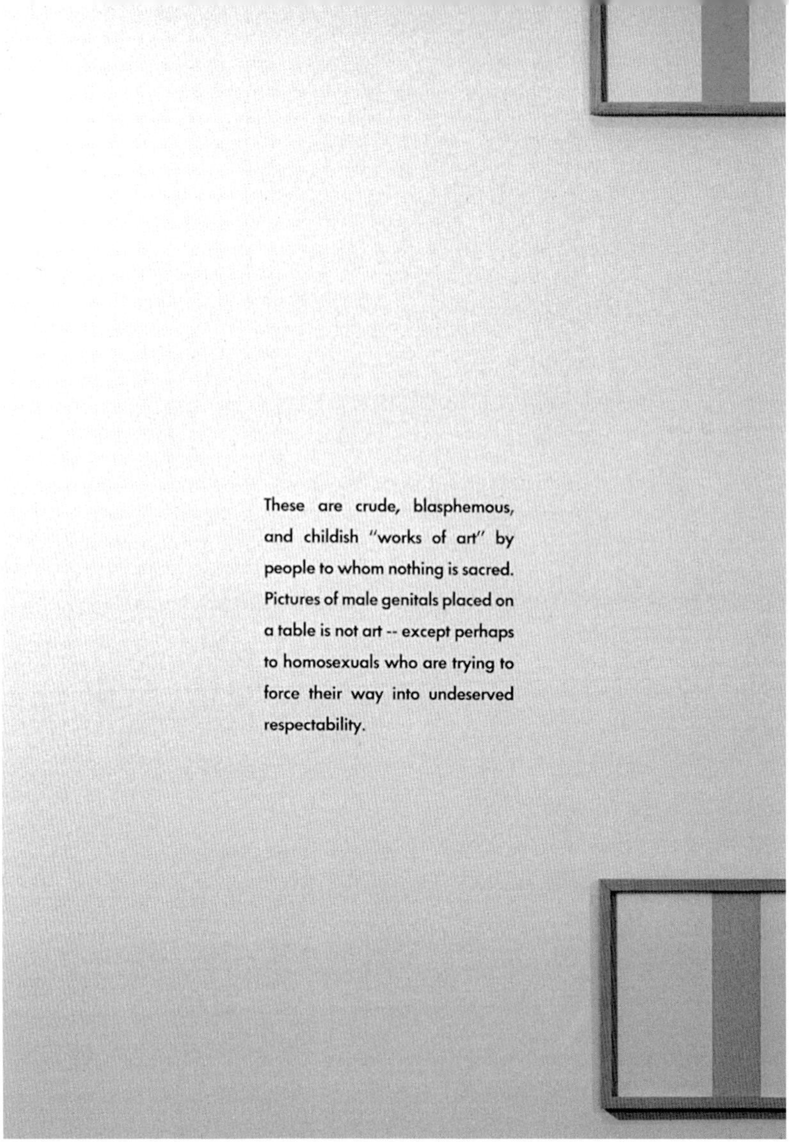

4.1 Andrea Fraser, *Notes on the Margin,* 1990 (detail, with untitled work by Daniel Buren). Installation of five wall texts quoted from congressional hearings on the work of Robert Mapplethorpe and Andres Serrano. Silk-screen on wall, dimensions variable. Courtesy the artist and American Fine Arts, Co. Photo: courtesy Gracie Mansion.

4

IT S ART WHEN I SAY IT S ART, OR . . .

This is a revised version of an essay first published in the November 1995 issue of Texte zur Kunst, *which was devoted to the question of artistic norms and competition. It was written as a reflection on the genre of the artistic manifesto.*

What motivates statements of artistic quality, relevance, and value? According to what logic are they justified? Can they be justified? To the extent that the artistic field is defined by competitive struggles over the definition of the artistic field—including its products and practices, discourses and values—the criteria imposed in such statements serve to reduce their objects to indifferent tokens in an economy of perpetual displacement. As structural linguistics describes the production of meaning in displacements along a signifying chain, or as Lacanian psychoanalysis describes the production of desire in displacement in demand, so the competitive struggles in the artistic field both ceaselessly produce the interests pursued through them and ensure that the object of those interests is never more than the arbitrary manifestation of a particular state of social or professional differentiation, that is, of distinction.

The developments in art of the past thirty years that determine my activity as an artist begin with minimal art's relative elimination of formal, properly aesthetic, relationships internal to the art object. Minimalism, in a sense, pushed those relationships out into the room. The composition of relationships between volumes and surfaces that had constituted the work of the work of sculpture became the organization of the relationship between the body of the viewer and an object in space.

During the 1960s and early '70s, first with institutional critique and then with political documentary and cultural activism, that space and those bodies came to be seen as socially defined according to economic status, race, or ethnicity, and their relationship came to be politically understood. With feminist practices in the '70s, that body became a gendered body. And, in the '80s, with the influence of psychoanalysis, that body became the site and support of a subject, and the relations on which works of art worked came to include the relations of identification and desire by which that subject is constituted.

Site specificity, as it emerged with minimalism and developed in post-studio practice, was defined by an insistence that both the art object and the procedures by which it is produced be determined by the particular context in which it is located. Again, with institutional critique, political documentary, and feminist practice, the investigation of what was first an essentially formal contingency gave way to an engagement with what I will call more radical forms of determination—social, historical, economic, sexual, and psychological—as they are imposed on and through cultural production by the structures and dynamics operative in a given context.

Before minimalism, art could be understood as a form of cultural production defined by an investigation and manipulation of two- and three-dimensional forms resulting in the creation of discrete, autonomous, aesthetic constructions. Over the course of the past thirty years, art has been redefined as the analysis of and intervention on the social relations of which such cultural production—and the symbolic systems of which they are a manifestation—is a transformed and misrecognized expression.

This is the historical version of the normative framework I apply when I consider different forms of artistic activity. I hold this particular trajectory as legitimate not on the basis of a teleological conception of art's evolution toward some imminent end, but on the basis of what I believe are the most fundamental shifts—I would even say innovations—of the art of the past thirty years; that is, those developments that I feel have come closest to engaging, challenging, reflecting upon, or transforming the structure of the field itself. Or, to put it another way, those practices that I believe have somehow managed to resist being reduced to the final function of simply reproducing the conditions and relations of their production.

I tend to consider art that does not follow this trajectory to be regressive or reactionary. I may enjoy a painting, a sculpture, a photograph, a video, a performance, or an installation as such—and may recognize it as a "good" painting, sculpture, etc. However, I can only recognize it as a form of artistic practice if the organizing principle of the work is not simply the exercise of a particular form of artistic competence but a determined means of immediate, practical, and material (as opposed to purely theoretical or symbolic) engagement with a given set of conditions that may include but necessarily exceed the art object (or construction or activity) itself. I then tend to evaluate the work according to its coherence with respect to this organizing principle—encompassing not only "form and content" but, more importantly, the conditions and relations of its production, presentation, and circulation—and the effect, or effectivity, of its mode of engagement.

This is simply how I understand artistic practice. Painting, sculpture, photography, video, performance, installation, etc.—to the extent that these media, as media, define a work or a practice as a sequence of works—I think of, rather, as forms of cultural production.

I consider most of the art that I see to be forms of cultural production. I define cultural production according to a very general understanding of anthropological concepts of culture. I understand culture, in the broadest sense, to be, first, the symbolic systems that provide for the integration and reproduction of social groups and, secondly, the process of acquiring the competencies and dispositions that compose those symbolic systems. I understand cultural production, whether legitimate or popular, generated for restricted or mass audiences, as the production of the objects, representations, narratives, discourses, and practices in which these competencies and dispositions are objectified and reproduced. Art, as legitimate cultural production, serves primarily as the objectified form of the competencies and dispositions of those who consume it, on one hand, and, on the other, of those who produce it, its discourse, and its practices of consumption. Among cultural consumers, art tends to function either as the domestic culture of those who appropriate it materially or as a form of legitimate public culture aspired to by those who appropriate it symbolically. Among cultural producers, art functions either as a formal, primarily professional culture or as the subcultural (or countercultural) manifestation of a group defined as much by a shared lifestyle and a history of social interchange as by a shared recognition of a history of previous practices.

I consider the function of art for both of these groups to be equally constitutive of legitimate cultural production. I do not believe that the meaning invested in art objects by art professionals can transcend the contexts in which they serve. "Aesthetic" producers may privilege the "direct experience" generated by an intimate, familiar, familial, domestic relation to art objects; "didactic" producers may privilege the more mediated and mediating reflection encouraged by public institutions. Yet any such intended experience can be little more than naive faith when invested in objects which, as discrete constructions, are predestined to circulate without restriction. Without restriction, that is, except that imposed by the distribution of the capital competencies and dispositions that constitute the conditions of their value and of their intelligibility. The transformation of this domestic and professional culture into public culture is one of the primary operations of museums and other public cultural institutions. It is also one of the primary mechanisms whereby dispositions acquired in privilege are imposed as universally legitimate within a public sphere, as the domestic culture of a particular class becomes the public culture of a city, a nation, or a "civilization." Yet if this mechanism can—and increasingly does—function just as well without a "patron" class, it is because the competencies and dispositions objectified in art objects express the culture of art professionals *as a class* as much as they might the culture of art collectors. Art professionals may have an even greater interest in the reproduction of their value.

Artists are, I would say, as cultural producers, engaged first and foremost in the reproduction of their own dispositions and competencies. I see most artworks as manifestations of particular technical or material means of artistic expression that have been learned, mastered, perhaps transformed to varying degrees, but are reproduced, fundamentally, as gratuitous, without requiring any justification other than that of perpetuating a particular form of practice, constructed as a value and end in and of itself. Such works are then evaluated primarily according to their interest or novelty as representative of particular artistic positions relative to other artistic positions, contemporary or historical. They are then presented by commercial or nonprofit organizations whose functions are often equally limited to that of legitimation, and which are equally committed to intensifying the demand for art and therefore its value and rarity.

The field of artistic production is a field of specialized production. Its existence as a field of specialized production implies that the means of production as well as appropriation of art objects and art discourse are not distributed equally. It also implies that the value of the competence possessed by art professionals depends upon its rarity, and thus that art professionals have an interest in maintaining and increasing (that is, of reproducing) their monopoly on that competence, an interest that is more or less inseparable from an interest in their professional, social, and historical status.

While the authority of the cultural competencies and dispositions possessed by art professionals may be challenged by those in positions of economic and political power, I do not believe that this in itself elevates the reproduction of those competencies to the status of a liberatory cause. This I hold true not only of the formal competencies recognized as artistic knowledge and technique, but also of those dispositions acquired by membership in a particular group, as well as those according to which such membership is imposed, such as subcultural style or even ethnic or gender identity.

Contemporary politicized forms of such cultural production, defined, for example, by identity politics, do not, I would say, depart much from the history of artistic activity as the site of struggles by artists to reproduce their legitimacy. While these struggles formerly revolved around status as determined by economic conditions and distance from social norms of behavior, they now encompass other forms of domination—according to gender, race, ethnicity, sexual orientation. But to the extent that they are located primarily in the field of art (as opposed to collectively based cultural activism working on representations and media in nonartistic sites), such symbolic struggles largely reproduce the hierarchical structuring they ostensibly oppose. This is because they often conceal or misrecognize the domination imposed by the specialization of cultural production and monopolization of cultural competence the artistic field itself represents. And while one may be happier about some groups representing and reproducing themselves than others, the logic of such preferences—and the politics that orient them—has very little bearing on the structure, function, and effects of legitimate cultural production itself.

Artistic practice, as I understand it, is something other than cultural production. Artistic practice resists, or aims to resist, functioning as the representative culture of a particular group—whether the makers, lookers, and buyers of art or any new or previously unserved constituency. It resists, or aims to resist, serving as the means of reproduction of particular competencies or dispositions. Instead, it functions, or aims to function, as analytical and interventionary. It can be distinguished from other analytical and interventionary practices—such as, for example, psychoanalysis, activism, and critical pedagogy—by its specific object of engagement: cultural production. It can be distinguished from academic disciplines that take cultural production as their object in that it engages this object not only substantively, as a symbolic system, but also on the level of the social relations and social structures of which this system is the site. Artistic practice works on the field of cultural production and, more specifically, on the effects of the specialization of cultural production and the consequent monopolization of cultural competence and cultural capital; on the imposition of legitimate modes of knowing about and being in relation to cultural forms and of appropriating and internalizing cultural properties. It works not to interpret this field, but to change it; not to change the nature of its products, but to change the structure of positions within it and the relations among the positions it structures. And if such change cannot, or can only barely, be achieved, artistic practice is the attempt to determine the conditions of its possibility.

According to Pierre Bourdieu, the artistic field—like any other field, according to his theory of social fields—can only be understood as "the product or prize of a permanent conflict": as a field of forces that is always also a field of struggles.[1] Struggles to determine the boundaries and membership in the field, struggles to define the form of capital according to which positions within it will be hierarchized, and struggles to determine the distribution of this form of capital are all variants of fundamentally competitive struggles among members to maintain or improve their positions relative to other producers. The artistic field, specifically, is constituted above all as "the site of struggles in which what is at stake is the power to impose the dominant definition of the [artist]," that is, the standards, the criteria, the norms according to which producers and their products will be evaluated.[2]

It's obvious: as an artist my interests and my aspirations have always been oriented toward accumulating as much authority, legitimacy, recognition, as I can. Inscribed, as Bourdieu might say, at the deepest levels of my artistic habitus is the sense of simple and immediate certainty that my professional status depends above all and especially in the long term on the degree to which I am able to influence others, that is, the degree to which my work, my position, becomes a model, becomes a kind of norm. And to the extent that the object of the normative framework I propose is the definition of art, or of artists, or of legitimate practice, I have entered into the race to the end of art history.

Yet the normative framework I propose to follow as an artist would attempt to reject such competitive struggles, to the extent that such struggles to maintain and improve one's professional position are fundamentally reproductive struggles. Competitive struggles not only reproduce the value of the capital that governs the field, affirming once again that the interests it proposes and the satisfaction it promises—recognition and remembrance, authority, legitimacy ("the fact of feeling justified in being what one is"), a kind of historical and cultural redemption—should be attainable. Competitive struggles also reproduce the structure of the distribution of this capital, reproducing through displacement the gaps and distances competition aims to close and thus guaranteeing that the sought-after will never be found. As Bourdieu writes, "what the competitive struggle makes everlasting is not different conditions, but the difference between conditions." This "structural gap and the corresponding frustrations are the very source of the reproduction through displacement which perpetuates the structure of positions while transforming the 'nature' of conditions."[3]

Is it possible to advance a normative framework for artistic practice that is not also a weapon in competitive struggles for dominance within the artistic field? The rejections and negations I perform in articulating a normative framework as above are, to me, patently violent. My stomach turns a little every time I reread this essay. On the other hand, however, refusals to hold and apply specific, articulated criteria often have less to do with maintaining neutrality or defending the free range of artistic experimentation than with protecting the social, economic, and symbolic capital that is usually the true basis, in such cases, for artistic legitimacy. It is less a refusal to admit a normative principle as such, than a refusal to admit a principle inconsistent with the principles upon which one's success actually depends, such as the credit accumulated as personal debts in social exchanges, or the safeguarding of cumulative investments made in the production of belief in the value of a given position. In the absence of any thematic, formal, stylistic, procedural, or ideological coherence, it is usually obvious what joins the set of artists supported by a dealer, critic, curator, or peer. Every judgment then becomes a referendum, not on the work, but on the dominance, the legitimacy, the authority, of the judge whose pronouncements must be defended all the more violently to conceal their fundamental arbitrariness: "It's art when I says it's art."

Notes

1. Pierre Bourdieu, "The Field of Cultural Production, or: The Economic World Reversed," in *The Field of Cultural Production* (New York: Columbia University Press, 1993), 34.

2. Ibid., 42.

3. Pierre Bourdieu, *Distinction: A Social Critique of the Judgment of Taste,* trans. Richard Nice (Cambridge: Harvard University Press, 1984), 164, 165.

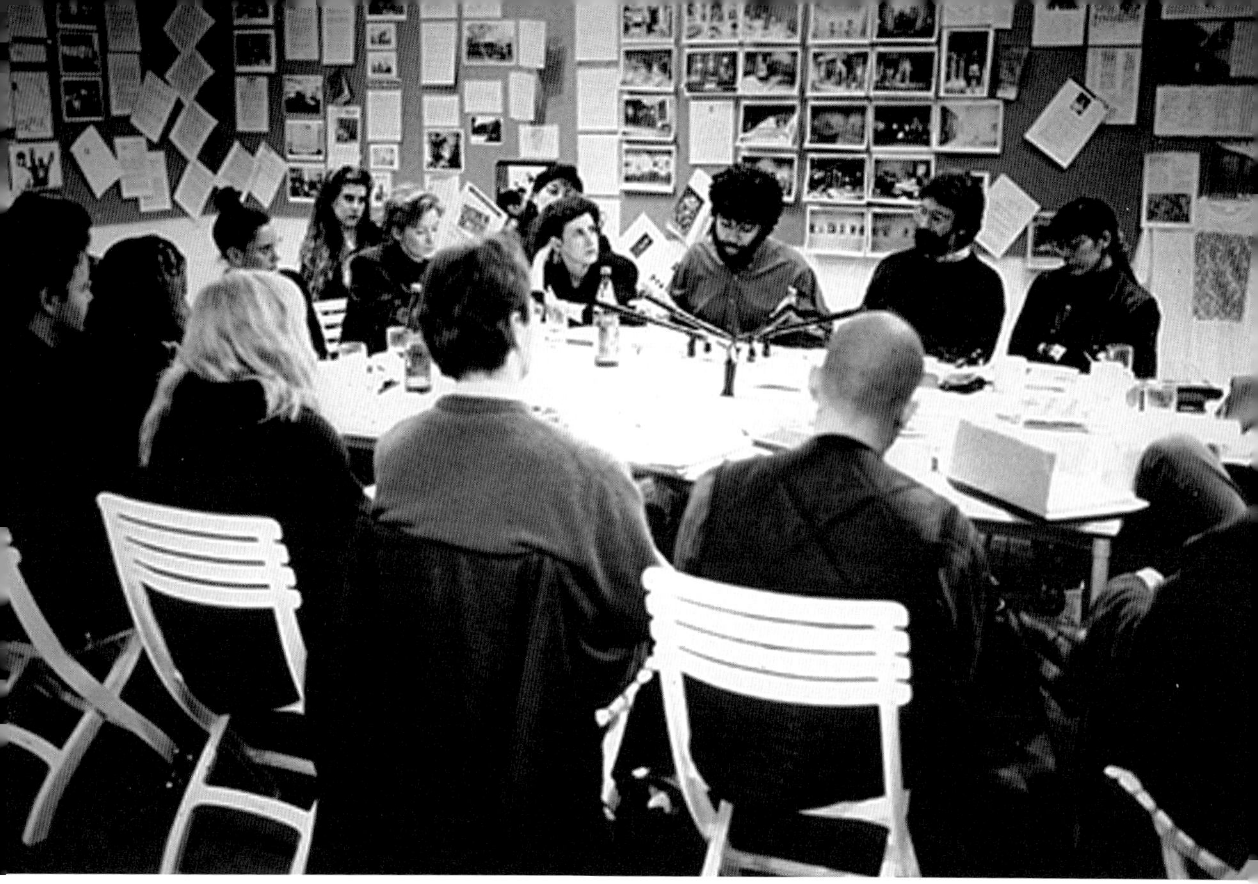

5.1 *Services*, organized by Helmut Draxler and Andrea Fraser, 1994. Working-group discussion at the Kunstraum der Universität Lüneburg, 1994.

5

WHAT S INTANGIBLE, TRANSITORY, MEDIATING, PARTICIPATORY, AND RENDERED IN THE PUBLIC SPHERE?

A revised version of an essay first published in the journal October *in Spring 1997, the text below served as an introduction to edited transcripts of the working-group discussions described in note 1.*

An artistic service?

> It appears to us that, related variously to institutional critique, productivist, activist, and political documentary traditions as well as post-studio, site-specific, and public art activities, the practices currently characterized as "project work" do not necessarily share a thematic, ideological, or procedural basis. What they do seem to share is the fact that they all involve the expense of an amount of labor that is either in excess of, or independent of, any specific material production and which cannot be transacted as or along with a product. This labor, which in economic terms would be called service provision (as opposed to goods production), may include:
>
> - the work of the interpretation or analysis of sites . . . ;
> - the work of presentation and installation . . . ;
> - the work of public education . . . ;
> - advocacy and other community-based work, including organizing, education, documentary production, and the creation of alternative structures. . . .
>
> —Helmut Draxler and Andrea Fraser, "Services: A Proposal for an Exhibition and a Topic of Discussion," 1993

The project *Services,* undertaken at the beginning of 1994, was a response to a specific situation and the largely practical and material concerns which arose as a result of that situation.[1] The introduction of the term "services" as a way of describing certain aspects of contemporary project work was largely strategic. It was not intended to distinguish a particular body of work as new or to function as a substitute for any of the labels at that time in use, from "institutional critique" to "post-studio art," "site-specific art," "context art," "community-based art," "public art," the more generic "project art," or the even more generic "cultural production." "Services," rather, was intended to identify one aspect of many, but not all, of the practices described with those terms: the status of the work, or labor, of which they consist and the conditions under which that work is undertaken. While most project work does, in the end, take a physical form, the contention of the proposal for *Services* was that, in addition to the work of production, all site or situationally specific projects involve "an amount of labor that is either in excess of, or independent of, any specific material production and which cannot be transacted as . . . a product." The strategic value of using the term "services" to describe that labor was that it provided a basis for identifying the value of that portion of an artist's activity which did not result in a transferable product. Motivating the project *Services* was the conviction that this dimension of contemporary artistic work, as something intangible in a field still dominated by the physical and visible, was going largely unrecognized and uncompensated. But the notion of "services" also provided the basis for understanding or describing important and troubling aspects of the relations these activities appeared to presuppose—relations that seemed to represent a significant shift in the status, meaning, and function of artistic activity.

Services was organized in response to the emergence of what appeared to be, by 1993, a consistent and durable demand for project work. The particularity of that demand—and what would render it durable—was the fact that it did not appear to be conditioned simply by the supply offered by a distinct artistic group. As noted in the proposal for *Services,* the practices characterized as "project work" did not seem to share a formal, procedural, thematic, or ideological basis. Nor could "project artists" be grouped along generational lines. Furthermore, many "project exhibitions"—exhibitions in which artists were asked to undertake work in response to specific sites and situations—consisted largely of artists with no history of situational or post-studio activity. The demand for project work, therefore, seemed to be based rather on something like a need for what it is that projects provide.

This need, if one may call it that, appeared to have a number of different dimensions, depending on the character of the given situation. The demand for community-based projects appeared to be related to a need by publicly funded organizations to satisfy the public service requirements of their funding agencies. The demand for institutional interventions appeared to be related to a need on the part of museum professionals to engage artists in a kind of collaborative effort at public education and institutional reflection. The demand for projects undertaken in response to specific curatorial concepts could be related to a need on the part of curators and their organizations to induce the "usual suspects" to produce something special in the context of the exponential expansion of contemporary art venues—and thus exhibitions—in the 1980s, as well as of the corps of curators, swelled by the graduates of at least a half-dozen new curatorial training programs.

This demand for project work had a number of important and troubling implications. It represented a state of affairs in which artists were undertaking projects not only for specific sites and situations, but also within specific relations to organizations and their representatives, curators, and other arts professionals. And it appeared to be the specificity of these relations—more than the physical or temporal specificity of the works themselves—that distinguished these contemporary "projects" from other forms of artistic activity.

The term "services" was introduced, above all, to describe these relations in their economic and social aspects. The emergence of the fee or honorarium as the standard form of compensation for project work appeared to mark less the emergence of a new form of practice than a shift in the character of that practice. Whether or not the result of a project is itself transferable—and most often it is, in some form—a fee is provided, generally, as compensation for that portion of the work that is assumed not to be transferable. Payment of a fee does not usually imply that the organization will own project results. In many cases, sponsoring organizations don't even have collections. When they do, the accessioning of objects resulting from projects usually remains a separate administrative procedure requiring a separate contract. The project fee is payment for the artists' work itself, not for a work of art: it is not an advance on an abstract value to be realized at a future date, but a payment for the final consumption of a value extinguished in some form of immediate use.

Whether or not a project is undertaken at the invitation of a particular organization and compensated with fee, whether or not it is a contractually defined response to an external demand, projects appear to be distinguishable from the broad range of post-studio practices by the degree to which they are constituted in relationship to externally determined interests or needs. Projects undertake to respond to (and perhaps, but not necessarily, satisfy) those interests and needs, not through the production of a utility embodied in an object, but through the execution of particular functions. These functions were identified in the *Services* proposal as including the work of interpreting, the work of presenting, arranging, and installing, the work of educating, and the work of advocating and organizing.

My attempt to produce a more complete account of the genealogy of artistic practice as service provision is represented by Part II of this essay. If certain artistic phenomena of the past five years can indeed be considered service provision, what definition of that term are they fulfilling? The very straightforward assertion of the proposal for *Services*—that all artistic work, or labor, which is not compensated through the sale of a tangible product must be considered a form of service provision—seems clear enough. Too clear, perhaps: the utility of the concept itself—beyond its strategic utility in justifying demands for compensation—seems almost exhausted in that clarity. Stepping beyond this basic definition of a service in the distinction between tangible and intangible products or production thereof, one immediately finds oneself mired in centuries of economic, sociological, and historical debates over whether services even exist as a distinct form of economic activity. Marx, for one, didn't think that they did. The term quickly evaporates as a structure or framework that can simply be applied for strategic, interpretive, and even descriptive use.

And yet "services" have been important as a theme in art at least since the late 1960s, particularly in performance and feminist art, and as a strategic element since the appropriation of institutional functions in practices of institutional critique. In addition to such strategic appropriation of service occupations, the practical or procedural appropriation of service positions has been a central aspect of artistic practice since the minimalists reduced (or expanded) their roles in the process of art making to (include) those of designers, engineers, managers, and administrators. The redefinition of artworks from physical, material products or goods to service products such as information and intellectual property is one way of understanding the "dematerialization of the art object" ascribed to conceptual art, as well as important aspects of artistic policies resulting from the critique of the commercial art apparatus, such as the "Artists' Reserved Rights Transfer and Sale Agreement" and many of the reforms advocated by the Art Workers Coalition. The introductions of service functions in art and the ethical dimension of the notion of service are evident in cultural activist and community-based practices. Finally, the emergence of specific, immediate service relations, as opposed to the abstracted relations of object production and exchange, can be seen as a consequence of post-studio practices, whether or not they result in a durable or tangible product (and most usually do). A specific site (or better, situation), always also includes a specific set of relations—within the process of site-specific production as well as within the site itself.[2]

The problem with the term "services" is equally apparent from this list of its seemingly appropriate applications: services as a category, considered in its economic, social, or political and ethical dimensions, separately or together, has no particular coherence. There is no consensus in economic or social thought as to what a service is. While the growth of what is generally considered the service sector in the twentieth century and particularly in the postwar period is quantitatively documented, the definitions of that sector, the features that distinguish it from an industrial or "productive" sector, remain fuzzy at best. Similarly, the social character of service occupations, which traverse the service and industrial sectors, however defined, range from corporate management, to the "independent" professions, to the lowest paid domestic and maintenance work. Services have traditionally been distinguished by their relationship to capital: Adam Smith considered payment for services as a form of final consumption and thus a reduction of capital rather than an investment. Consequently, services were long considered resistant to industrial organization and limited either to individual exchange (as of personal services), or public sector provision (as of the social services responsible for a large part of postwar service sector growth as it is generally defined). Yet the privatization of formerly public (or nonprofit) services, such as health care, and the increasingly industrial organization of both personal services and those traditionally rendered by "independent" professionals, such as doctors in HMOs, has revealed the fallacy of such definitions. These contemporary phenomena can also lay to rest any lingering sympathies for the optimistic predictions of Daniel Bell and others that service sector growth portends the coming of a postindustrial society.[3]

One very general explanation for the heterogeneousness of the category services may be that, given the focus of classical economists, as well as Marx, on industrial production and the accumulation of capital, services were always simply everything else: everything that was not material production or extraction; that was not or did not result in a durable, transferable product; that was not productive of profit: "the domestic servant, the musician, the actor, the painter, the physician, the teacher, and the priest."[4] In a similar way, perhaps, one may be able to reflect on the presence in contemporary art of service products, service positions, service functions, and, above all, service relations only on the basis of the difference between these and the character and status of those products, positions, functions, and relations that had hitherto more or less exclusively defined artistic activity. The shift in the character of artistic activity, whether or not the term "service" conclusively describes it, can nevertheless be seen as related to those attributes with which services have traditionally been distinguished from other economic forms: the intangible as opposed to tangible product or production thereof; the position of organizing or mediating the production and circulation of goods; the execution of functions that cannot appear as values independently of their use; and work undertaken in an immediate relation to a client, consumer, or user in which there is little or no physical or temporal distance between production and consumption and in which the use-value produced often involves the user's direct participation.

Considering these definitions, one could conclude that almost every significant attempt by artists of the past thirty years to transform the conditions and relations of their activity, whether through the redefinition of artworks or of the competencies required to produce them, has resulted in a tendency toward forms of work (or working) that include an aspect of service provision. If one considers services simply as a negative category, a catchall for everything that was not of primary interest to classical economists, such a conclusion might be less far-fetched. However, it would also be meaningless—unless, that is, one considers the emergence of artistic service provision not as an instance of art reflecting or emulating the historical conditions of a "service economy," but rather as resulting from a self-conscious artistic critique of the cultural commodity, of the exploitation of art for economic and symbolic profit, and of the structures of artistic practice and of the artistic field which provide for the creation of the value thus appropriated. Whether the shift to service provision, if it has in fact occurred, represents the failure of the critique of the political economy of art or the realization of at least some of its goals would remain in question.

The term "services," therefore, may not be particularly useful as an interpretive framework in understanding the impact of economic or historical structures on art, or even shifts in thematic, procedural, or ethical paradigms in art. Rather, it is useful, I would say, first, for what it requires: a genealogy of contemporary practices that traces, not the visible, visual manifestations of the positions artists represent, but the very positions they construct for themselves and the economic conditions and social relations that those positions presuppose and impose. Second, it is useful for what it emphasizes: that these conditions and relations, at least in those dimensions that distinguish them from commodity production and exchange, entail a significant transformation of one of the central characteristics of artistic activity and the artistic field: that is, artistic autonomy. Third, it is useful for what it implies as to the character of this transformation.

Notes

1. *Services: The Conditions and Relations of Service Provision in Contemporary Project-Oriented Artistic Practice* was organized by Helmut Draxler and me at the invitation of Beatrice von Bismarck, Diethelm Stoller, and Ulf Wuggenig at the Kunstraum der Universität Lüneburg. The opening of the exhibition, in January 1994, followed two days of working-group discussions between artists and curators involved with "project work." Participants in the working-group discussions included Judith Barry, Ute Meta Bauer, Ulrich Bischoff, Iwona Blazwick, BüroBert (Jochen Becker and Renate Lorenz), Susan Cahan, Clegg & Guttmann, Stephan Dillemuth, Renée Green, Christian Philipp Müller, Fritz Raumann, and Fred Wilson. In addition to videotapes of the working-group discussions, the exhibition contained the documentation (photocopies, photographs, slides, videotapes, and audiotapes) that working-group participants brought to support their presentations. It also contained "historical" material—usually also in photocopy form—collected by Draxler and myself. This material did not present a complete genealogy of "services" or "project work," but was intended rather to function as an expanding archive documenting individual or collective efforts in the past thirty years in which artists and curators have sought to transform the material conditions of their activities. The material Draxler and I collected focused on groups such as the Art Workers Coalition and Artists Meeting for Cultural Change; events such as the cancellation of Hans Haacke's exhibition at the Guggenheim Museum and the unionization of the Museum of Modern Art; and the contracts, statements, and project descriptions generated by artists such as Daniel Buren and Michael Asher.

   Following the presentation at the Kunstraum der Universität Lüneburg, the material in the exhibition circulated to the Kunstverein München; the Künstlerhaus Stuttgart; Sous-sol, École supérieure d'art visuel, Geneva; the Depot, Vienna; and, in its last incarnation in January 1995, the Provinciaal Museum, Hasselt. Additional discussions, sometimes including original working-group participants, sometimes with new participants, were scheduled during each presentation of the project.

2. The distinction I make here between service positions, service products, service functions, and service relations has been adapted from J. I. Gershuny and I. D. Miles, *The New Service Economy*. Gershuny and Miles distinguish between "service industries," which "cover all those firms and employers whose major final output is some intangible or ephemeral commodity"; "service products"—the

intangible or ephemeral commodities themselves—which "are not all necessarily produced by service industries"; "service occupations," which are "present across the whole range of industries, and are involved in 'non-production' activities ranging from data-processing to repair and maintenance, from cleaning and catering to education and health-care"; and "service functions," which "involve individuals in service work" but not necessarily "within the money economy." See Gershuny and Miles, *The New Service Economy* (New York: Praeger, 1983), 3–4, 23. From this framework I have subtracted "service industries," which are not my concern here, and added "service relations," a term which I use to describe those aspects of service provision implied by Jean Baptiste Say's definition of services as "values consumed at the moment of production" itself.

3. An analysis of Adam Smith's views on services can be found in Jean-Claude Delaunay and Jean Gadrey, *Services in Economic Thought: Three Centuries of Debate* (Boston: Kluwer Academic Publishers, 1992). Harry Braverman offers a similar interpretation in *Labor and Monopoly Capital: The Degradation of Work in the Twentieth Century* (New York: Monthly Review Press, 1974). In *The Coming of the Post-Industrial Society: A Venture in Social Forecasting* (New York: Basic Books, 1973), Daniel Bell advanced the idea that, because services are somehow resistant to industrial organization and private sector provision, the expansion of the service sector would result in the emergence of a postindustrial society. Bell thus contradicts the argument made by Ernest Mandel in *Late Capitalism* (London: Verso, 1972). According to Mandel, far from "representing a 'post-industrial society,'" the "penetration of capital into the so-called services sector" instead "constitutes *generalized universal industrialization*." "The *private* relationship between the seller of specifically qualified labour power and the spender of private revenues, which still predominated in the nineteenth century . . . , becomes increasingly converted into a *capitalist,* but at the same time objectively socialized, service business" (*Late Capitalism,* 387–388, 385; italics in original).

4. "These are the most usual illustrations" of services in the first half of the nineteenth century, according to Delaunay and Gadrey, *Services in Economic Thought,* 15–16.

6

WHAT'S INTANGIBLE, TRANSITORY, MEDIATING, PARTICIPATORY, AND RENDERED IN THE PUBLIC SPHERE? PART II

The following essay is a revised version of a text originally written in 1996 as the second part (indeed, the bulk) of the essay of the same name published in October *in Spring 1997.*

The Critique of Artistic Autonomy

> This is the crux of the problem. . . . In this country, under American-style capitalism, a man who owns a work has complete legal and unalterable possession of it.
> —Barnett Newman, Art Workers Coalition Open Hearing, 1969

> **1.** A work of art by a living artist would still be the property of the artist. . . .
> **2.** The artist would be consulted when his work is displayed. . . .
> **3.** The museums, collectors, or publication would compensate the artist for use of his art. This is a rental, beyond the original purchase price . . . : the principle of a royalty would be used. . . .
> **4.** An artist would have the right to retrieve his work from a collection if he compensated the purchaser. . . .
> **5.** When a work is resold from one collector to another, the artist would be compensated with a percentage of the price.
> —Sol LeWitt, Art Workers Coalition Open Hearing, 1969

> Artists should attach binding conditions to the sale of their work. Such conditions should include the condition that the work may not be re-sold. . . . Another condition should be made universal and should be enforced systematically, rigorously, and with a constant eye to filling loop-holes out of which the force of the condition drains: that condition is, *no owner may in any way enrich himself through the possession of the work of art.*
> —Carl Andre, Art Workers Coalition Open Hearing, 1969

That the critique of the autonomy of the art object had, by the late 1960s, become a rejection of more than Greenbergian formalism is evident in the speeches made at the Art Workers Coalition's Open Hearing in April 1969. At issue was the fact that the autonomy of art objects—as discrete and separable from both artist and viewer, from both the site of production and the site of presentation or consumption—determines their "materiality" not only in their physical "presence" but also as commodities.

Artistic autonomy can be considered in terms of four different though interrelated dimensions. Artistic autonomy has a specifically aesthetic dimension: the freedom of artworks from rationalization with respect to specific use or function, whether moral, economic, political, social, material, or emotional. Second, it has an economic dimension: the emergence of the relatively anonymous bourgeois market and, with it, the artistic commodity; the consequent separation of sites of production and consumption and, with it, the separation of production from the demands it meets or satisfies in the places and processes of consumption. Third, artistic autonomy has a social dimension: in Pierre Bourdieu's analysis, the autonomy of any field is relative to that field's capacity to impose "its own norms on both the production and the consumption of its products" and to exclude norms and criteria dominant in other fields—especially those of the economic and political fields.[1] Finally, this social dimension of artistic autonomy implies a fourth, political dimension: the freedom of speech and conscience and the right to dissident opinion.

Bourdieu describes two mechanisms through which the products and practices of the relatively autonomous field of art are brought into the service of external interests and functions. The first is heteronomization: the imposition within the field of art of interests and values dominant in other fields, particularly economic and political interests. Such heteronomization can function directly, as instrumentalization, or indirectly, through the devaluation of specifically artistic criteria through the influence of economic and political (or social) criteria.

A second mode of "use" proceeds through what Bourdieu calls "the logic of homologies": that is, through parallels between the dynamics, structure, and interests of the field of art and those of what he calls the field of power—of dominant classes understood as the locus of monopolies of political, social, and cultural as well as economic capital.

If the critique of the production and exchange of art objects as commodities—like the critique of the studio and the museum—emerged out of a critique of the autonomy of the artwork, it was not just as a challenge to aestheticism. Rather, it was rooted in a recognition of the partial and ideological character of that autonomy and an attempt to resist the heteronomy to which artists and artworks are subject by the apparatus that supports their legitimacy and through which that legitimacy is appropriated as symbolic and economic profit. The critique of the art object's autonomy in this sense was less a rejection of artistic autonomy than a critique of the *uses* to which artworks are put: the economic and political interests they *serve*. The statements made at the Art Workers Coalition Open Hearing indicate that a central element of rejections of the commodity form in art of the late 1960s was an attempt to resist such use.

The late 1960s produced at least three different strategies of resistance. One strategy was represented by the AWC and other groups developing counterhegemonic practices of cultural and community-based activism: that of reforming the art institutions and commercial art apparatus that oversaw the circulation, presentation, and consumption of artworks. The second and third strategies of resistance were directed at art—artistic practice and artistic products—and not just at institutions and the market. They include conceptual art's dematerialization of the art object in language and action and the temporalization of artworks in specific times and spaces in what came to be called post-studio practices. A fourth set of strategies, represented by institutional critique, emerged as a combination of these three.

Service Products: Conceptualism and Intangible Value

> The labour of a manufacturer adds, generally, to the value of the materials which he works upon, that of his own maintenance, and of his master's profit. The labor of a menial servant, on the contrary, adds to the value of nothing. . . . [It] does not fix or realize itself in any particular subject or vendible commodity. His services generally perish in the very instant of their performance, and seldom leave any trace or value behind them.
>
> —Adam Smith, *An Inquiry into the Nature and Causes of the Wealth of Nations,* 1776

A primary focus of the AWC was developing policies to defend claims by artists to proprietary rights over their works even after they are sold. These policies were to safeguard both economic and artistic interests. The AWC came into existence in January 1969 when a group of artists and critics supported a protest by kinetic sculptor Takis over the way one of his works, owned by the Museum of Modern Art, was exhibited in the museum's "Machine" show. Takis's claim that as the producer of the work he had the right to determine when, where, and how it was exhibited, even if he no longer owned it, evolved into the AWC's broader critique of the circulation and exchange of artworks as commodities. It also led to agitation for museum reform that continued to be directed primarily, if largely for strategic reasons, at MoMA.

In most of the reforms sought by the AWC, the status and character of artwork and artistic competence were not in question. One of the AWC's founding principles was to eschew a particular artistic orientation. The goal of protecting artwork from misuse was to be accomplished through legal and organizational rather than artistic means. At the same time, however, many of the AWC's most active members, including Carl Andre, Hans Haacke, Lucy Lippard, and Gregory Battcock, were pursuing or supporting artistic practices that questioned the bases of the value of artworks within commercial and social markets. Haacke's work about physical systems from the 1960s challenged the durability of artworks. Lippard and Battcock were among the earliest critics to identify the "dematerialization of the art object." Andre's stack and scatter work had already been identified, in a 1967 review by Dan Graham, with the rejection not only of the autonomy of the art object, or even the commodity form, but of all forms of possession and use: "The component units possessed no intrinsic significance

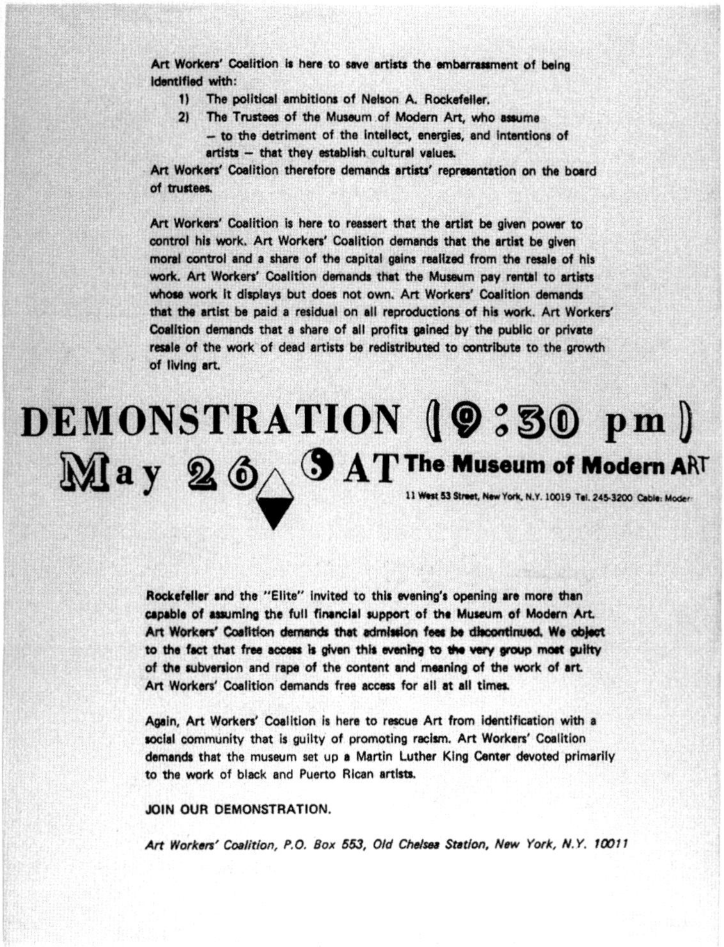

Art Workers' Coalition is here to save artists the embarrassment of being identified with:

1) The political ambitions of Nelson A. Rockefeller.
2) The Trustees of the Museum of Modern Art, who assume – to the detriment of the intellect, energies, and intentions of artists – that they establish cultural values.

Art Workers' Coalition therefore demands artists' representation on the board of trustees.

Art Workers' Coalition is here to reassert that the artist be given power to control his work. Art Workers' Coalition demands that the artist be given moral control and a share of the capital gains realized from the resale of his work. Art Workers' Coalition demands that the Museum pay rental to artists whose work it displays but does not own. Art Workers' Coalition demands that the artist be paid a residual on all reproductions of his work. Art Workers' Coalition demands that a share of all profits gained by the public or private resale of the work of dead artists be redistributed to contribute to the growth of living art.

DEMONSTRATION (9:30 pm)
May 26 AT The Museum of Modern ART
11 West 53 Street, New York, N.Y. 10019 Tel. 245-3200 Cable: Moder

Rockefeller and the "Elite" invited to this evening's opening are more than capable of assuming the full financial support of the Museum of Modern Art. Art Workers' Coalition demands that admission fees be discontinued. We object to the fact that free access is given this evening to the very group most guilty of the subversion and rape of the content and meaning of the work of art. Art Workers' Coalition demands free access for all at all times.

Again, Art Workers' Coalition is here to rescue Art from identification with a social community that is guilty of promoting racism. Art Workers' Coalition demands that the museum set up a Martin Luther King Center devoted primarily to the work of black and Puerto Rican artists.

JOIN OUR DEMONSTRATION.

Art Workers' Coalition, P.O. Box 553, Old Chelsea Station, New York, N.Y. 10011

6.1 Art Workers Coalition flyer, 1971.

beyond their immediate contextual placement, being 're-placeable.' Works are unpossessible by the viewer in the monetary sense, [in] the sense of an artist being possessed of a vision or of satisfying personal inner needs of the viewer."[2] The economic and political dimensions of these artistic tendencies may have had their most explicit expression in the activities of the AWC.

One of the most consistent arguments to be found in the documents of the AWC is that artworks serve interests that are contrary to those of artists. Artworks, even the most aesthetically autonomous, are used. Artists must take such use into account, if not for reasons of conscience, artistic or political, then for reasons of self-interest—hopefully, a radical self-interest, a self-interest with an analysis.

Many of the statements at the Open Hearing describe such *use* as a *misuse*. Artworks are subject to price speculation and manipulation by profiteering galleries and "commercial middle-men" who reduce art to objects of conspicuous consumption and artists to producers of luxury commodities: "servants of the wealthy" and "toadies of the upper middle-class elite" whose livelihood depends on their capacity to provide for "THE ENTERTAINMENT OF ISOLATED RICH PERSONS"; "RICH PERSONS" who control museums—as well as "ALL [other] legitimate communicative agencies"—and who are "waging war in Viet Nam" and calling "the cops at Columbia" and "justifying their slaughter . . . by their precious, conscious support of ART."[3]

With the recognition that even the most aesthetically autonomous artworks are used and that their commodity form conditions this use, many of the policies advocated by the AWC were oriented toward controlling such use. Whereas the transfer of artworks as merchandise implies "complete legal and unalterable possession," artist after artist at the Open Hearing proposed legal mechanisms for retaining at least some proprietary rights over works after they are sold. These included not only the right to a percentage of appreciated value realized in resale but also royalties from reproductions and fees from exhibitions (even when the exhibitor owns the work). That these models are all drawn from the legal and economic conditions of intellectual property was noted. Artists, Alex Gross stated, "are only asking for the same return from their work as is received by writers, composers and film-makers in the form of copyrights and royalties."[4] Ian Whitecross took up the same theme: "It can be objected that art is different since it is intrinsically valuable as a unique object whereas music and literature have value only in their idea and not in their physical form—yet, one can maintain that the sale of an art work conveys only the right to private and personal enjoyment thereof and not the right to financial gain, personal publicity or public acclaim."[5] In 1969, these arguments began developing into the "Artists' Reserved Rights Transfer and Sale Agreement." The final version of the Agreement, written by attorney Robert Projansky and published in *Studio International* in April 1971, was designed, according to Seth Siegelaub, "to remedy some generally acknowledged inequities in the art world, particularly artists' lack of control over the use of their work."[6]

Some of the participants at the Open Hearing also noted that protecting the proprietary rights of artists was not very radical, accepting as it did the principle of private ownership. However, what was radical about the AWC's proposed protections was the duplicitous condition of art's value that they uncovered: they implied a radical splitting of artwork into tangible and intangible value. And this in turn implied a redefinition of artwork from a commercial product or good to a service product—in this case, intellectual property.

Instead of complete and "unalterable" possession, the exchange of services—even service products—generally implies specific and limited use. Compensation for the production of durable goods can always function as an advance on value to be appropriated in sale and resale—that is, on profit. Compensation for services, on the other hand, such as fees and royalties, are only the cost (or a portion of the cost) of final consumption.

One of the earliest distinctions between goods production and service provision, made by Adam Smith, relates less to the tangible or intangible character of the product of labor than to the social character of labor itself: whether or not that labor produces profit. For Smith, a service is a product that contains only use value and no exchange value: it adds "to the value of nothing."[7] It may have been precisely this condition—which rendered services suspect for Smith—that the artists of the AWC aspired to in considering their work intellectual property: as Andre stated, "no owner may in any way enrich himself through the possession of the work of art."[8] From this perspective, one can understand how artists of the late 1960s saw in the condition of service products, relations, positions, and functions a means of protection from, and even resistance to, forms of exploitation (of themselves and others) consequent to the production and exchange of cultural commodities.

The substitution of service products for material products, of ideas for things, already accomplished by conceptual art in the years before the Open Hearing, did not in fact do away with any of the basic property relations that more traditional forms of artistic production had operated within. But eliminating such relations may not actually have been the aim of many of conceptual art's most prominent proponents and practitioners. In his acknowledgments for his first book of *Statements,* published in 1968 by Seth Siegelaub, Lawrence Wiener notes that "certain specific statements are reproduced with the kind permission of the people who own them."[9] In a 1970 essay Jack Burnham quotes Siegelaub as saying: "My interest as a businessman isn't in circumventing the commercial system. I've just made pages of a book comparable to space. . . . Artists having their work go out as printed matter can be just as viable as selling Nolands."[10] And while Lucy Lippard laments conceptual art's failure to resist "general commercialization" in her 1973 postscript to *Six Years: The Dematerialization of the Art Object,* she describes her early hopes for such resistance as pinned, not on the efforts of the artists so much as the (initial) unattractiveness to collectors of ephemera like Xerox sheets which, she supposed, would "forcibly" free conceptual art from "the tyranny of a commodity status and market-orientation."[11]

Conceptual art nevertheless questioned what the AWC did not: the ways in which the character of artworks and artistic practice itself presupposed the forms of symbolic and economic appropriation to which they are subject. The AWC's institutional critique was largely directed at the art apparatus as exterior to artistic practice, which was generally considered separable from the contexts in which it functioned (hence the solution was to impose restrictions on that apparatus, externally, by contract). For conceptual art, however, definition of the conditions and relations of exchange became an integral part of art itself.

If the AWC attempted to protect artworks contractually, conceptual artists reduced artworks themselves to contracts that often described not only objects or actions, but the conditions under which they would be produced or undertaken. In his 1969 *Duration Piece #15,* Douglas Huebler offers a reward for information leading to the arrest of a man wanted by the FBI which is to decrease from $1,100 to $0 over the course of a year. If the piece is purchased within that time period, the new owner assumes all responsibility for payment of any claims. Huebler specifies: "The price for this piece is $1,100: from that sum I will reimburse its owner any money that he pays as a reward." In the proposal for *Location Piece #14,* also 1969, which describes the process of generating 24 photographs from 24 locations at longitudes divisible by 15, Huebler specifies: "The owner of this work will assume the responsibility for fulfilling every aspect of its physical execution."

In another example, Lawrence Weiner's often-cited "instructions" may be significant less because the "receiver" may include any reader than because the "receiver" also, explicitly, includes the buyer. "People, buying my stuff, can take it wherever they go and can rebuild it if they choose. If they keep it in their heads, that's fine too."[12]

As in the AWC's contract, the predominant orientation of conceptualism was not to refuse to sell an artwork, but to control it. Even in her optimistic preface to *Six Years,* Lippard predicts not the disappearance of collectors but rather their replacement by people "less interested in possession." These she characterizes as "patrons."[13] It seems that conceptual art was to revolutionize the political economy of art by returning collectors to the more altruistic motives of patronage projected onto art's premarket past.

Service Relations: Site Specificity and Temporalization

> Immaterial products [are] values consumed at the moment of production.
> —Jean Baptiste Say, *A Treatise on Political Economy,* 1803

The idea of the return of the patron can also be found in Joseph Kosuth's "Art After Philosophy": "When someone 'buys' a Flavin he isn't buying a light show, for if he was he could just go to a hardware store and get the goods for considerably less. He isn't 'buying' anything. He is subsidizing Flavin's activity as an artist."[14] With the substitution of "subsidizer" for collector, the compensation an artist receives is less payment for a product than payment for artistic activity itself. Kosuth implies that Flavin's rejection, as a minimalist and with the readymade, of specifically artistic competencies and the production of unique aesthetic compositions is what turns art collectors into art subsidizers. What Kosuth doesn't mention, however, is that Flavin was one of the first artists of the 1960s to sell his work not just as an object but also as a certificate. The fluorescent tubes that constitute a Flavin are destined to die, making collectors the proud owners of specifications for the work's reproduction with new generations of materials.

In another reference to Flavin, Douglas Huebler wrote in a statement for *Prospect '69:* "Anyone could produce an Andre or a Flavin for instance. At the same time, I believe that the collector is someone who enters into a conspiracy with the artist that is beyond the issue of accessibility, an agreement that the sensibility is an important one. This agreement may be really what the owner had that is original."[15] Huebler implicitly recognizes that a rejection of artistic competencies and the production of unique objects does not necessarily undermine the value of art. Rather, such value depends on the symbolic conditions of an artistic position: on the degree to which a work's underlying principles are recognized as unique, legitimate, and historically relevant.

If Andre and Flavin did transform the conditions of artistic value, their doing so may have had little to do with their rejection of artistic competencies and products.[16] The "return of the patron" their work implied had less to do with the disappearance of objects with specifically artistic value than with the emergence of a specific relation: the "conspiracy" that Huebler describes in his statement and inscribes in his contractual works. But while the works of Huebler and other conceptualists explicitly project and circumscribe specific relations to collectors, the works of Andre and Flavin do not. If Kosuth and Huebler nevertheless cite Andre and Flavin as precedents in redefining artistic exchange, it is because the specific relations implied by their practices are established within the form of their activity itself: the introduction, through practices restricted to the variable arrangement of ready-made materials, of a specific relation not only within a site but within a process of production. This was the challenge to the circulation and exchange of artworks developed in post-studio and site-specific practices in the 1960s and '70s.

The implications of post-studio practice for the social conditions of artistic activity are hard to miss in one of the texts that introduced the paradigm of site specificity, Robert Smithson's "Towards the Development of an Air Terminal Site," which opens as follows:

> Since July, 1966 I've been rendering consultation and advice as an "artist consultant" to Tippetts-Abbett-McCarthy-Stratton (Engineers and Architects). The project concerns the development of an air terminal between Fort Worth and Dallas. From time to time, after studying various maps, surveys, reports, specifications and construction models, I meet with Walther Prokosch, John Gardner and Ernest Schwiebert in order to discuss the overall plan. I have engaged in these discussions not as an architect or engineer, but simply as an artist.[17]

Remarkable in this description is not only that Smithson describes himself as an "artist consultant" but that he describes his client and the individuals he is working with so specifically. It reveals that a specific site, even when engaged only in its physical aspects, always also implies a specific set of relations, whether social, economic, or subjective. Those relations are not only relations within a site engaged or thematized by a site-specific work, but also the relations an artist constructs or enters into as a condition of working in that site.

The production of artworks on site instead of in a studio, even when not motivated by a critique of the commodity and even when not resulting in the elimination of transferable objects, has the effect of reducing the temporal and physical distance between the processes of production and consumption. As Daniel Buren recognized in "The Function of the Studio," that distance requires the production of durable and movable objects that conform to the conditions of commodities and entails the abstraction of those objects from their sites of production in circulation and exchange.[18] It also requires the abstraction of relations of exchange themselves. This abstraction is the difference between the artist-patron relationship defined by specific commissions and the artist-collector relationship that emerged with relatively anonymous bourgeois art markets and that introduced the economic dimension of artistic autonomy. What post-studio practice represented, therefore, was a radical shift in the conditions not only of the autonomy of the art object, but the autonomy of artistic practice itself.

One aspect of Buren's critique of the studio and museum was that the distance between sites of production and consumption, explicitly closed by post-studio activity, are only, in fact, apparent: the museum "makes its 'mark,' imposes its 'frame' (physical and moral) on everything that is exhibited in it . . . all the more easily since *everything that the Museum shows is only considered and produced in view of being set in it.*"[19] Buren recognized that the instrumentalization of art for economic and symbolic profit is conditioned by the autonomy of the artwork itself. This autonomy allows the art object to become "what even its creator had not anticipated, serving instead, as is usually the case, the greater profit of financial interests and the dominant ideology."[20] Buren also appeared to recognize that this ideological use depends not only on the autonomy of artworks, but on the autonomy of the aesthetic itself. While the former allows for the appropriation of artworks for economic profit, the latter, by foreclosing determined functions, consigns artworks to ideological use. While the autonomy of artworks as commodities may allow them to produce economic profit, the

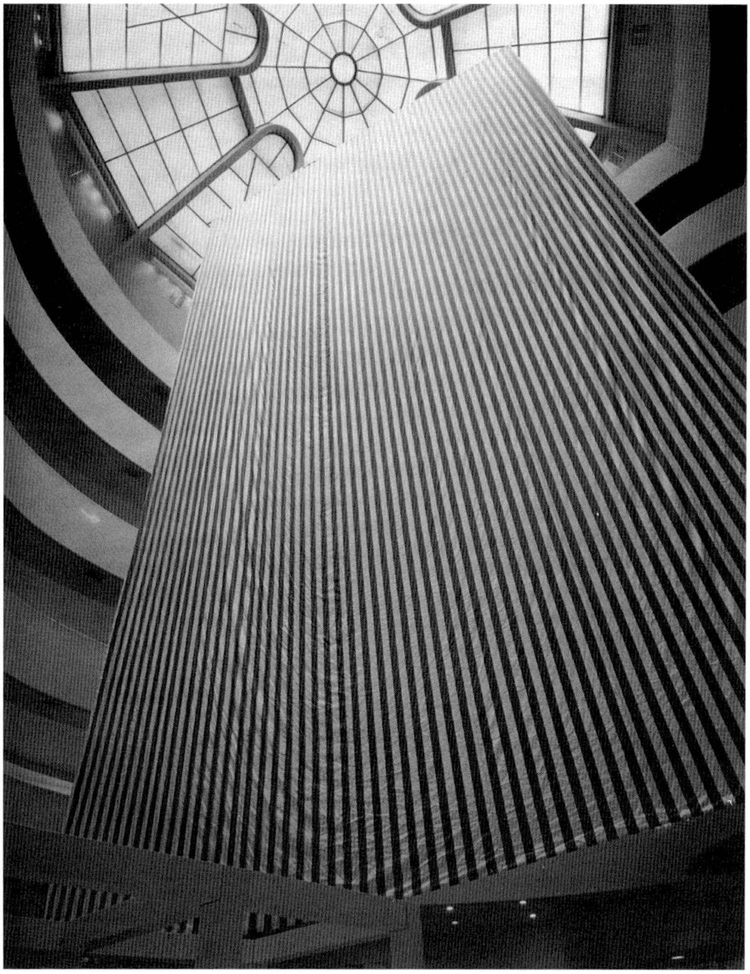

6.2 Daniel Buren, *Photo-Souvenir: Peinture-Sculpture (Painting-Sculpture)*, acrylic on fabric, work in situ at the Guggenheim International Exhibition, 1971, Solomon R. Guggenheim Museum, New York. Photo: Robert E. Mates and Paul Katz.

autonomy of art as aesthetic construct is what allows it to produce the symbolic profit of social and cultural legitimacy.

It may have been precisely this profit in legitimacy that Huebler was describing when he wrote about the "conspiracy" (of taste) that underlay exchanges between collectors and conceptualists or minimalists. In a text published at the same time as Huebler's statement, Buren was writing—"in conscience of the danger that, in art, a form/thing . . . can become, even if it is physically, aesthetically, objectively insignificant, an object of reference and of value"—of the need to develop "a method of work." This method should be allied, not to "any particular inspiration" (or sensibility), but to "a specific system" that he characterizes as "*indicative* or *critical*. Among other things . . . of its own process."[21]

The rejection of commodity production in the dematerialization of the art object or its temporalization in specific sites did not necessarily imply a rejection of economic relations. But did it imply the return of relations of patronage, as texts by Lippard and Kosuth seem to suggest, or the emergence of a new set of relations? Both conceptual art, by projecting its consumption in contractual works, and post-studio practice, by eliminating the distance between sites of production and consumption, substituted specific for generalized relations of exchange. But what would turn those specific relations into patronage? The answer may be found in the absence of a direct exchange of quantities of value: the absence not only of the deferred exchange value of an object of investment but also, within aesthetic paradigms of gratuitous production and disinterested consumption, of function and use. The determinedly critical function of Buren's "method" is what distinguishes the relations established in his post-studio approach from those of patronage that much conceptual and site-specific work seemed to evoke, from the extravagant subsidies of the Dia Art Foundation to the support provided by Virginia Dwan, a wealthy gallerist who made many of the most ambitious earthworks of the period possible.

Buren's engagement with specific sites implicitly addressed the social and economic relations underlaying "the false discretion of . . . depersonalized architectures."[22] However, it was left to Michael Asher to develop a system that both revealed the relations constitutive of a site and redefined the place of his own practice within them.

Asher's 1973 and 1974 exhibitions at commercial art galleries are notable not just as interventions on the "commercial adaptation" of aesthetic production within the gallery space, but because they formalize Asher's situational practice itself as a form of resistance to that adaptation. Writing about his 1973 exhibition at the Heiner Friedrich Gallery in Cologne in which he painted the ceiling throughout the entire gallery (including offices, hallways, storage, etc.) a tone slightly darker than the floor, Asher notes: "In this work, the viewer could see the relationship between the gallery's office space activities and the gallery's exhibition space activities, which visibly appeared as opposed functions in that the fixed nature of the work (the whole gallery) came into opposition with the commercial functions of the gallery." However, besides making those opposed functions visible, the work also performed its own opposition by stipulating that the ceiling be painted over after the one-month duration of the exhibition. (The gallery did not meet this condition.)

Service Occupations: Institutional Critique and Cultural Mediation

> The apparently homogeneous notion of the expansion of the services sector, that is typical of late capitalism, must therefore be reduced to its contradictory constitutive elements. This expansion involves:
> 1. The tendency towards a general extension of intermediate functions . . .
> —Ernest Mandel, *Late Capitalism*, 1972

The first time Asher received a fee for his work was for the "Spaces" exhibition organized by Jennifer Licht at the Museum of Modern Art in late 1969. "Spaces" was also the first time MoMA compensated artists for participating in an exhibition that did not result in the museum's ownership of an artwork. The fees that artists received for "Spaces" were only and explicitly in compensation for generating temporary installations specifically for the exhibition.

It wasn't Asher who requested a fee for his participation, but probably the collaborative group Pulsa. Pulsa, whose members were trained as architects and engineers, may simply have transferred practices standard in these fields to their relations with the museum. For the museum, the request could not have come as a complete surprise—MoMA had been fending off AWC demands to provide fees for showing existing works for almost a year. The museum may have found the logic of providing fees for temporary site-specific installations easier to follow.

While "Spaces" does not appear to have been considered a particularly important exhibition at the time, it was noted as an example of the new curatorial practices emerging around conceptual and other "dematerialized" art. "Spaces" conformed to noted aspects of those practices: artists were selected, rather than specific works, and artists participated with works that were produced specifically for the exhibition and ceased to exist after it closed.

These practices were perhaps most evident in Lippard's and Siegelaub's curatorial activity. Lippard's exhibition concepts entailed a new level of curatorial determination in formulating not only the themes but also the procedures, sites, and situations that artists would work within. Writing about Lippard's 1969 Seattle exhibition, "557,087," Peter Plagens noted: "There is a total style to the show, a style so pervasive as to suggest that Lucy Lippard is in fact the artist and that her medium is other artists."[23] In "On Exhibitions and the World at Large," Siegelaub describes the new tendency as the organizing of "exhibitions in which the general conditions are proposed to the artists and the decisions about specifics are left entirely to them."[24] Lippard describes her 1970 exhibition "Groups" as an "experiment in dealing with an imposed experience."[25]

By early 1970, Jack Burnham could write that the fact that gallery and museum exhibitions were "increasingly planned, not through the selection of existent work, but on the basis of submitting proposals" was a *reason* for the emergence of conceptual art rather than a response to it.[26] In any case, it's clear that the shift conceptual and post-studio practices accomplished from abstract and generalized conditions of production and circulation to specifically determined relations of exchange was also being implemented by new curatorial practices. While conceptual and post-studio practices implied a new relationship between artists and curators, those relationships were also emerging through developments taking place within museums and museum professions themselves.

Siegelaub wrote that conceptual art would reduce the art world to "two types of people: artists and everyone else."[27] What seems to have been building was, rather, a new level of identification among artists, critics, and museum professionals: a "collaboration of people and flexible adjustment of roles and areas of responsibility," as Licht wrote in her *Spaces* acknowledgments.[28] However, the meaning and character of that collaboration was soon called into question. Battcock's 1970 review of MoMA's "Information" show echoes Buren's "The Function of the Museum." Artworks, Battcock writes, "are perceived within a frame of reference." In the case of "Information," "the museum is our frame of reference for the art works and interacts with them in providing the meaning." However, Battcock continues, one "result from the new frame of reference concept is that art works have to be made specifically *for* the Museum of Modern Art, and that's what's wrong. They should have been made *against* it."[29]

Half a year before the formation of the AWC, another group of artists and activists occupied the Palais des Beaux-Arts in Brussels and attempted to supplant its administration. Marcel Broodthaers's participation in that occupation is widely evoked as a precedent to his establishment, in September 1968, of the *Musée d'Art Moderne, Département des Aigles, Section XIXème Siècle* in his Brussels studio and his appointment of himself as director.[30]

In its first incarnation, which lasted a year, the interface of Broodthaers's museum with officially chartered institutions was limited to the inaugural address given by Johannes Cladders, director of the museum of Mönchengladbach. Broodthaers's own appropriations of the functions of a museum director were limited to scheduling discussions and issuing open letters under his museum's letterhead. In two of its later incarnations—the 1970 *Section XIXème Siècle (Bis)* and the 1972 *Section des Figures (Der Adler vom Oligozän bis Heute),* both at the Städtische Kunsthalle Düsseldorf—his interaction with museums and their representatives and his appropriation of their functions were greatly extended. The art postcards and empty shipping crates arranged in his Brussels studio were supplanted by objects borrowed from first one museum and then over a dozen museums. Broodthaers's reversal of his initial reversal—from the site of reception to the site of production back to the site of reception—established a set of relations that went well beyond those implied by creating an installation specifically for (or against) a museum. His appropriation of a museological position was no longer purely discursive but became unavoidably intertwined with the mediating functions, practices, and protocols of chartered museums themselves. These included not only Broodthaers's catalogues and captions and the selection and arrangement of objects on loan, which were oriented toward scrambling the classificatory systems and shattering the linguistic transparency those formats and functions presuppose and impose. In fact, all the procedures of securing loans, ensuring their care, registering their circulation, etc., were now also superimposed on Broodthaers's "museum fiction," not only as its object, but also as the very real condition of its possibility.

It was left to Louise Lawler to identify the entire range of functions, sites, and procedures of art presentation as the object and material of artistic engagement: not only the installation of art objects and the mechanisms of publicity and exchange, but also the economic relations that underlie and orient those functions. Her *Untitled: Black/White* artist book of 1978 and her 1983 *Gift Certificate* for Leo Castelli Gallery not only thematize the economic value of artworks but work on the construction of value directly, making the act of valuation in purchase constitutive of the works themselves. Direct engagement with economic relations also underlay Lawler's 1982 arrangement of works by gallery artists at Metro Pictures. If the entire arrangement was sold, Lawler would receive a 10 percent commission on the total value of the work. Lawler's collection installations can thus be distinguished from those of Broodthaers in that she engaged not only the procedures and functions of art mediation, but also the economic conditions and social relations according to which those functions are defined. Yet, unlike the value of the artist books and gift certificate, Lawler's commission was not explicitly constituted as a part of the work.

The ambivalence that marks Lawler's approaches to the economic aspects of her work has everything to do with problems of artistic autonomy. With an art consultant's commission for a gallery show or a curator's fee for a museum installation comes a question of the difference between taking up institutional functions as an artistic intervention and executing the functions of an institutionally defined position.

Service Functions: Community-Based Art and Participatory Public Culture

> A service is nothing more than the useful effect of a use-value, be it of a commodity, or be it of labor.
> —Karl Marx, *Capital,* 1867

I can only speculate on why MoMA decided to compensate artists for participating in "Spaces." If the demands of the AWC for exhibition fees and royalties played some part, it may have been through the direct involvement of curator Jennifer Licht herself in some of the AWC's initiatives.

As the AWC's struggles with MoMA unfolded, the museum as an institution became increasingly differentiated in the group's discourse. Although the AWC initially attacked the curators for mispresenting Takis's sculpture, the group gradually began to identify the board of trustees as the locus of power within the institution and to address the professional staff as potential allies. This change eventually led to the direct collaboration of MoMA's professional staff (against the

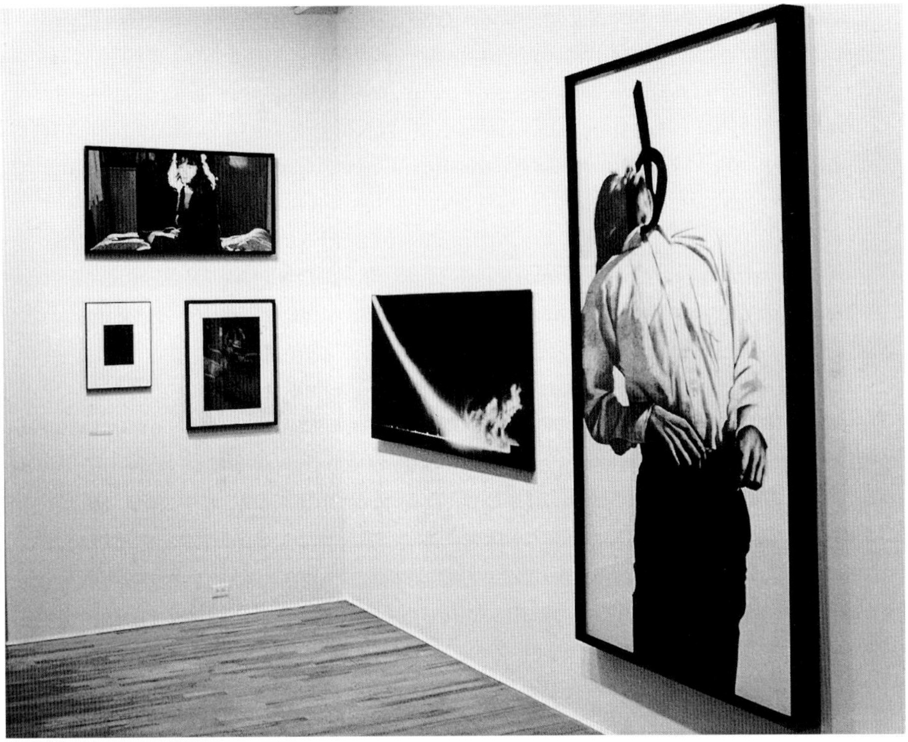

6.3 Louise Lawler, installation view of an arrangement of works by gallery artists at Metro Pictures, New York, 1982. Photo: Louise Lawler.

wishes of management) in such AWC initiatives as the My Lai protest poster. Such collaboration represented not only a growing understanding of museums by the AWC, but also a growing assertion of autonomy by museum professionals from the interests and demands of the museum's management and board. Such assertion of autonomy can be seen as culminating in two events of 1971. The first was the unionization of MoMA's professional staff, a first in the United States. The second event was curator Edward Fry's support of Hans Haacke's exhibition at the Guggenheim against the director's decision to cancel it; Fry was subsequently dismissed for that support.

The unionization drive at MoMA was widely supported by artists, writers, and filmmakers, who signed petitions and joined picket lines. The primary issues in the unionization drive at MoMA were not wages and benefits but staff participation in determining museum policy. A specific policy at issue was MoMA's decision to respond to a budget crunch by cutting back on public services. The strikers' focus on public services may have been strategic, but what it implies is fundamental: MoMA's staff would define their obligation as being to serve not the museum trustees who ostensibly employ them, but the public that supports the museum through tax deductions and for whose benefit the museum exists as a charitable institution. The fact that the contract won by the staff required the museum to seek government funding indicates that the organizers considered it in their interest to make this public support even more direct.

One can see the unionization of MoMA as a conclusive step in the transformation of curators from the personal art advisors of collectors and museum founders (or even the "gentlemen" curators themselves) to independent professionals. Among the contractual guarantees of "professional self-respect" that MoMA's staff won through collective bargaining were paid sabbaticals, research leaves, and tuition funds. Unlike the directly public museums of Europe, long defined as scientific institutions, in the private, nonprofit museum of the United States this assertion of professional autonomy required recourse to the public sector and a substitution of an ethos of public service for one of personal service to museum patrons.

If the shift in the status of museum professionals due to unionization also had an impact on the relations between artists and museums, it may have been because that shift was consistent with the demands of artists themselves. At the AWC's Open Hearing, many participants were already calling on museums to recognize their public responsibilities. A statement prepared jointly by Hollis

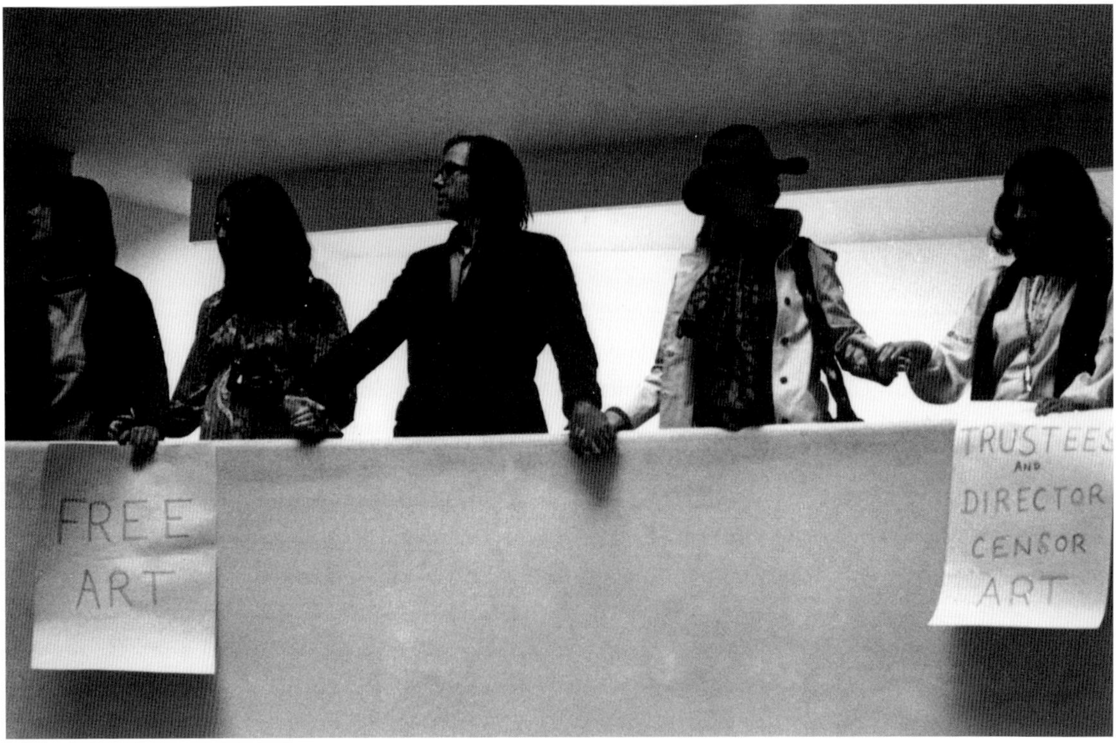

6.4 Demonstration at the Guggenheim Museum, New York, organized in protest against the cancellation of Hans Haacke's retrospective, May 1, 1971. Courtesy Hans Haacke. Photographer unknown.

Frampton, Mark Jacobs, and Michael Snow and a letter to MoMA director Bates Lowry by Tom Lloyd and Faith Ringgold challenged the museum's denial of public obligation by analyzing its tax base as a nonprofit institution. Asserting that the responsibility of museums "comprehends public service," Lloyd and Ringgold called on MoMA to set up a "program embodying cultural identification for blacks and Puerto Ricans," and they questioned its past commitment to the stated aim of providing programs "adapted to the needs of smaller communities."[31]

Most of the demands by Open Hearing participants that museums recognize public service obligations and meet the needs of more diverse communities implied that the gaps between artists and publics were by-products of the elitist character of museums: their plaques to patrons, their entrance fees, their locations, their work-day hours, their exclusion of art by African-American and Hispanic artists. However, there were already intimations of a demand addressed to artists as well: a critique of the art world, the art market, and artworks produced for that apparatus. In the few years following the Open Hearing, the impulse that led to calls for museums to serve diverse communities found an outlet in the development of cooperatives and alternative spaces and in initiatives for community cultural centers spearheaded by artists themselves. The cultural activism represented by the AWC itself and the closely related Guerrilla Art Action Group (and in Europe by such actions as the occupation of the Palais des Beaux-Arts in Brussels and demonstrations at the 1968 Venice Biennale) emerged as a distinct form of artistic activity, along with what is now referred to as community-based art.

What the activist and community-based activities of the early 1970s shared with at least some minimalist, post-studio, and conceptual art was a critique of the commodity status of art objects and their appropriation for economic and symbolic profit. Post-studio and conceptual artists sought to resist such appropriation by pursuing a critique of the partial and ideological character of artistic autonomy while at the same time adopting literally heteronomous forms, procedures, and relations. Implicit in activist and community-based practice, on the other hand, was an acknowledgment and acceptance of the function of art as common culture in representing the interests and serving the needs of particular communities. The obvious homologies between the fields of producers and consumers of art belied art's universality as well as its autonomy. If apparent freedom from the interests of taste and the needs of representation, from economic and other forms of rationalization, itself predisposed autonomous art to represent the freedoms afforded by privilege, then so-called "high" or "elite" culture was nothing other than the culture of elites.

Rather than continuing to serve the interests of the "community" constituted by art insiders (makers, lookers, and buyers), the artists engaged in activist and community-based practices proposed instead to serve their own and other communities of artists, women, African-Americans, Hispanics, neighborhood residents. If post-studio and conceptual artists sought to resist commodification by producing intangible or untransferable works, artists engaged in activist and community-based practices followed a similar course but with a difference: their immaterial and site-specific interventions functioned primarily or exclusively within the public sector as well as within the public sphere.

The Critique of Artistic Autonomy Revisited

Benjamin Buchloh concluded his 1989 essay on conceptual art by linking "the achievement of Conceptual Art"—including its "transformation of audience and distribution" and "abolition of object status and commodity form"—to what he saw as "a profound and irreversible loss," one that represented yet another, perhaps the "last of the erosions . . . to which the traditionally separate sphere of artistic production had been subjected in its perpetual efforts to emulate the regnant episteme within the paradigmatic frame proper to art itself."[32]

In many ways, a genealogy of conceptual art and contemporaneous practices within the framework of services seems to confirm Buchloh's thesis because it brings into clearer focus the myriad points of artistic emulation and appropriation of the "regnant episteme" of a terciarized late capitalist society. These would now include not only the administrative procedures identified by Buchloh, but a whole range of practices and competencies, products, positions, and relations that continue to emerge within the ever expanding field of intermediary and mediating functions that Ernest Mandel identified as one of the dominant features of late capitalism. At the same time, such a genealogy may also make it possible to identify some of the fundamental contradictions that have defined so much critical practice since the 1960s: that a critique of the social and economic uses to which art is put would result in the pursuit of a form of pure use value; that the rejection of the role of "servants of the wealthy" would result in the adoption of the economic conditions and social relations of service provision; that the discovery of the partial and ideological conditions of artistic autonomy would lead to an embrace of heteronomous positions, functions, and relations.

The critique of the autonomy of the art object resulted, first for minimalism and then site-specific art, in the production of works that were physically and conceptually dependent on their particular placement. The critique of the autonomy of the artist as represented by the free play of expression and experimentation resulted in the adoption by minimalists and conceptualists of the systematic procedures that Buchloh called administrative and Rosalind Krauss called obsessional. The critique of the commodity status of the art object did lead some conceptual artists to eschew the art market, but it led many more to reduce the artwork itself to a contract that projected and circumscribed—and, one could argue, further reified—its conditions of exchange. The critique of the autonomy of artistic production in the preserve of the studio resulted in the post-studio practices of Buren, Asher, and others, in which the artwork as well as the motive for its production itself became determined by the conditions under which the artist works. And finally, the critique of the instrumentalization of art and art institutions by political and economic interests resulted in (self-) instrumentalized political documentary practices, like that of Hans Haacke, on the one hand, and the appropriation of instrumental institutional functions, such as exhibition organizing, in the work of Marcel Broodthaers and Louise Lawler, on the other.

But what in fact is the "paradigmatic frame proper to art itself"? What these artists revealed, above all, was that this frame, in its very paradigmatic propriety and artistic discretion, in its traditions of separateness, was "itself" the most mythified of all the "mythical forms of perception and hierarchical modes of specialized experience" that constituted the aesthetic field.[33] What they tore away was the veil on which this myth was projected, which maintained an illusory separation between the paradigmatic and epistemic forms that constitute art's symbolic systems and the practical and economic relations that constitute its material conditions.

At issue is not just the emulation of administrative practices and service relations as a strategy of critical engagement or secondary mythification, much less an aesthetic construct. These artists demanded of artistic practice something much more profound. What they constituted as the fundamental practice of art was nothing less than work on the conditions and relations of production of artistic practice itself: not only the symbolic transformation of artistic positions, and not only what Bourdieu calls "position-takings," but their material transformation as well; the transformation not only of the positions artists represent within the paradigmatic frame of an aesthetic system, but the very positions they occupy and the economic conditions and social relations that produce those positions and which they in turn reproduce. It is not possible to evaluate the work of Hans Haacke, or Lawrence Weiner, or Daniel Buren, or Michael Asher, or Marcel Broodthaers, or Louise Lawler, or of any of the artists whose work proceeds from theirs, without taking into account not only the visible, visual manifestations of their practices, but also their policies; not only the artistic positions they manifest, but also the positions they construct for themselves within the network of relations that constitutes the fields of their activities.

The material arrangements that artists of the past thirty years have endeavored to put into place, both to secure the means to continue their activities and as an integral part of their works, are not only conceptual systems. They are also practical systems that fulfill, or fail to fulfill, the principles of artistic positions on the level of their social and institutional conditions. Far from functioning only as ideology critique, they have aimed to construct a less ideological form of autonomy, conditioned not by the abstraction of relations of consumption in the commodity form, but by the conscious and critical determination, in each particular and immediate instance, of the uses to which artistic activity is put and the interests it serves. And it is in this sense that the substitution of literally heteronomous service relations for ideologically autonomous relations of commodity production and consumption can be seen, not as the final erosion of the traditionally separate sphere of art but as the first step in an effort to move beyond the perpetual replay of the dialectic of negation and institutionalization to which the critique of ideological use is consigned so long as the artistic positions that artists take are considered in isolation from the social and material conditions of the art they make.

Notes

1. Pierre Bourdieu, *Distinction: A Social Critique of the Judgment of Taste,* trans. Richard Nice (Cambridge: Harvard University Press, 1984), 3.

2. Dan Graham, "Carl Andre," *Arts Magazine* (December/January 1967–68), 34.

3. The comments in quotation marks are cited from the statements made by Bruce Brown, Frederick Castle, and Gregory Battcock at the Art Workers Coalition Open Hearing, as represented in a collection of manuscripts distributed by the AWC after the event, 4, 7, 47.

4. AWC Open Hearing, 112–113.

5. Ibid., 76.

6. Seth Siegelaub, "Artists' Reserved Rights Transfer and Sale Agreement," *Studio International* (April 1971), 142. The Agreement itself is reproduced on pages 186–188. It was also reproduced in the catalogue of Documenta V.

7. Adam Smith, *An Inquiry into the Nature and Causes of the Wealth of Nations* (New York: Modern Library, 1985), 136.

8. "A Reasonable and Practical Proposal for Artists Who Wish to Remain Free Men in These Terrible Times," AWC Open Hearing, 32.

9. Lawrence Weiner, *Statements* (New York: Louis Kellner Foundation and Seth Siegelaub, 1968), n.p.

10. Seth Siegelaub, quoted in Jack Burnham, "Alice's Head: Reflections on Conceptual Art," *Artforum* (February 1970), 48.

11. Lucy Lippard, postscript to *Six Years: The Dematerialization of the Art Object* (New York: Praeger, 1973), 263.

12. Lawrence Weiner, quoted in Ursula Meyer, *Conceptual Art* (New York: E. P. Dutton, 1972), 217. Weiner first presented his "instructions" in Seth Siegelaub's exhibition "January 5–31, 1969" (of that date):

    With relation to the various manners of use:

    1. The artist may construct the piece
    2. The piece may be fabricated
    3. The piece need not to be built

    Each being equal and consistent with the intent of the artist the decision as to condition rests with the receiver upon the occasion of receivership.

13. Lippard, preface to *Six Years,* 8.

14. Joseph Kosuth, "Art after Philosophy," *Studio International* (October 1969), 137.

15. Douglas Huebler, *Prospect '69* (Düsseldorf: Kunsthalle Düsseldorf, 1969), 26.

16. Andre made his opinions clear, at least with regard to the latter point, in 1976: "The most farcical claim of the conceptualizing inkpissers is that their works are somehow antibourgeois because they do away with objects. In fact, doing away with objects and replacing them with such reifications of abstract relations to production as stockshares, contracts, liens, options, and paper money itself (which is nothing but the fetishization of the idea of exchange value severed from even the dream of production) is exactly the final triumphant form of the bourgeois revolution." Carl Andre and Jeremy Gilbert-Rolfe, "Commodity and Contradiction or Contradiction as Commodity," *October* 2 (Summer 1976), 103.

17. Robert Smithson, "Towards the Development of an Air Terminal Site," *Artforum* (June 1967). Quoted here from *The Writings of Robert Smithson,* ed. Nancy Holt (New York: New York University Press, 1979), 41.

18. Buren writes that work produced in a studio "makes its passage, in order to exist, from one refuge to another. It should therefore be portable, manipulable if possible, by whoever (except the artist himself) assumes the responsibility of removing it from its place of origin to its place of promotion." Daniel Buren, "The Function of the Studio" (1970), in AA Bronson and Peggy Gale, eds., *Museums by Artists* (Toronto: Art Metropol, 1983), 63.

19. Daniel Buren, "The Function of the Museum" (1971), in Bronson and Gale, *Museums by Artists,* 58.

20. Buren, "The Function of the Studio," 63.

21. Daniel Buren, "Beware!," first published as "Mise en Garde!" in the catalogue *Konzeption/Conception* (Leverkusen: Städtisches Museum, 1969). Quoted here from *Studio International* (March 1970), 101, 102.

22. Daniel Buren, "The Function of Architecture" (1975), in Bronson and Gale, eds., *Museums by Artists,* 73.

23. Peter Plagens, "557,087," *Artforum* (November 1969). Quoted here from Lippard, *Six Years,* 111.

24. Seth Siegelaub, "On Exhibitions and the World at Large," interview with Charles Harrison, *Studio International* (December 1969), 20.

25. Quoted from Lucy Lippard's description of the project in "Groups," *Studio International* (March 1970), 93. The entire project was presented at the School of Visual Art, New York, November 3–20, 1969.

26. Burnham, "Alice's Head," 41.

27. Siegelaub, "On Exhibitions and the World at Large," 20.

28. Jennifer Licht, acknowledgments in *Spaces* (New York: Museum of Modern Art, 1969), n.p.

29. Gregory Battcock, "Informative Exhibition at the Museum of Modern Art," *Arts Magazine* (Summer 1970), 26.

30. See for example, Benjamin Buchloh, "The Museum Fictions of Marcel Broodthaers," in Bronson and Gale, eds., *Museums by Artists;* and Douglas Crimp, "This Is Not a Museum of Art," in *Marcel Broodthaers* (Minneapolis: Walker Art Center, 1989).

31. Tom Lloyd and Faith Ringgold, AWC Open Hearing, 64, 61.

32. Benjamin Buchloh, "Conceptual Art 1962–1969: From the Aesthetic of Administration to the Critique of Institutions," *October* 55 (Winter 1990), 143.

33. Ibid., 143.

7

TO QUOTE, SAY THE KABYLES, IS TO BRING BACK TO LIFE

This tribute to Pierre Bourdieu was first published in October *and* Texte zur Kunst *in their Summer 2002 issues.*

> Doomed to death, that end which cannot be taken as an end, man is a being without a reason for being. It is society, and society alone, which dispenses, to different degrees, the justifications and reasons for existing; it is society which, by producing the affairs or positions that are said to be "important," produces the acts and agents that are judged to be "important," for themselves and for the others—characters objectively and subjectively assured of their value and thus liberated from indifference and insignificance.
> —Pierre Bourdieu, "A Lecture on the Lecture," 1982

I am sitting at a desk at the Collège de France, in an office a few doors down from the office Pierre Bourdieu occupied until a few months ago. I found my way here through the intervention of Inès Champey, who often played the role of mediating my contact with Bourdieu when he was alive. (Bourdieu was the only person to whom I ever sent unsolicited work, but even after we met I remained too shy to call him directly.) Marie-Christine Rivière, Bourdieu's secretary of many decades, graciously responded to my need to consult English translations of his writings. Inès thought this would be the easiest place to find them.

I've been trying to write this short text for over six weeks now. I want to attribute my difficulty to the fact that I'm traveling and don't have access to my library. But the painful irony is that the task of writing a memorial essay about Bourdieu has become a test, not only of my understanding of his work, but of my success in internalizing it.

I haven't been able to find copies of tributes Bourdieu himself wrote. I'm looking through the essays collected in *Language and Symbolic Power*. I wonder if he would have counted the tribute as one of the "rites of institution" he described as serving to consecrate arbitrary differences—the difference, for example, between a significant and an insignificant life.[1] But there is nothing arbitrary to me about Bourdieu's significance in my own life. I'm looking through *Outline of a Theory of Practice*. I wonder if he would have analyzed the tribute as an exchange within a symbolic economy where debt is repaid as recognition.[2] The language of honor and the achievements of great men are foreclosed to me. I'm looking through the essays collected in *Practical Reason*. I wonder if he would have considered the tribute a form of production of symbolic capital that serves to structure the perception of particular properties according to modes of classification generated by the field in which those properties are constituted as legitimate stakes. Or would he have considered the tribute an occasion to practice a "*realpolitik* of reason," pressing the symbolic capital accumulated in the cultural field into the service of struggles against symbolic domination?[3]

Perhaps he simply would have said, as he did when accepting the Ernst Block Prize, that the many eulogies written about him are "really too generous," attributing to "my individual personality alone a number of properties or qualities which are also the product of social conditions."[4]

No, I won't betray him now, by honoring him. No, I won't betray him now, by failing to honor him.

Having come to Paris, where Inès has shown me dozens of tributes published in France, and to the Collège de France, where a meeting of Bourdieu's colleagues and collaborators happens to be taking place in the next room, I'm acutely aware of the arbitrariness of being delegated to write this essay, as well as the arbitrariness of my knowledge of Bourdieu's work itself. I have only a secondhand sense of the impact of his activism of the past decade. I'm not a sociologist or an ethnographer or a philosopher. I can't evaluate his research or theory in its intellectual context. Sitting here, I find myself retreating to the first-person narrative (running the risk of individualizing an experience that is only, as Bourdieu liked to say, after Bachelard, "a particular instance of the possible").[5] Theoretical overviews and artistic applications will have to wait. The tools of universalization are lost to me. Sitting here, I find myself reduced once again in my own mind to the high school dropout whose desperate efforts to compensate for educational failure led me to scour bookshops obsessively, without order, without syllabi. As Bourdieu described the autodidact's knowledge—I'm searching through my borrowed copy of *Distinction* for the passage—what I know of his work is no more than "a collection of unstrung pearls, accumulated in the course of an uncharted exploration" with no other connection than a "sequence of biographical accidents."[6]

My encounter with Bourdieu was just such an accident. Had I syllabi I might never have bought *Distinction,* as Bourdieu was on no reading list I ever received in my mid-1980s art education, despite its infusion with postwar French theory. I was very young. His work became my second language.

He writes: the "autodidact's relations to culture, and the autodidact himself"—in later works Bourdieu took to using feminine pronouns—is a negative product of the educational system as "the sole agency empowered to transmit the hierarchical body of aptitudes and knowledge which constitutes legitimate culture, and to consecrate arrival at a given level of initiation."[7] Above all, he continues, "the autodidact, a victim by default of the effects of educational entitlement, is ignorant of the right to be ignorant that is conferred by certificates of knowledge."[8]

Sitting here in the Collège de France brings back the memory of the acute anxiety I once felt when confronted with legitimate culture—in academic contexts, in France generally, in museums and galleries. I credit Bourdieu with freeing me, or helping me free myself, from the sense of illegitimacy—what he later called symbolic violence—imposed by legitimate culture, "a product of domination predisposed to express or legitimate domination."[9] Against a legitimacy Bourdieu described so simply as "the fact of feeling justified in being (what one is), being what it is right to be,"[10] *Distinction* exposed the paralyzing experience of illegitimacy with liberating clarity: the muting and mutilating violence of cultural judgments, the crushing authority of consecrated competence, the anguish that filled the gap between knowledge and recognition, the sense of imposture, the disfiguring force of aspirations structured according to socially and materially foreclosed possibilities.

But *Distinction,* as a product of Bourdieu's relational, reflexive sociology, also made it impossible for me to imagine symbolic domination as a force that exists somewhere out there, in particular, substantive, institutions or individuals or cultural forms or practices, external to me as a social agent or as an artist—however young and disempowered I may have felt.

"Reflexive analysis," Bourdieu says in *An Invitation to Reflexive Sociology,* "teaches that we are the ones who endow the situation with part of the potency it has over us." It allows us to step back and monitor "the determinisms that operate through the relation of immediate complicity between position and dispositions," between the social fields in which we exist and the internalized schemes of perception and appreciation, classification and hierarchization, interest and practice produced in those very fields, which he called habitus.[11]

Bourdieu was explicit in describing one of the aims of his work as producing a habitus disposed, "as a matter of practical logic," to act reflexively. If reflexivity, for Bourdieu, was the condition of the possibility of liberation from symbolic domination, he also saw it as the condition of social science, as what stands between scientific truth and theoretical distortions which, more often than not, result in the reproduction of conservative doxa.[12]

Bourdieu defined reflexive methodology as the full objectification, not only of an object, but of one's relation to an object—including not only the schemes of perception and classification one employs in one's objectifications, and not only one's interest in objectifying, but the social conditions of their possibility.[13] The principle of reflexivity seemed to orient every turn of Bourdieu's practice, from choosing to do ethnographic fieldwork in Algeria during the Algerian war—where he already questioned the "practical privilege" of the observer[14]; to pursuing ethnographic study first of his hometown in France and then, in *Distinction,* of France itself; to his study of the production and exploitation of the very forms of capital that he himself held as a consecrated intellectual, in *Homo Academicus* and *The State Nobility;* to his work on *Masculine Domination;* and finally, to challenging in his activism the profound if often unconscious complicity that exists between increasingly heteronomous intellectuals and neoliberalism's "theodicy" of competence, which they share.[15]

One of the most important elements of Bourdieu's analysis of the cultural field (including such subfields as the arts, the humanities, and the sciences) is that it occupies a dominated position in the dominant field—or what he also called the field of power. He described this condition as one of the foundations of the ambivalence of artists and intellectuals. In our own experiences as a "dominated faction of the dominant faction," as well as in the homology between our condition and the condition of dominated classes, we may find our politics. But in our own interests in maintaining and improving our relative position, invested even in our struggles against the dominant, we also tend to reproduce the conditions of domination—our own and that of others.[16] As Bourdieu wrote in *Distinction,* "one may choose to emphasize either the complicities which unite them in hostility or the hostilities which separate them in complicity";[17] but the structural homologies that exist within the field of power between the holders of cultural capital and the holders of economic and political capital consign artists and intellectuals to their place within "divisions of the labor of domination"—material and symbolic. They are homologies that political self-proclamations tend most often only to mask.

It is, above all, from the structural ambivalence of the cultural field that the necessity of reflexive cultural practice arises. According to our position "as dominated among the dominant," reflexive analysis does not only demand of cultural practice a politics. It also—to evoke a term Bourdieu used only rarely and with caution—demands an ethics: a limit on the exploitation of a form of power we may or may not subjectively experience but nevertheless objectively manifest as holders of a relative monopoly on forms of socially and institutionally recognized competence.

It was Bourdieu's reflexivity, even more than the explanatory power of his account of the cultural field (and my experiences in it) that turned me into an adherent. As an artist, I perceived an immediate sympathy between his reflexive sociology and site-specific institutional critique—they are practices I now see as differing only in the different tools they employ and the different fields in which they function. While I have never been in the position to evaluate the scientific truth claims of Bourdieu's work, I do see reflexivity as the condition of the truth of any critical practice. It may be the only thing that stands between critique, intervention, even possible transformation, and the reproduction of the relations of domination expressed and legitimized in the cultural field. If we, as artists and intellectuals, are to exercise our historically won freedoms by speaking truth to power, then it is first of all to the truth of our own power that we must speak. Any other critical practice, or critical theory, is simply bad faith. Bourdieu provided not only the tools for understanding that truth, but an exemplary performance of its practice. Cultural fields confer an extraordinary autonomy, he wrote somewhere, especially when you use that autonomy not as a weapon against others or an instrument of defense, but as a weapon against yourself, an instrument of vigilance.

I'm reaching for "A Lecture on the Lecture," which Bourdieu delivered in 1982 on his induction into the Collège de France. It begins: "One ought to be able to deliver a lecture, even an inaugural lecture, without wondering what right one has to do so: the institution is there to protect one from that question and the anguish inseparable from the arbitrariness of all new beginnings."[18] With that question Bourdieu stepped away from the protection, the consecration, the justification, provided by the institutions of cultural legitimacy. And in that distance he created the only opening through which I can imagine being able to enter them.

Notes

1. Pierre Bourdieu, "Rites of Institution," in *Language and Symbolic Power,* ed. John B. Thompson, trans. Gino Raymond and Matthew Adamson (Cambridge: Harvard University Press, 1994), 118.

2. See Pierre Bourdieu, "Structures, Habitus, Power: Basis for a Theory of Symbolic Power," in *Outline of a Theory of Practice,* trans. Richard Nice (Cambridge: Cambridge University Press, 1977).

3. See Pierre Bourdieu, "The Economy of Symbolic Goods" and "The Scholastic Point of View," in *Practical Reason* (Stanford: Stanford University Press, 1998).

4. Pierre Bourdieu, "A Reasoned Utopia and Economic Fatalism," *New Left Review* 227 (January/February 1998), 125.

5. See, for example, "The Practice of Reflexive Sociology (The Paris Workshop)," in Pierre Bourdieu and Loïc Wacquant, *An Invitation to Reflexive Sociology* (Chicago: University of Chicago Press, 1992), 233–234.

6. Pierre Bourdieu, *Distinction: A Social Critique of the Judgment of Taste,* trans. Richard Nice (Cambridge: Harvard University Press, 1984), 328.

7. Ibid.

8. Ibid., 329.

9. Ibid., 228.

10. Ibid.

11. Bourdieu and Wacquant, *An Invitation to Reflexive Sociology,* 136.

12. For a good introduction to Bourdieu's notion of reflexive sociology, see Loïc Wacquant, "Epistemic Reflexivity," in Bourdieu and Wacquant, *An Invitation to Reflexive Sociology,* 36–46.

13. See also Bourdieu's discussion of "participant objectivation" in *An Invitation to Reflexive Sociology,* 68, 253–260.

14. Bourdieu, *Outline of a Theory of Practice*, 1.

15. Pierre Bourdieu, "The 'Globalization' Myth and the Welfare State," in *Acts of Resistance*, trans. Richard Nice (New York: New Press, 1998), 42–44.

16. See Pierre Bourdieu, "The Field of Cultural Production, or: The Economic World Reversed," in *The Field of Cultural Production* (New York: Columbia University Press, 1993).

17. Bourdieu, *Distinction*, 316. See also the section on "The Correspondence between Goods Production and Taste Production," 230–244.

18. Pierre Bourdieu, "A Lecture on the Lecture," in *In Other Words*, trans. Matthew Adamson (Stanford: Stanford University Press, 1990), 177. The title of this tribute, as well as the epigraph, can be found in the same text on page 196.

PUBLIC

PRIVATE

INSTITUTIONS,

OBJECTS

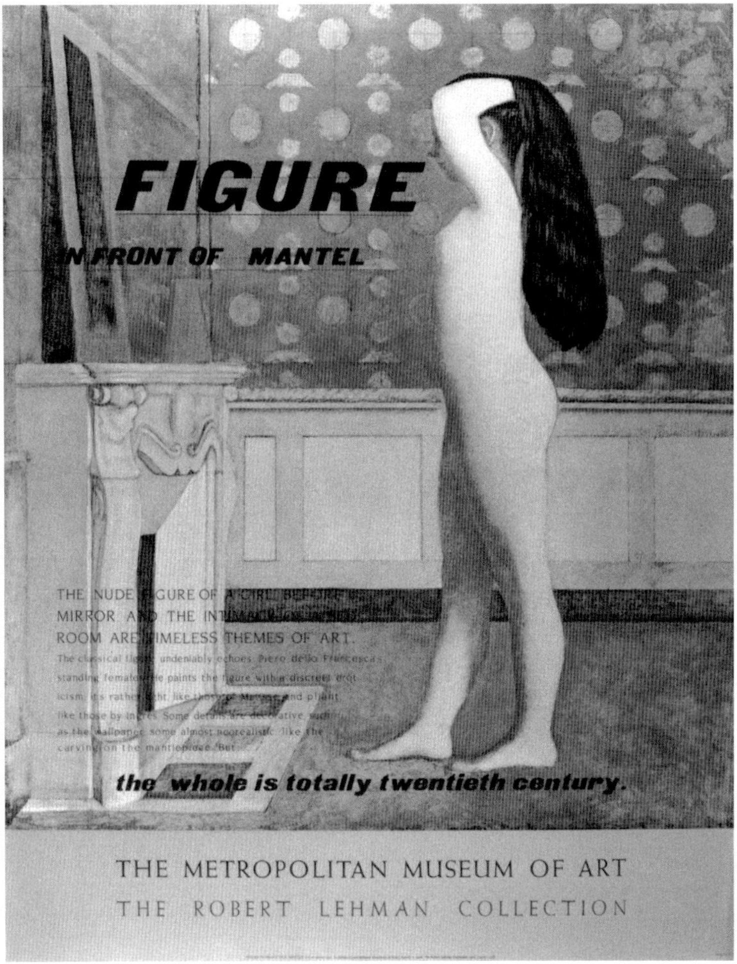

8.1 Andrea Fraser, *Four Posters,* 1984 (detail). Posters purchased at the Metropolitan Museum of Art gift shop with text from the museum's object labels silk-screened over the reproductions. Courtesy the artist and American Fine Arts, Co.

8

NOTES ON THE MUSEUM S PUBLICITY

"Notes on the Museum's Publicity" was first published in the Fall 1990 issue of the journal Lusitania.

According to the National Endowment for the Arts, in order for an institution to qualify as a museum in the United States it must, among other things, have "permanent facilities open to the public on a regularly scheduled basis" and be "a nonprofit tax-exempt organization."[1] The nonprofit tax-exempt status of an art museum—even and particularly including its income-generating activities, such as merchandising—depends on the museum's primary charitable purpose of "providing educational experiences for the public."[2] This educational purpose is conceived of as accomplished in the first instance, not in any actively educational programs or practices, but simply in the presentation of art to the public: not only "on a regularly scheduled basis" (like any commercial art gallery), but specifically by "a nonprofit tax-exempt organization."

It would seem, then, that the museum's nonprofit tax-exempt status is what qualifies the artworks it presents to be the object of the educational experiences on which its tax-exempt status depends. This apparent tautology can be resolved by introducing a single displacement: it is not tax-exempt status as such that conditions the educational value of the art objects presented in museums, but the philanthropic gestures through which those objects find their way into the private nonprofit sphere.

So I arrive at the rather contradictory logic of the private nonprofit art museum's status as a public institution. The economic aspect of the art museum's publicity is conditioned by the fact that it is publicly subsidized, often directly through municipal support and state and federal grants, and always indirectly through its tax-exempt status and the deduction on income taxes allowed for contributions to charitable organizations. (Under the Tax Reform Act of 1969, the taxpayer's share of every $1,000 donated to a tax-exempt organization was estimated at 60 to 70 percent.)

Yet this economic publicity is predicated on, and at the same time concealed by, the much more highly publicized privacy of the bankers and investors, lawyers and industrialists, executives and corporations on whose philanthropic engagement nonprofit organizations depend.

Public subsidy is provided no such publicity. The charitable deduction is invisible; municipal support generally funds the most menial, least visible aspects of the museum's operations—utilities, building maintenance, and security. There are no plaques reading "This light bulb was given to the museum by the City of New York."

The museum's purpose is not only to publicize art, but to publicize art as an emblem of bourgeois privacy. Its purpose, in a sense, is to publicize privacy. It is in this, it would seem, that the museum's educational function consists.

Of course, this has always been the logic of American public policy. Public provision, if it must exist to maintain stability in a population subject to the violent vacillations of a capitalist economy, should exist always only as a promise and never as a right: a promise perpetually retreating into the private sector. The history of this retreat is marked by a trail of institutions and organizations operating in the name of public education. When art museums began to be established in numbers in the United States, in the last quarter of the nineteenth century, what limited public relief programs that existed were being systematically dismantled and privatized. Some of the proponents of privatization founded museums and libraries, others established Charity Organization Societies. Like museums, these Societies would offer only things of the mind and spirit. Instead of providing material relief, they sought to educate.

Of what did this education consist? Not schooling, not training, but rather "friendly visits" that aimed "to regenerate character" and "involved the direct influence of kind and concerned, successful and cultured, middle- and upper-class people upon the dependent"[3]—education by example; education by identifications structured within public policy and institutional discourse.

If the museum's publicity has the function of structuring popular identification with bourgeois privacy, it does so first simply through the museum's visibility and accessibility: open "on a regularly scheduled basis," it offers up what was formerly the content of homes to public display. Second, as "a nonprofit tax-exempt organization," often with direct municipal subsidy, the museum imposes popular investment in itself, inasmuch as the museum comes to that population already with the population's economic support. Third, on this, the museum's real "debt" to the public, is superimposed a symbolic debt of the public to it: a debt produced by the philanthropic gestures of the patrons who provide it with much more visible support. The museum thus draws a population into a cultural contract, obliging that population to make itself "worthy" of capital's gifts. Finally, after indebting a population to it and thereby obliging that population to enter it, the museum offers to it, as its own, what it has already turned into "public" culture.

If culture consists of the narratives, symbolic objects, and practices, with which a particular group represents its interests and its experience, its history and possible futures, fine art represents the interests and experiences first of the professional community of primarily middle-class artists who produce it, and second of the bourgeois patrons who collect it and re-present it in museums with their names alongside those of its producers. The museum, as a public institution, offers up fine art as a general public culture, a national or even universal civic culture, and turns it into the single cultural currency that can be traded by members of the civic community.[4] The museum's patrons are represented as being in primary and privileged possession of this cultural currency, while all of the symbolic objects produced outside of the specialized sphere of publicized artistic activity are banished to the oblivion of individual lives, without authority to represent "public" experience.

Notes

1. National Endowment for the Arts, *Museums USA* (Washington, D.C.: U.S. Government Printing Office, 1974), 4. Other criteria used to determine whether an organization is a museum include: facilities open at least three months per year, an operating budget of a minimum of $1,000 (in 1971–72), ownership of at least part of the collection exhibited, and at least one full-time paid employee with academic training.

2. Ibid., 25. In the late nineteenth century, the educational purpose of museums was articulated as improving public morals by improving public taste. These days, one more often hears the more modest promoting public awareness of art.

3. Walter I. Trattner, *From Poor Law to Welfare State: A History of Social Welfare in America* (New York: Free Press, 1974), 97.

4. Art museums, like public schools historically, may in this way function to foster a material impoverishment of the cultural practices they exclude. In New York City, for example, the aim and direct effect of instituting a public school system—or rather, a public school tax—in the mid nineteenth century was to prevent most immigrant Irish from sending their children to Catholic parochial schools, for which they would have to pay again. Thus public schools functioned to break down community organizations by forcing a mass investment in a public sphere controlled, of course, by an American-born Protestant bourgeoisie. See David Nasaw, *Schooled to Order: A Social History of Public Schooling in the United States* (New York: Oxford University Press, 1979), for example 54–55.

9

MUSEUM HIGHLIGHTS: A GALLERY TALK

"Museum Highlights: A Gallery Talk" exists in a number of different forms, each with the same script but very different frames. As a live performance in the form of a museum tour, it existed for audiences at the Philadelphia Museum of Art in the winter of 1989. Later, it was recorded as a videotaped introduction to the museum. The form presented here, with stage directions, epigraphs, and extensive footnotes, was first prepared for publication in the journal October *in Summer 1991.*

> Posters, placards, signs, symbols must be distributed, so that everyone may learn their significations. The publicity of punishment must not have the physical effect of terror; it must be an open book to be read. Le Peletier suggested that, once a month, the people should be allowed to visit convicts, "in their mournful cells: they will read, written in bold letters above the door, the name of the convict, his crime and his sentence. . . ." Let us conceive of places of punishment as a Garden of the Laws that families would visit on Sundays . . . a living lesson in the museum of order.
> —Michel Foucault, *Discipline and Punish,* 1977

> In every home in Philadelphia, youth will be taught to revere the things that are housed here.
> —Mayor Harry A. Mackey, at the opening of the new Pennsylvania Museum building, March 27, 1928

The West Entrance Hall of the Philadelphia Museum of Art, February 5, or 11 or 12 or 18 or 19, 1989. Two or three dozen museum visitors are waiting in the southeast corner of the visitor reception area; some are waiting for a Contemporary Viewpoints Artist Lecture by Andrea Fraser; some are waiting for one of the Museum's many guided tours; some are just waiting for friends.

At three o'clock, Jane Castleton enters the West Entrance Hall and begins to address whoever appears to be listening. She is dressed in a silver and brown houndstooth check double-breasted suit with a skirt just below the knee in length, an off-white silk button-down blouse, white stockings, and black pumps. Her brown hair is gathered into a small bun held in place with a black bow:

Good afternoon, uh, everyone? Good afternoon. My name is Jane Castleton, and I'd like to welcome all of you to the Philadelphia Museum of Art. I'll be your guide today as we explore the museum, uh, its history, and its collection.

Our tour today is a collection tour—it's called "Museum Highlights"—and we'll be focusing on some of the rooms in the Museum today, uh, the Museum's famed period rooms; dining rooms, coat rooms, et cetera, rest rooms, uh—can everyone hear me? If you can't hear me, don't feel shy; just tell me to speak up. That's right. As I was saying, we'll also be talking about the visitor reception areas, and various service and support spaces, as well as this building, uh, this building, in which they are housed. And the Museum itself, the Museum itself, the "itself" itself being so compelling.[1]

Of course, we'll only be able to visit a small portion of the Museum on our tour today; its over two hundred galleries contain hundreds of thousands of art objects spanning the globe and centuries. But, just to give you a general idea, uh, to help you orient yourself, this may be your first visit, your very first visit to the Museum today—welcome again.

This is the West Entrance Hall. Uh. Opposite, of course, is the East Entrance, where we'll be going shortly. This is really the center of the Museum which—as you can see on these maps here—consists of a long central building with wings extending back at each end. It's four stories high including a basement.

This West Entrance Hall provides access to the ground floor of the South Wing that houses some of the Museum's public facilities that we'll be visiting, uh, later on today.

Jane walks to the information desk in the center of the West Entrance Hall.

It also houses the Museum's brand-new combination information desk, admissions desk—I hope that all of you have paid your admission fee—and, uh, membership desk. If you're a Museum Member, of course, you don't have to pay an admissions fee.

Membership, you know, "plays a vitally important role in the life of the Museum. . . . Many Members indicate that they joined the Museum because they perceive it to be an institution of the highest quality, one of the world's great repositories of civilization. They see it as a place apart from the mundane demands of reality where an individual can fortify his or her linkage with the creative forces of the world, old and new."[2]

And, uh, if you're a Museum Member, you'll also be able to use the Members Only Lounge located on the balcony directly above my head and to the right, as you see.

I myself did not pay an admission fee. Uh. I'm not a Museum Member, nor am I a Museum employee. I'm a visiting lecturer, a guest of the Division of Education. Uh, I am also, like the Board of Trustees and the Museum Guides, a volunteer.[3] It is thus my privilege, my privilege, as a guest, as a volunteer—and, shall I say, as an artist—to be able to express myself here today simply as a unique individual, an individual with unique qualities.

And I sincerely hope that I express my best qualities—as do we all, if I may say so. That's why we're here.[4]

Let's move on to the East Entrance, shall we. Follow me, if you will. To the elevator . . .

Jane leads the group to the elevators.

Uh, here we are. We're going to the second floor.

When the group reassembles on the second floor in the Great Stair Hall, Jane continues.

Is everyone here? All right, let's continue.

This is the Great Stair Hall, and, as you can see, we're on the second floor, just inside the East Entrance. As I said earlier, this is really the center of the Museum, and it provides access to the Museum's collections. To my right is the South Wing where the American art is generally kept to itself on the first floor, with the South Asian, Near and Far Eastern, and Medieval art on the second floor. To my left is the North Wing where you'll find European and Twentieth-Century Art on the first floor and, on the second floor, more European art and the Period Rooms that we'll be talking about later today.

Uh. The Philadelphia Museum of Art is one of the oldest art museums in the United States. It was originally the Pennsylvania Museum and School of

Industrial Art and it was established in 1877, 1877. Uh, that was in Memorial Hall, not this building.[5] This building opened to the public in 1928. It wasn't originally supposed to be the new home of the Pennsylvania Museum. It was first envisioned about 1907 as, uh, just as a, as "a great building [to be the] terminal feature of the [Benjamin Franklin] Parkway. The purpose of the building was secondary."[6]

But an art museum is not just a building, not just a collection of objects. An art museum—particularly a municipal art museum like our own—is public institution with a mission, with a mandate. And the Philadelphia Museum of Art, uh, like all public institutions, was the product of a public policy.

What was that policy?

Well, writing about *The New Museum and Its Service to Philadelphia* in 1922, the Museum wrote that, uh, they wrote: "We have come to understand that to rob . . . people of the things of the spirit and to supply them with higher wages as a substitute is not good economics, good patriotism, or good policy."[7]

Like the other municipal institutions of the day—uh, the Zoological Garden and the Aquarium also, of course, in Fairmount Park; the new free library on the Parkway; the new municipal stadium; Camp Happy, "for undernourished children"; Brown's Farm, for "dependent and abandoned children"; the new House of Correction; the new Hospital for Mental Diseases at Byberry; the new General Hospital at Blockly; the Hospital for Contagious Diseases at Blockly; the Hospital for the Feeble-Minded at Blockly; the Home for the Indigent at Blockly;[8] the Commercial Museum next to Blockly, where homeless men were sometimes housed, "dedicated to economic education"—now the Philadelphia Civic Center; the poorhouses of Germantown, Roxborough, and Lower Dublin. . . .[9]

Called living tombs and social cemeteries, vile catchalls for all those in need, squalid warehouses for the failures and cast-offs of society,[10] no one would enter the poorhouse voluntarily. The receipt of public assistance was made into a ritual of public degradation so abhorrent that even the meanest work for the meanest wages was preferable.[11]

Jane walks to a window and leans against the grand piano standing in front it.[12]

The Municipal Art Gallery "that really serves its purpose gives an opportunity for enjoying the highest privileges of wealth and leisure to all those people who have cultivated tastes but not the means of gratifying them." And for those who have not yet cultivated taste, the Museum will provide "a training in taste."[13] But, above all, the Municipal Art Gallery should be "generous enough to fitly symbolize the function of art as the expression of all that is noblest in either the achievements or the aspirations of humanity . . . 'where there is no vision the people perish.'"[14]

Jane throws open the curtains covering the window and reveals a perfect vista of the Benjamin Franklin Parkway.

And just look at this view! Magnificent!

"If we do not possess art in a city, or beautiful spots in the city, we cannot expect to attract visitors to our home town."[15]

Jane gestures toward group.

"Because young people in particular are drawn to the area, Philadelphia attracts a huge labor pool of college-educated and trained technical people. And, due to its old manufacturing traditions, skilled laborers are also plentiful."[16]

Jane leaves the window and walks through and past the group. She gestures generally as she walks.

"The climate is healthy. Quality space is available and affordable. . . . The systems for success are in place and working well. But even more important, Philadelphia is livable.

"You can choose from 5 professional sports teams, a world class symphony, 100 Museums, the largest municipal park system in the country, and a restaurant renaissance the whole world is talking about."[17]

Plus: "8 million square feet of new commercial office space. . . . High-tech, Health Care, Medical Publishing and Printing, General Business Services, Financial Services, Heavy Manufacturing [and] Fashion."[18]

I'd like to move on now to the galleries where we'll be talking about some of the Museum's period rooms, uh, as I mentioned earlier, the Museum's famed period rooms. If you'll just follow me, please.

Jane leads the group through the European Art galleries to one of the Museum's period rooms.

And here we are.

This is the Grand Salon from the Château de Draveil. It's French, uh, eighteenth century.

Few eras in history were more preoccupied with "living in style" than eighteenth-century France.

Notice "the chaste style, characteristic of the later years of Louis XVI's reign . . . revealed here in the simplicity of the broad surfaces, in the slender proportions of their frames, and in the classical ornaments . . . carved with the most extreme crispness and brilliance . . . of great beauty and refinement . . . unusual interest . . . of the utmost delicacy."[19]

Next, I'd like to talk about another period room. It's just across the gallery. If you'll follow me, please.

Jane walks across the gallery to another period room, entered through a short, narrow corridor that also contains the door to the Men's Room.

Uh, this is a Paneled Room from England, dating from 1625. It contains seventeenth century Dutch paintings, and was installed in the Museum in 1952, uh . . .

And in here, this is the Men's Room.

"What a difference there may be on opposite sides of a thin partition-wall! On this side of the wall is a family inclined to dirt and disorder because of its unperfect social education. . . . Cleanliness of persons or rooms is wholly forgotten. The floors become littered with filth, for no one feels the desire or obligation to have it otherwise. The rights of property are disregarded or are only respected through fear and personal force.

"On the other side of the wall, only a few inches away, the floor, neatly carpeted, is spotless. The center-table holds a . . . lamp, [and] a vase with fresh grasses. . . . There are pictures on the walls, of . . . landscapes [and] the family. . . .

"One may find a bureau turned into a shrine.

"It stands to reason that slovenly and destructive occupants are not accorded the same attention that is given to . . . those who are clean and careful and prompt in their payments."[20]

Jane leaves the Paneled Room.

"The public, who buy clothes and table china and wall paper and inexpensive jewelry, must be forced to raise their standards of taste by seeing the masterpieces of other civilizations and other centuries."[21]

Here for example . . .

Jane gestures around the gallery.

"Imposing architectural installations . . . provide noble settings within the Museum's . . . galleries."[22]

Jane walks north into the next gallery. Then, addressing The Birth of Venus *by Nicolas Poussin:*

"Resplendently . . . amazingly flawless . . . sumptuous. . . . This figure is among the finest and most beautiful creations. . . . An image of exceptional rhythm and fluidity."[23]

Jane walks across the room to address Saint Luke *by Simon Vouet.*

"This is the most spectacular . . . prized for their clear, bold patterns and relatively few yet strong and harmonious . . . of the more than one thousand works collected by the celebrated Philadelphia Lawyer . . . monumental, sculptural . . . in an austere setting . . .

Jane walks north into a gallery containing The Four Seasons *attributed to Augustin Pajou. As she walks:*

["Steady, thrifty, forehanded and domestic in their habits . . . independent and self-helpful . . . quietly self-assured."][24]

Addressing The Sacrifice of the Arrows of Love on the Altar of Friendship *by Jean Pierre Antoine Tassaert:*

"One of the most jarring and emotionally effective interpretations. . . . The writhing, enchained, muscular . . . majestic, frenzied . . . [vast and vigorous . . . perfectly complimented Europe's opulent palaces and churches . . .]

[Let's move on to the next gallery, shall we . . .]

Jane walks north into the next gallery. Gesturing generally:

"One of the most complex yet graceful compositions of the seventeenth century . . .

Addressing Cabinet *attributed to Adam Weisweiler:*

"This charming group of dancing maidens . . . graceful, life-size, mythological . . . a creation of almost visionary splendor. The sweeping and surging . . . exaggerated, lunging . . . at once so splendidly theatrical and so obviously individualized . . .

Jane walks back into the gallery containing The Four Seasons. *She addresses the group:*

["Though she was from 'out of town' her background was similar to theirs, and she fit in to the routine of afternoons 'at home,' the Tuesday box at the Academy of Music, the opening night of the Oil Painting Show . . ."][25]

Speaking generally:

". . . where the best qualities of taste were sustained until late in the century . . .

Addressing a guard's stool in the corner of the gallery:

"In scale and complexity . . . the most ambitious undertaking . . . in the great European tradition . . . abundance and grace . . . free from time and change . . ."

Addressing The Four Seasons: Autumn as Bacchus:

And here . . .

"American, mother, three brothers distinctly subnormal, herself mentally deficient, violent, undisciplined and lacking in every qualification of motherhood, shiftless, irresponsible. . . . Her second husband is one of the most degraded, of a low and vicious family . . . extremely backward and incorrigible . . . father being of less than average intelligence . . . generally . . . regarded by all who have dealt with her as weak . . . and a dangerous character on account of her immoral propensities . . . grossly low condition . . . unable to learn . . . of no service in the home, and constantly . . . given to self abuse . . . almost entirely nude . . . stretched out on floor with a dirty, blackened pan. . . ."[26]

Addressing the group:

I want to be graceful.

Rituals of family and love and orderliness.

Jane walks back to gallery with The Birth of Venus. *Speaking generally:*

"Gentle, private . . . charm and originality. . . . Total restraint . . . utilitarian . . . rectilinear . . ."[27]

Addressing The Birth of Venus:

"Lower class culture: there is a substantial segment of present-day American society whose way of life, values, and characteristic patterns of behavior are the product of a distinctive cultural system which may be termed 'lower class.'"[28]

Jane walks back into the gallery between The Grand Salon *and the Paneled Room. Speaking generally as she walks across the gallery:*

"Plain grace . . . harmony and perfection . . . impressive . . . severely formal, yet tender . . . vigorous . . . humble . . . joyful . . ."[29]

"Shiftless, lazy, unambitious . . . ; chronic poor . . .

Addressing Rape of the Sabines *by Luca Giorgano:*

"unable to 'make a go of it' because of character deficiencies or lack of skill . . . ; [If you'll just follow me . . .] 'the new poor'; 'multi-problem families'; 'the culture of poverty'; 'disreputable poor,' 'paupers,' 'cannot cope,' 'make noise,' cause trouble and generally 'create problems' . . . 'lower-lowers.'"[30]

Addressing an exit sign above door at the far end of the gallery:

"Firm in painting, delicate in color and texture, this picture is a brilliant example of a brilliant school."[31]

Or over here . . .

Jane exits the gallery, leaving most of the group some distance behind her. She continues into the Medieval art galleries, walking back toward the Great Stair Hall. Speaking generally:

"Unstable and superficial interpersonal relationships . . . low levels of participation . . . little interest in, or knowledge of, larger society . . . sense of helplessness and low sense of personal efficiency. . . . Low 'need achievement' and low levels of aspirations for the self.

Turning to address the group:

["The love of beauty is one of the finer things that makes life worth living."][32]

Again speaking generally:

"Jobs at the lowest level of skills . . . unskilled . . . and menial jobs . . .

Gesturing toward various parts of the gallery:

"in hotels, laundries, kitchens, furnace rooms, nonunionized factories and hospitals . . ."[33]

"Scattered brick houses . . . dreary warehouses . . . blank walls and junk yards . . . drab, enclosing . . . sometimes blue. . . ."[34]

Jane walks through the doors to the Great Stair Hall. She stops and turns to address group:

Really! I mean . . . Here for example . . .

Jane moves in the direction of the stairs as she speaks, gesturing generally at benches, the stone railing, tapestries, etc.

"You take your ordinary, barnyard room, so to speak, the familiar room that you have lived in, that you never thought of as a work of art, and somehow, insensibly, you pull it about, you put a chair in a different place, you arrange the mantelpiece, get rid of half the impedimenta of the mantelpiece—you know how most people load up the mantelpieces—you simply strip it and you put one or two things there and you put them in the right place . . . an artist will do that. . . . Well, that's what a museum does, I think, for all of us."[35]

I'd like to continue on now to the first floor.

Jane descends the Great Stair with the group. At the second landing she begins speaking, gesturing in various directions around the Great Stair Hall as she walks. When she reaches the bottom of the stair she walks around it to the left.

As I mentioned earlier, it "consists of a center building, with wings at each end extending back. . . . It is four stories high, including the basement. . . .

"The inmates are lodged in rooms of about 22 feet by 45 feet (of which there are 42) from 20 to 24 persons in each room, and are classed according to their general character and habits, separating the more deserving from the abandoned and worthless, and thus removing the most obnoxious feature consequent to such establishments. The Americans are generally by themselves; so are the Irish; and the Blacks also have their separate apartments.

"[It] also contains a penitentiary, a hospital for the sick and insane, several large buildings for work shops, school rooms, lodging rooms for children, and the various out-houses of a large and well regulated establishment. . . ."[36]

She stops in front of Diego Rivera's Liberation of the Peon, *which is hung outside the door to the coat room underneath the stair.*

And isn't this a handsome drinking fountain!

Jane walks into the Coat Room, gesturing toward the drinking fountain at the far end. Addressing the drinking fountain:

Hmm, ". . . a work of astonishing economy and monumentality," "it boldly contrasts with the severe and highly stylized productions of this form." [Uh, notice, uh . . .] "The massiveness . . . the vast [uh] . . . most ambitious and resolved!"[37]

Graceful, mythological, life-size . . .

I want to be graceful.

Jane leaves the coat room, gesturing for the group to follow her.

You know—come along. You know "each individual, no matter how untutored, [can find] a thousand objects (or better still, just one . . .) so obviously perfect and so directly in the line of [her] own half understood striving for perfection that . . ."[38]

Here for example . . .

Jane walks to David Smith's Two Box Structure. *Standing next to it, she holds her arm outstretched.*

Notice how the light catches the fabric, the tiny houndstooth checks of the suit, and silvers the fabric a little more brightly, as it falls about the arms, the legs, uh, just below the knee, and creases slightly at the waist, double-breasted.

But look at the face. The skin is broken. She turns her head away slightly.

Jane begins walking to the stairs leading to the West Entrance Hall, still speaking.

While her dress and bearing may suggest an upper-class, uh, lady, the discriminating, uh, the discriminating, viewer, will notice that her hands are scarred and poorly manicured, and her teeth have not been straightened.

I'd like to move on to the West Entrance now.

Half way down stairs to the West Entrance Hall, Jane turns to address the group.

"The museum's task could be described as the continuous, conscientious and resolute distinction of quality from mediocrity."[39]

"Hunger is the best sauce, and everything that is eatable is relished by people with a healthy appetite; but a satisfaction of this sort shows no choice

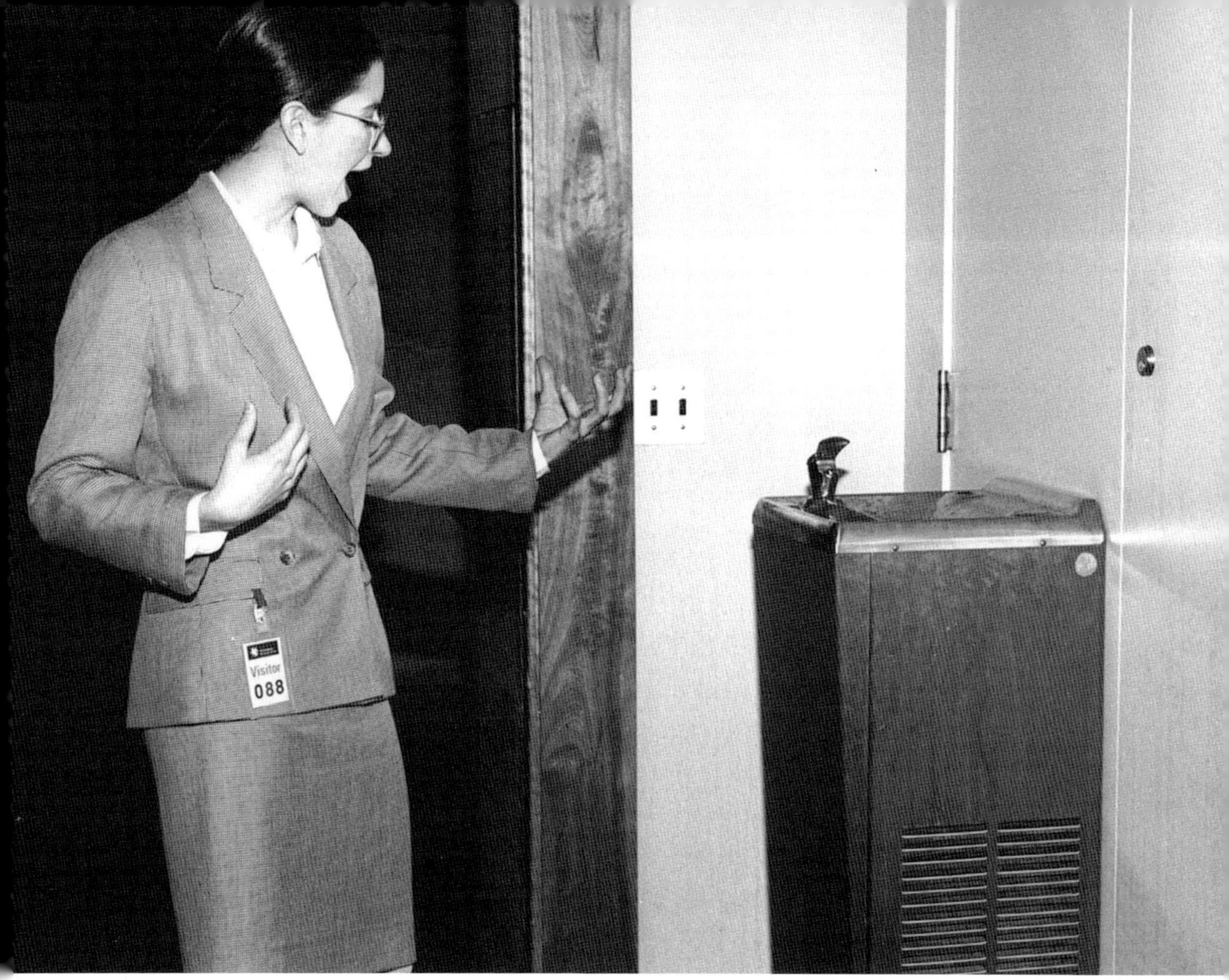

9.1 Andrea Fraser, *Museum Highlights: A Gallery Talk*, 1989. Live performance at the Philadelphia Museum of Art, Philadelphia. Courtesy the artist. Photo: Kelly & Massa Photography.

directed by taste. It is only when the want is appeased that we can distinguish which of many men has or has not taste."[40]

In the West Entrance Hall:

"Still, it takes very little to produce a perfect plate of fruit and cheese." Here for example . . .

Addressing one of two Nymphs Holding Aloft a Platter Charged with Fruit *by Claude Michel (known as Clodion):*

". . . hunks of sharp white Vermont cheddar served in rough hewn blocks, and a single perfect apple are elegant in their simplicity and preferable . . .

Turning to address the second of the Nymphs:

". . . to such daunting combinations as chicken medallions with avocado."[41]

Jane walks away from the Nymphs. *She walks past the coat room and into a corridor with rest rooms, telephones, the Art Sales and Rental Gallery, and some contemporary art. She speaks while walking, turning occasionally to address the group.*

"I heard at a Sunday Brunch not long ago. . . . Everybody, it seems, now has horror stories:

"A man with a magnificent house on Delancey Place says he can't keep flowers outside, because every morning he finds the pots overturned and his sidewalk covered with filth and litter.

"Another man tells of seeing a street bum [who seems to have taken over every available nook, cranny, and stairwell] sprawled in front of Nan Duskin on Walnut Street, in our prime retail location. Nobody could move this bum, not even the police.

"A woman who has always been a patron of the Art Museum can't believe what a shambles the landscaping there has become . . .

". . . there is no longer anyplace to escape [no civilized oasis]."[42]

Jane stops at the end of the corridor and turns to address the group.

This corridor houses some of the Museum's public facilities: the coat room, rest rooms, telephones, uh . . . it doesn't really have a name, but, uh, down the hall here . . .

Jane walks down an adjoining corridor toward the Drawing and Print Galleries opposite the Museum Shop.

Down the hall here we have the Muriel and Philip Berman Drawing and Print Galleries. They were named as part of the Museum's Donor Recognition Program. The Museum you know provides prospective donors with a veritable cornucopia of Named Space Opportunities.

Here for example . . .

Jane walks across the corridor to address the Museum Shop.

. . . for $750,000 you could name the Museum Shop.

You know, I'd like to name a space, why, if I had $750,000 I would name this shop um . . . Andrea. Andrea is such a nice name.

Jane walks a few feet further down the corridor and stops again to address the group.

This is our Museum Shop, Andrea, named in 1989 by Mrs. John P. Castleton, a onetime Museum guide and eternal art appreciator. Jane, as she was called, always liked to say that "patronage creates a personal sense of ownership in a beautiful home of the arts and unites the most enlightened spirits of the community in a high devotion to the public good."[43]

"Did you know her? To know her was to love her. She was special . . . with her long stride and tailored profile, a [blond] of medium height dressed in understated refinement, incredibly 'finished.' She often carried a briefcase . . . apologizing. . . . Her voice surprised . . . deep and husky and resonant with emotion . . . drawing out and lingering over the vowels . . . a serious student, humble, hungry, analytic. She read . . . and would look and invite us to look. . . . There was time to . . . see more clearly."[44]

Jane is silent for a moment and then continues speaking as she walks past the Museum Shop and on through the series of harshly lit and empty corridors that lead to the Museum's cafeteria.

"The Museum wants and needs an informed, enthusiastic audience whose . . . knowledge of the collections and programming continue[s] to grow."[45]

The Museum says: here you will find "satisfaction," you will find "contentment," you will find "pleasure," here you will find "the finer things that make life worth living," here you will be liberated "from the struggle imposed by material needs," here you will find your "ideal beauty," you will find "inspiration," here you will find "a place apart," you will find "standards," here you will find "civilization. . . ."[46]

Jane stops just outside the cafeteria.

Oh, I've known happiness, intense happiness, exquisite happiness, here in the museum, beside these tiles, or across the room from those or, or over here, between these two.

It's nice to feel alive.

I'd like to live like an art object. Wouldn't it be nice to live like an art object . . .

A “sophisticated composition” of “austere dignity,” “vitality and immediate quality”; a “strict formality softened by an exquisitely luminous atmosphere. . . .”[47]

How could anyone ask for more.

Graceful, mythological, life-size . . .

Jane enters the cafeteria.

“This room represents the heyday of colonial art in Philadelphia on the eve of the Revolution, and must be regarded as one of the very finest of all American rooms.”[48]

Jane moves through the room as she speaks, gesturing at tables, chairs, trash bins, cafeteria patrons, etc.

Notice “the architectural decoration. . . . [It] combines the classical vocabulary of broken pediments and fluted pilasters familiar in English house design, with the flamboyant, asymmetrical plaster ornamentations derived from the French Rococo style. The beautiful upholstered sofa, Chippendale style chairs, and marble-top table show the variety of form for which Philadelphia furniture makers were justly famous.”[49]

And . . . “This room was much frequented by Washington while Commander-in-Chief and President.”[50]

Jane leaves the cafeteria and walks back the way she came.

“Stately men and women—above all things stately—measured, ordered, with a certain quiet elegance about them . . . sober color, dignified composition, the arrangement . . . that is simple, fine, and sympathetic to us all . . . [certain habits of good drawing . . . things which I like to call the ‘good manners of painting’] . . . a little more measure, a little more calm, a little more serenity . . . dignity and a certain technical rectitude . . . taste, the sense of measure and decorum. . . .

“Well, frequent this museum of yours and get in contact with tradition. You drink in the tradition that exists [here] and that is . . . piled up [here], all the epochs, all the great ages. You will feel with me that these touchstones, these standards, after all, are not pedantic things [but] standards for a cultivated, governed, discriminating instinct.”[51]

Let’s not just talk about art. Because finally, the Museum’s purpose is not just to develop an appreciation of art, but to develop an appreciation of values.

“By appreciation of values we have in mind the ability to distinguish between the worthy and the unworthy, the true and the false, the beautiful and the ugly, between refinement and crudity, sincerity and cant, between the elevating and the degrading, the decent and indecent in dress and conduct, between values that are enduring and those that are temporary,”[52] between . . .

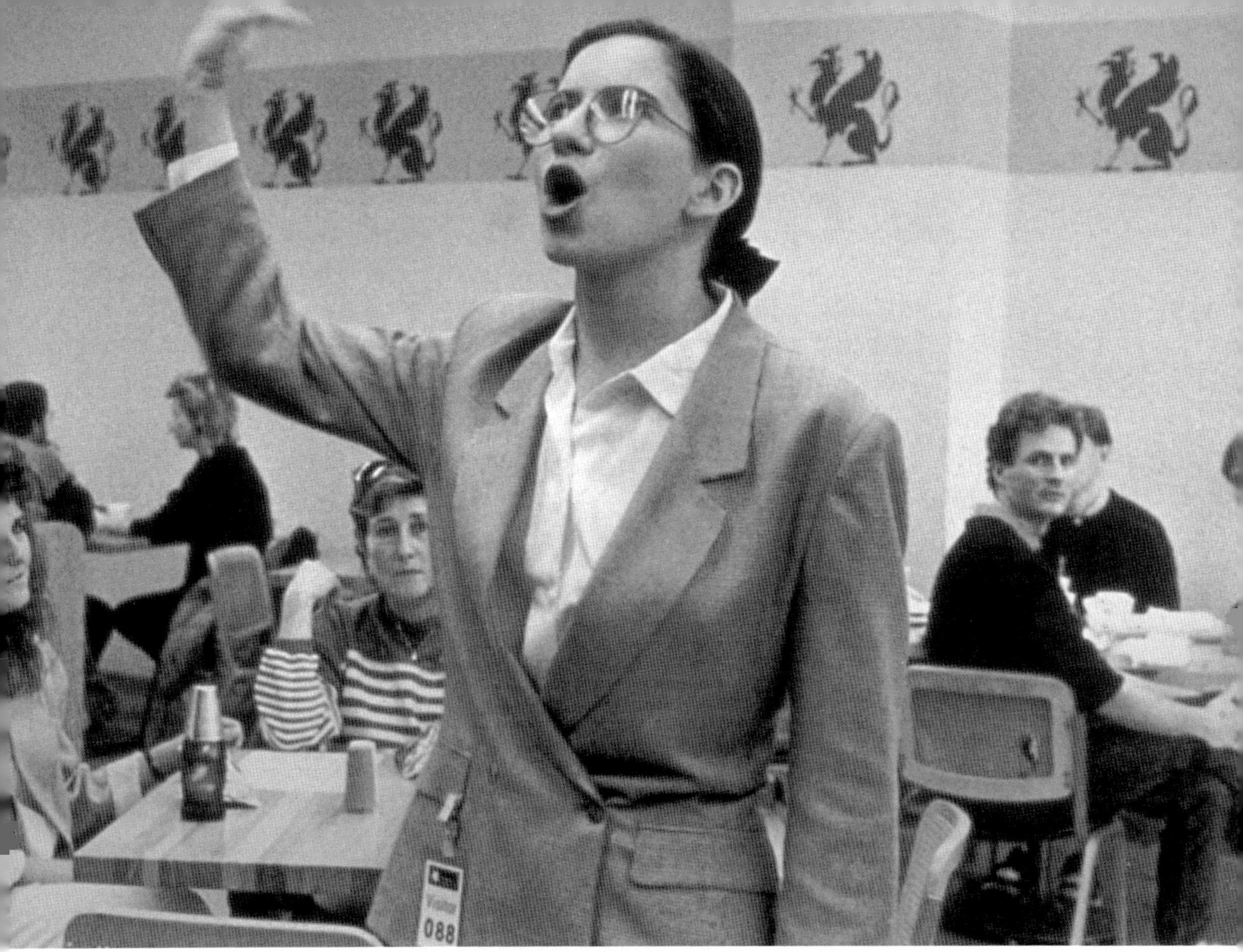

9.2 Andrea Fraser, *Museum Highlights: A Gallery Talk*, 1989. Live performance at the Philadelphia Museum of Art, Philadelphia. Courtesy the artist. Photo: Kelly & Massa Photography.

Here . . . over here . . . between . . .

Jane walks quickly back into the corridor with the telephones, coat room, rest rooms, Art Sales and Rental Gallery, etc. She moves around the corridor, gesturing to these things as she refers to them.

. . . here, the ability to distinguish between a coat room and a rest room, between a painting and a telephone, a guard and a guide; the ability to distinguish between yourself and a drinking fountain, between what is different and what is better and objects that are inside and those that are outside; the ability to distinguish between your rights and your wants, between what is good for you and what is good for society.

Well, that's the end of our tour for today.

Thank you for joining me and have a nice day.

Notes

1. *Museums Highlights: A Gallery Talk* was developed as part of the Contemporary Viewpoints Artist Lecture Series, which was organized by the Tyler School of Art of Temple University and funded by the Pew Charitable Trusts. The performance owed its existence to Hester Stinnett, the director of Contemporary Viewpoints, who invited me to Philadelphia, and to Danielle Rice, the Philadelphia Museum of Art's Curator of Education, who supported the performance from within the Museum. I would also like to thank Donald Moss for his comments on various drafts of this script, Allan McCollum for first calling the activities of docents to my attention, and Douglas Crimp, at whose request the script was first prepared for publication in *October* magazine.

2. Robert Montgomery Scott and Anne d'Harnoncourt, "From the President and the Director," *Philadelphia Museum of Art Magazine* (Spring 1988).

3. This is partly true. For the first performance, I received an honorarium from Contemporary Viewpoints. The following four performances were "voluntary." Providing the services of a guide in the galleries and at the information desk, a volunteer docent is not just someone who gives tours for a small percentage of the museum's visitors; she is the museum's representative. Unlike the members of the museum's nonprofessional maintenance, security, and gift shop staff whom visitors come in contact with, the docent is a figure of identification for the primarily white, middle-class audience. And unlike the museum's professional staff, the docent is the representative of the museum's voluntary sector. The Philadelphia Museum of Art, like many municipal or civic museums in the United States, is a hybrid of public and private nonprofit, volunteer and professional. The city owns the building and provides municipal employees for its security and maintenance; volunteer trustees own everything in the building and govern a private nonprofit corporation that engages other volunteers and hires a professional staff. While docents are usually trained by the professional staff, I would say that they aspire less to professional competence than to what Pierre Bourdieu calls the "manner of relationship to legitimate culture" that marks those to whom the objects within the museum belong(ed), a manner

that really only can be acquired through an "imperceptible learning" over "time and applied by those who can take their time" (*Distinction: A Social Critique of the Judgment of Taste*, trans. Richard Nice [Cambridge: Harvard University Press, 1984], 66, 71, 72).

4. While Jane is a fictional docent, I would like to consider her less as an individual "character" with autonomous traits than as a site of speech constructed within various relations constitutive of the museum. As such, Jane is determined above all by the status of the docent as a nonexpert volunteer. As a volunteer, she expresses the possession of a quantity of the leisure and the economic and cultural capital that defines a museum's patron class. It is only a small quantity—indicating rather than bridging the class gap that compels her to volunteer her services in the absence of capital; to give, perhaps, her body in the absence of art objects. Yet it is enough to position her in identification with the museum's board of trustees and as the museum's exemplary viewer.

5. The Pennsylvania Museum and School of Industrial Art was a product of the Centennial Exposition held in Philadelphia in 1876. In 1893 the School of Industrial Art moved to a "property formerly belonging to the Institution for the Deaf and Dumb." The Pennsylvania Museum maintained a large study collection of decorative arts. By 1910 it began to be derided as a "mixed up collection of industrial exhibits and curiosities, as well as art, in . . . the cluttered gloom of Memorial Hall" (Nathaniel Burt, *Perennial Philadelphians* [Boston: Little Brown, 1963], 344). "Occupied by specimens of Industrial Art," Memorial Hall was considered unsuitable "for the exhibition of paintings and fine art" (*Report of the Commissioners of Fairmount Park for the Year 1912*, 9).

6. George and Mary Roberts, *Triumph on Fairmount* (Philadelphia: J. B. Lippincott, 1959), 24.

7. Anonymous, *The New Museum and Its Service to Philadelphia* (Philadelphia: Pennsylvania Museum and School of Industrial Art, 1922), 19. Art museums began to be established in large numbers in the United States in the last quarter of the nineteenth century. At that time there was a general movement, spearheaded by bankers and industrialists, to tighten public relief and reorganize public policy. The primary aim of this movement was to eliminate all direct outdoor or extra-institutional public relief which, Francis Fox Piven and Richard A. Cloward write, "was making it possible for some of the poor to evade the new industrial assault" by providing a choice between work under any conditions and starvation (*The New Class War* [New York: Pantheon, 1982], 64). Direct material relief would be limited to the poorhouse, where "'discipline and education' should be 'inseparably associated with any system of relief'" (Michael B. Katz, quoting Josephine Shaw Lowell, *In the Shadow of the Poorhouse* [New York: Basic Books, 1986], 71).

8. According to the *Report of the Committee on Municipal Charities of Philadelphia* (1913), Blockly was "a reproduction on a large scale of conditions often found in country almshouses," an overcrowded and "unscientific massing of several types of dependents" (11). In 1928, the year that the new Pennsylvania Museum on the Parkway opened to the public, Philadelphia's Home for the Indigent was described in municipal reports as follows: "In this division of the bureau is the City's poor of both sexes; some who have served their apprenticeship in crime and shady transactions, as lax in caring for their bodies as their morals, acquainted with the usages and customs of reformatories and prisons, graduates from the House of Correction and similar institutions, having 'sold their birthright for a mess of pottage,' and when unable to continue the customary mode of existence owing to age or infirmities, have drifted into the home and become a public charge" (*The Fourth Annual Message of W. Freeland*

Kendrick, Mayor of Philadelphia, Containing the Reports of the Various Departments of the City of Philadelphia for the Year Ending December 31, 1927, 244).

9. This list was compiled from *The First Annual Message of Harry A. Mackey, Mayor of Philadelphia, Containing the Reports of the Various Departments of the City of Philadelphia for the Year Ending December 31, 1928*.

10. Nineteenth-century descriptions of nineteenth-century poorhouses quoted in Walter I. Trattner, *From Poor Law to Welfare State* (New York: Free Press, 1984), 59.

11. The establishment of public institutions, particularly poorhouses, as deterrents to their use and goads to work at menial jobs at below subsistence wages is an idea that was perhaps first codified in England in the 1834 *Report from His Majesty's Commissioners for Inquiring into the Administration and Practical Operation of the Poor Laws:* "Into such a house no one will enter voluntarily; work, confinement, and discipline, will deter the indolent and vicious; and nothing but extreme necessity will induce any to accept . . . the sacrifice of their accustomed habits and gratifications." Quoted in Francis Fox Piven and Richard A. Cloward, *Regulating the Poor* (New York: Random House, 1971), 33–34.

12. Where Mrs. Robert Montgomery Scott is wont to give impromptu recitals.

13. The Museum Fund, *A Living Museum: Philadelphia's Opportunity for Leadership in the Field of Art* (Philadelphia: Pennsylvania Museum and School of Industrial Art, 1928), 2, 17.

14. Fairmount Park Art Association, *Forty-Second Annual Report of the Board of Trustees* (1913), 18. I would like to consider the art museum, then, as one term in an organization of public institutions, and of publicity, into a system of incentives and disincentives, goads and deterrences. Composed of coupled ideas, paired and opposing representations, this system might function similarly to what Foucault described in *Discipline and Punish* as the tactics of nineteenth-century penal reform: "Where exactly did the penalty apply its pressure, gain control of the individual? Representations: the representations of his interests, the representation of his advantages and disadvantages, pleasure and displeasure. . . . By what instrument did one act on the representations? Other representations, or rather couplings of ideas (crime-punishment, the imagined advantage of crime-disadvantage perceived in the punishments); these pairings could function only in the element of publicity: punitive scenes that established them or reinforced them in the eyes of all." Michel Foucault, *Discipline and Punish: The Birth of the Prison*, trans. Alan Sheridan (New York: Vintage Books, 1979), 127–128.

15. Joseph Widener, "Address," in *Fairmount Park Art Association, Fifty-Sixth Annual Report of the Board of Trustees* (1928), 44.

16. Philadelphia Industrial Development Corporation, "How a Unique Combination of Location, Lifestyle and Low Costs Is Sparking a Regional Economic Boom in the Nation's Birthplace," *Business Week*, 18 April 1986, 27.

17. Philadelphia Industrial Development Corporation, "Philadelphia Is a Decision You Can Live With," *Business Week*, 18 April 1986, 13.

18. Philadelphia Industrial Development Corporation, "How a Unique Combination," 27.

19. Fiske Kimball, "Six Antique Rooms From the Continent," *Pennsylvania Museum Bulletin* 24 (October/November 1928), 7. (Kimball was the Parkway Museum's founding director.)

20. Octavia Hill Association of Philadelphia, *Good Housing that Pays* (Philadelphia, 1917), 83.

21. *The New Museum and Its Service to Philadelphia*, 5.

22. The following descriptions (except those otherwise footnoted) were taken in the order that they appear from *Introduction to the Philadelphia Museum of Art* (Philadelphia: Philadelphia Museum of Art, 1985).

23. I would like to consider the following descriptions as representations not of paintings, but of the museum's ideal visitor—representations of her interests, representations of her advantages and disadvantages, pleasures and displeasures. They are representations less addressed to than constructing the museum's audience—constructing out of a heterogeneous field of different, conflicting interests, a homogeneous public. They would do so by taking hold of those interests, wants, needs, desires; taking hold of them and representing them, reforming them, directing them, and determining the space, the language, and the logic in which they can be articulated.

24. Descriptions of Philadelphians from Burt, *Perennial Philadelphians*, 108, and John Lukacs, *Philadelphia: Patricians and Philistines 1900–1950* (New York: Farrar, Straus & Giroux, 1981), 72.

25. A description of Mrs. Eli Kirk Price. Price, according to George and Mary Roberts, was responsible for getting the new Fairmount Museum building on the city plan. See Roberts and Roberts, *Triumph on Fairmount*, 21.

26. Department of Public Health and Charities of Philadelphia, *The Degenerate Children of Feeble-Minded Women* (1910), 2–8: "THE HISTORIES OF THESE FEEBLE-MINDED WOMEN AND THEIR FEEBLE-MINDED CHILDREN ARE PRACTICALLY THE SAME. THEIR UNFORTUNATE BIRTH, HELPLESSNESS, PAUPERISM AND RUIN IS PART OF A CONTINUOUS SERIES WHEREBY THE COMMUNITY IS CONSTANTLY SUPPLIED WITH THE ELEMENTS OF DEGENERACY."

27. *Introduction to the Philadelphia Museum of Art.*

28. Walter B. Miller, quoted in Chaim I. Waxman, *The Stigma of Poverty: A Critique of Poverty Theories and Policies* (New York: Pergamon Press, 1977), 26.

29. *Introduction to the Philadelphia Museum of Art.*

30. Z. D. Blum and P. H. Rosi, "Social Class Research and Images of the Poor: A Biographical Review," in Patrick Moynihan, ed., *On Understanding Poverty* (New York: Basic Books, 1969), 350.

31. This sentence is the complete description of a painting in "The Display Collections: European and American Art," *Pennsylvania Museum of Art Handbook* (1931), 65.

32. Museum Fund, *A Living Museum*, 27.

33. Blum and Rosi, "Social Class Research," 351.

34. Description of the approach to Philadelphia's Twentieth Street Station on a train. From Roberts and Roberts, *Triumph on Fairmount,* 17.

35. Royal Cortissoz, "Life and the Museum," Fairmount Park Art Association, *Fifty-Seventh Annual Report of the Board of Trustees* (1929), 55.

36. Philadelphia Board of Guardians, "Report of the Committee Appointed by the Board of Guardians of the Poor of the City and Districts of Philadelphia to Visit the Cities of Baltimore, New York, Providence, Boston, and Salem (1827)," in David Rothman, ed., *The Almshouse Experience: Collected Reports* (New York: Arno Press, 1971), 8.

37. *Introduction to the Philadelphia Museum of Art.*

38. *The New Museum and Its Service to Philadelphia,* 20.

39. Alfred H. Barr Jr., from a Museum of Modern Art plaque.

40. Immanuel Kant, *Critique of Judgment,* trans. J. H. Bernard (New York: Hafner Press, 1951), 44.

41. Fran R. Schumer, "Salad and Seurat: Sampling the Fare at the Museums," *New York Times,* 22 April 1987, C1.

42. D. Herbert Lipson, "Off the Cuff," *Philadelphia Magazine,* December 1988, 2.

43. Museum Fund, *A Living Museum,* 19.

44. *The Weekday Museum Guides Twenty-Fifth Anniversary 1960–1985* (Philadelphia: Philadelphia Museum of Art, 1985), 2.

45. Scott and d'Harnoncourt, "From the President and the Director."

46. From Scott and d'Harnoncourt, "From the President and the Director"; Museum Fund, *A Living Museum;* and *The New Museum and Its Service to Philadelphia.*

47. Descriptions of art in *The Metropolitan Museum of Art Guide* (New York: Metropolitan Museum of Art, 1983), 18, 20.

48. "The Display Collections: European and American Art."

49. *Guide* (Philadelphia: Philadelphia Museum of Art, 1977).

50. *Pennsylvania Museum of Art Handbook* (1931).

51. Cortissoz, "Life and the Museum," 53.

52. Edwin C. Broome, "Report of the Superintendent of Schools," *One Hundred and Tenth Report of the Board of Public Education for the Year Ending December 31, 1928,* 275–276.

10

A LETTER TO THE WADSWORTH ATHENEUM

"A Letter to the Wadsworth Atheneum" was written to the museum's curator of Contemporary Art, Andrea Miller-Keller, during the preparation of the performance Welcome to the Wadsworth. *The letter circulated informally within the museum when it was received in March 1991. It was first presented publicly (along with the videotape of the performance) at the exhibition "What Happened to the Institutional Critique?" organized by James Meyer at American Fine Arts, Co., New York, in 1992.*

It isn't easy for me to describe at this point exactly what my performance at the Wadsworth will be. In the interest of helping you prepare your essay on my project, I have outlined below my interpretation of the Atheneum in the Hartford context. The performance, in any case, will be based on this analysis.

Let me begin by saying that the Wadsworth Atheneum is a tough nut to crack. I have come to see art museums as compromise formations set up to protect the interests of one class while responding, in a displaced way, to the demands of another. In this way they're like symptoms; they cover over conflict with displaced representations. Such representations exist as seams, which I then try to unstitch. But I can't find any seams in the discourse of the Wadsworth Atheneum. I can't find any representations that even covertly recognize class conflict. In the museums I have studied in the past, such covert recognition comes into play in representations of a public other than the museum's patron class; the public for or against which the institution constitutes itself—the public, for example, that a museum is founded to educate.

The Wadsworth Atheneum is and always has been, like other art museums in the United States, an educational institution. But unlike most late-nineteenth-century municipal museums, the Atheneum's conception of its educational purpose does not appear to have been defined by an interest in reforming its public's culture. Indeed, as far as I can tell, until the 1970s the Atheneum had no interest in a public: no interest, that is, in those who were not already disposed to the culture of the museum's patron class.

Why was this so? Perhaps it was because in the mid nineteenth century the Hartford "community" was so homogeneous that there was no "public" in this sense. Perhaps it was because in the late nineteenth century Hartford's ethnic communities were not large or strong enough to develop the Tammany Hall that the Metropolitan Museum's founders organized to challenge. Perhaps it was because the early dominance of service sector industries in Hartford did not give rise to the kind of class conflict that threatened bourgeois hegemony in other, larger cities in the late nineteenth century. Perhaps it was because by the time class and racial conflicts produced militant community organizations in the 1960s, all of the affluent whites had already moved to the suburbs. Perhaps it was because Hartford's Yankee identity was so strong, and so narrow, that the city's affluent simply would not recognize that they had interests that were in conflict with those of others.

All of this implies that the Atheneum was not founded to engage in the social control through public cultural re-education that defined other nineteenth-century American art museums. But it also implies that, at least in its cultural institutions, social conflict in Hartford is not recognized, not represented—even as a by-product of an attempt to repress it.

The absence of representations of conflict in the discourse of the Atheneum would not have struck me if it did not also appear to characterize Hartford as a whole. For example, all the texts I read about Hartford published outside of the region tell of the city's severe racial conflicts and dire economic distress, while all the texts I read published within the region offer glowing reports. In the Hartford Collection at the Hartford Public Library there seem to be no files on the many oppositional community groups mentioned in *New York Times* articles. The index to the *Hartford Courant* contains no references to articles about the opposition to urban renewal projects that I have read about elsewhere.

Similarly, within the Atheneum itself, in all of the published material I have found on A. Everett Austin Jr., the Atheneum's director from 1927 to 1945, there is no mention of the circumstances under which he left the museum. In the files I have found on Carl Andre's *Stone Field* and Alexander Calder's *Stegosaurus* there is no documentation and almost no mention of the well-known local opposition to the public placement of these sculptures.

I'm sure that local representations of urban conflict in the Hartford area exist. My point is that they seem to be excluded from public discourse, or at least from the discourse of public institutions and public space in the downtown area. This seems to be a consequence not simply of the usual suppression, but rather of a nonrecognition of the fact of social alterity; of the not just different but conflicting interests that constitute the social field.

If the Atheneum was not founded for an "other" public, for whom was it founded? I think that the philanthropic gestures with which most late-nineteenth-century municipal museums were founded had the purpose of obligating a public to the museum and its patrons. They were gifts that functioned to create a social debt. With the Atheneum, I have the sense that the patrons' gifts were rather offered to satisfy historical obligations of a patriotic or familial nature. Its patrons were paying debts to their fathers, their brothers, their husbands; to the hometown they had in other ways abandoned; in the case of Daniel Wadsworth, perhaps to redeem the wealth his father amassed (profiteering on his position as the Chief General of Supply, some say) during the Revolutionary War. If the Atheneum is, as it appears to be, a series of memorials, it would not be far-fetched to say that its intended audience is less the living than the dead. Rather, I would say, its audience is not the dead, but the same.

The prevalence of memorials in downtown Hartford, including those that make up the Atheneum, indicates a particular conception of a public and of public space on the part of those who created them. It indicates, first, that Hartford imagines itself to be, or wants to present itself as, a kind of preindustrial community consisting only of one or two very large families—now including corporate families. Public space is the field across which these families address each other and represent their common history. Everyone else is a visitor whom one might treat kindly but whom one really doesn't want in one's home, and need not address. They're simply not members of the "community."

The prevalence of historical plaques amidst the destruction of actual historical sites in downtown Hartford indicates a similarly narrow conception of urban "community"—but here along historical rather than demographic lines. It is as if these "families" need save nothing of the past for posterity because they, their ancestors, and their progeny are one and the same. Those who build the new buildings are the same as those who built the buildings being torn down.

They are not obliged to preserve their past, but only to maintain the markers that stimulate a common memory of 350 years.

The destruction of historical landmarks may be an economic necessity in a city dependent on property tax revenues, but this necessity is probably ensured by the same people who protest the destruction—those who continue to leave the city, who continue to vote against an income tax, who fight against legislation that would create a "community of interests" by requiring the suburbs to carry some of the city's economic burdens. These markers and memorials, including parks, which constitute much of the tax-exempt property that makes up almost half of Hartford's area, contribute greatly to the city's economic distress.

If Connecticut's Yankees want to have their cake and eat it too, the question remains whether this has the purpose—or only the consequence—of ensuring that the city goes without bread. In the state with the highest per capita income in the United States, the tax code and zoning laws ensure a scarcity that requires sacrifices to be made; that produces crises and requires coming-to-the-rescues by private interests; that creates "difficult choices," perhaps, between money for museums and for public housing. Does this impoverishment of the public sphere have the aim of protecting private interests such as real estate or of maintaining a cheap labor pool? Or is it simply the result of an unusual autonomy of interests in which the affluent white population is going along reproducing itself by itself and there just happens to be a large and desperately poor black and Hispanic population on the periphery?

While the latter is obviously not true in fact (the tobacco industry in the Connecticut River Valley actively recruited up to 8,000 people a year from Puerto Rico, partly with federal aid, until the 1970s), it seems to be fact in effect, the consequence of the relative autonomy provided a class by a service economy and an incredibly tenacious Yankee identity. It seems that the affluent of the Hartford area will go to great lengths to preserve the integrity of that identity, avoiding, or not recognizing, the conflicts that would belie its autonomy. It will abandon the city on which that identity depends—all but the downtown. It will celebrate pluralism and cultural diversity—from the homogeneous safety of the suburbs.

Postwar Hartford's supply-side urban renewal projects seem to have been geared toward ensuring that the affluent members of corporate families could continue to support their identity with a historic hometown without ever having to deal with urban conflict and real social alterity. In the suburbs conflict is barred and equity questions need never be asked. The highway system allows people to travel from these suburbs to the city center without ever having to come in contact with the urban poor. Downtown renewal projects are oriented exclusively to suburban residents and aim to create an urban fiction of the conflict-free security that they feel at home.

One urbanist wrote: "A business trip down I–84 to the Aetna or the Civic Center is easier than a journey of conscience, across lines of class and race and history, to North Hartford or Frog Hollow." Yet there is, I would say, an abundance of conscience in Hartford. That's part of the problem. It's a conscience that refuses to recognize common and conflicting interests and instead constructs its object as a purely external entity.

It seems that Hartford's "business leaders" are finally beginning to realize (perhaps since the demise of tobacco and manufacturing in the 1960s and '70s) that it is not in their interest to abide by a large population of urban poor—it no longer functions to keep wages down but rather to keep taxes up. Similarly, perhaps, the Wadsworth Atheneum seems to have realized in the 1960s or '70s that it needed to broaden its audience in order to broaden its funding base. The old family money was no longer enough. Corporations were interested in blockbuster shows, the larger audiences for which would make their patronage worthwhile in public relations terms. Public agencies began to require more tangible evidence of public service when funding museums. The discourse of the Atheneum began to represent and be addressed to a public, that is, to audiences not already disposed to the culture of the museum's patron class.

The question that remains is, how did a museum produced by a community so resistant to conflict develop such progressive programming as Matrix and the Lions Gallery, or acquire the Simpson collection? Is it enough to point to the "Austin legacy," or to James Elliott, or to you?

First of all, the Atheneum's early involvement with contemporary American art does not appear to have been the product of the aspiration for a more cosmopolitan, or European, cultural disposition that marks other nineteenth-century American museum collections. That A. Everett Austin Jr. represented such aspirations was, I imagine, one of the reasons he was forced to leave. If the museum prior to Austin had the function of memorializing the traditional culture of a particular traditional (Yankee) community, Austin's orientation would amount to a negation of that function in preference to a more individualized and individualizing relationship to culture.

Whatever the reasons why these modern and contemporary programs developed, it seems fairly clear to me why they have survived—and why Austin did not. If Hartford's affluent have exhibited an extraordinary talent for disidentifying themselves out of interclass conflict, the problem with Austin was intraclass; he was of the same affluent New England stock as the Atheneum's trustees, he married into their families, and yet he did not share their values. A snag of some size. The current contemporary art programs, on the other hand, could be described as interclass. They present the culture of others: individuals with particular visions, or sensitivities, or experiences, or problems, that are not really like "ours"—they're not in conflict with ours, but they are interesting to come and see. Ours is a pluralistic community of "practical idealists." We just prefer to live in the suburbs.

Multicultural programs may support the same conception of culture as that with which the Atheneum was founded: the traditional culture of traditional communities. They are separate but equal—as representations. Their juxtaposition admits no common field of interest, no struggle, no inequity.

Thinking about Hartford and the Atheneum, I am reminded of a story I once read. An Englishwoman who traveled in West Africa in the late nineteenth century writes in her autobiography of a missionary group arriving in a village. They are greeted warmly and given a hut. The next morning the missionaries wake up to find that the village has moved away, leaving them stranded in the middle of the jungle.

What are the implications of all of this for what I will do at the Atheneum? One possibility could involve a progression from a rhetorical identification of the museum with fantasies of, and desires for, a homogeneous, conflict-free social field to a breakdown of these representations in, for example, suburban fears of urban violence. Such representations could be presented in aesthetic terms, in judgments of taste about an environment, judgments that have a particular social and historical character. I could situate myself as the subject and then perhaps as the object of these fantasies and fears and judgments. This could be accomplished, for example, by first identifying myself as a Daughter of the American Revolution (one of my paternal ancestors was an aide to Lafayette and could actually have visited Jeremiah Wadsworth's house), and then as a woman of Puerto Rican descent (on my mother's side). The challenge will be to construct myself as a figure of identification rather than an object of interest and an outsider.

I don't know how helpful all of this is for you. It's been very helpful to me. I know that none of the above would be appropriate for your Matrix brochure—it would scare people away from the performance. It would probably be best if you wrote the kind of statement that you usually write without making specific references to the themes suggested here. Perhaps you might focus more on the function of the Matrix program and of the presentation of contemporary art at the Atheneum. You might write more about the form of my work or in general about efforts by contemporary artists to move away from art-making defined as a specialized activity of talented individuals and toward a practical engagement with social relations and representations—engagements that may take up the forms in which those relations exist in everyday life.

Well, that's all for now. Good luck!

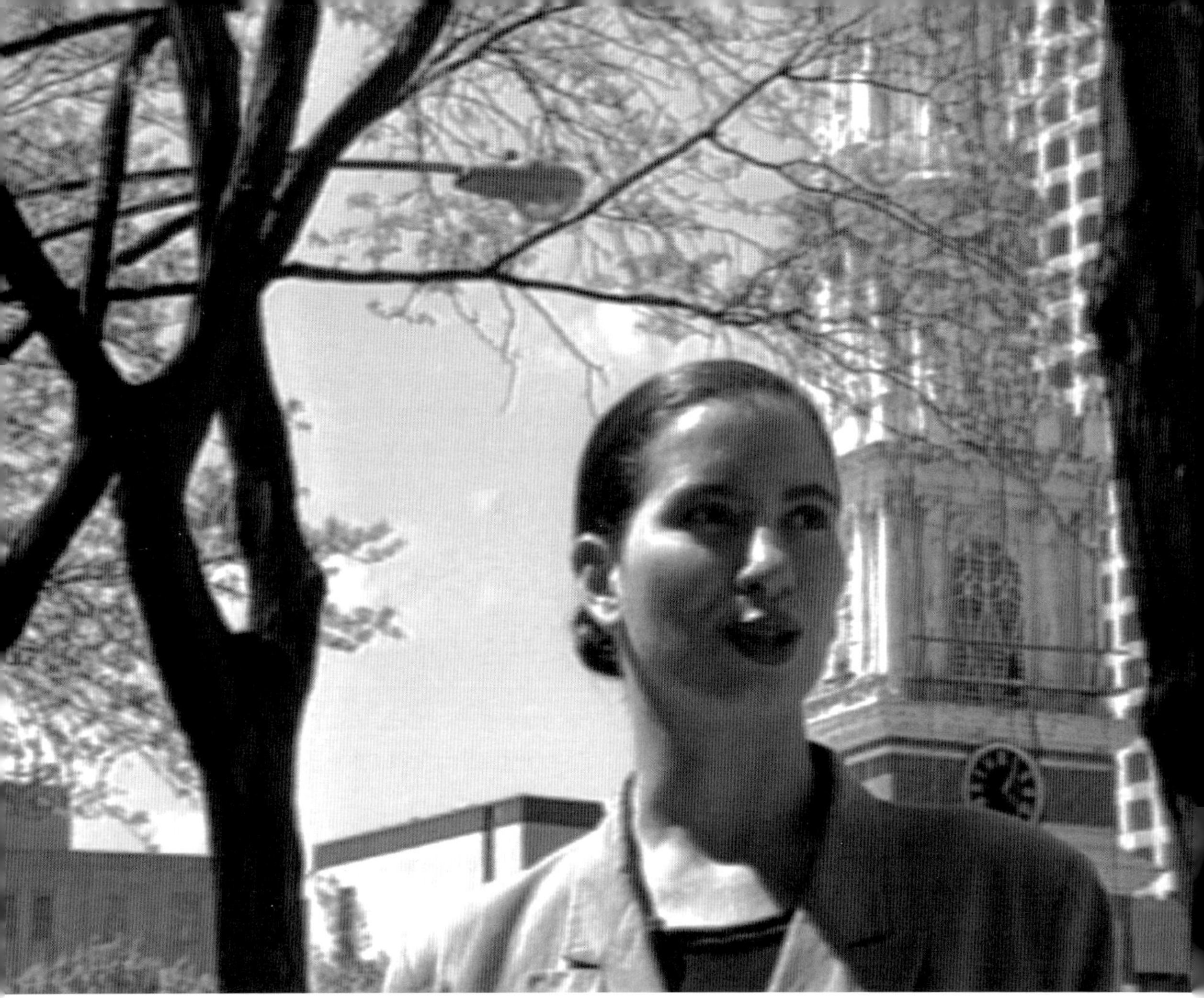

11.1 Andrea Fraser, still from *Welcome to the Wadsworth*, 1991. Videotape of live performance at the Wadsworth Atheneum, Hartford, Connecticut. Courtesy the artist.

11

WELCOME TO THE WADSWORTH

It is the main lobby in the Wadsworth Building of the Wadsworth Atheneum, on a Saturday or Sunday in April 1991. At one o'clock, Andrea Fraser enters the lobby from the A. Everett Austin Gallery in the James Lippencott Goodwin Building. She comes to a stop near a sign announcing museum tours by the artist Andrea Fraser, organized by the museum's Matrix program, and begins to address the visitors milling around the lobby.

Excuse me, uh, excuse me . . . are any of you waiting for Andrea Fraser's museum tour, "Welcome to the Wadsworth"?

You are? Well, good.

Good afternoon. I'm Andrea Fraser and, uh, welcome to the Wadsworth.

I'm an artist. I live in New York. I've been invited here today by the Matrix program to give you a tour of your museum.

I'm glad to be here.

The Wadsworth Atheneum is the oldest continuously operating public art museum in the United States. Its founding in 1842 predated by more than thirty years the first art museum building boom in the United States, when the Metropolitan Museum of Art, the Philadelphia Museum of Art, and half a dozen other encyclopedic civic museums were founded.

The Wadsworth was and remains, I think, atypical of major art museums in the United States in many ways. While these late-nineteenth-century civic museums were founded on European models largely with collections of European painting, the Atheneum's collection during the first seventy-five years of its existence consisted almost entirely of American art—even contemporary New England art.

Every museum represents something very particular in the community in which it exists. Every museum defines culture and its purpose as an institution according to its own history and according to the interests of its founders, its trustees, and patrons.

The founding of the Atheneum was, I think, above all else, a patriotic gesture and an investment in the culture and history of the United States and of the region.

Hartford was one of the earliest European settlements in New England, and downtown Hartford is filled with historical markers. If you'll follow me . . .

She leads the group out of the front entrance to the Atheneum, speaking as she walks.

The first time I came to Hartford to visit the Atheneum, one of the first things I noticed was the number of memorials, monuments, named spaces, and commemorative plaques between Union Station and the Atheneum.

She stops on the front steps of the Atheneum and gestures out over downtown Hartford with its parks, historic buildings, insurance offices, and, directly in front of the Atheneum, a large bus shelter normally crowded with young and elderly city residents.

If you just look out here, across the street you'll see Bushnell Plaza, and behind that is Bushnell Park. Both are named after Hartford's nineteenth-century clergyman and reformer, Horace Bushnell. A few blocks to the left of Bushnell Park is Bushnell Memorial auditorium. It was dedicated by his daughter to "perpetuate in the community the spiritual, cultural and civic influence of a great man."[1]

Let's see . . . directly to the left of the Atheneum is Burr Mall. It was dedicated by Ella Burr McManus to her father, the long-time publisher and editor of the *Hartford Times*. Down Gold Street here is Trumbull Street, named after Connecticut's Revolutionary-era governor, Jonathan Trumbull. Up Trumbull Street is Goodwin Square. Across the intersection here is Center Church and Ancient Burying Ground. And up Main Street, of course, is the Old State House with its statue of Thomas Hooker, who founded Hartford in 1636.

And this is just to name a few.

Hartford is a city that's proud of its history and its heritage and wants to represent it.

This pride is embodied in the Atheneum in many ways, the most obvious of which is its form as a series of memorials.

She walks down the steps and gestures up toward the Wadsworth Building.

The five buildings that make up the Atheneum include the original Atheneum building—just behind me—which is referred to as the Wadsworth Building, after the museum's founder. Counterclockwise from the Wadsworth Building is the Colt Memorial, then the Morgan Memorial, then—at the corner of Prospect Street and Atheneum Square—the Avery Memorial, and directly behind the Wadsworth Building is the museum's most recent addition. It's named after James Lippencott Goodwin.

While it's quite common for museum buildings to be named after major patrons, what's unusual about the Atheneum is that its buildings are not just named after patrons but were built specifically in memory of patrons or by patrons in memory of loved ones who sometimes had no interest in art themselves.

As memorials, they represent a strong public and private commitment to preserving the memory of past generations, and they address the community in which they exist almost as a family that holds those memories in common.

The early history of the Wadsworth Atheneum is as much the story of its namesake and founder, Daniel Wadsworth.[2]

Daniel Wadsworth was the descendant of one of Hartford's first settlers, and his family had played an important role in Connecticut history. It was Daniel's great-great-great-uncle Joseph Wadsworth who hid the Connecticut Charter in the Charter Oak, and Daniel's father, Jeremiah, was the army's Chief General of Supply during the Revolutionary War.[3]

If you'll follow me.

She begins to walk around the Wadsworth Building toward Atheneum Square North.

The Wadsworth Building stands on the site of the historic Wadsworth family home, the home in which Daniel Wadsworth was raised. It was built by Daniel's grandfather, and occupied by his father Jeremiah until his death.[4]

The house was moved to make room for the Atheneum, and later torn down, but outside the museum is a plaque installed by the Daughters of the American Revolution commemorating the site of the house. It reads in part:

GEORGE WASHINGTON
WAS ENTERTAINED BY
COLONEL JEREMIAH WADSWORTH IN HIS HOME ON
THIS SITE, ON JUNE 30, 1775
. . .

ON SEPTEMBER 21, 22, 23 1780
WITH LAFAYETTE, GENERAL LENOX, AND GOVERNOR
JONATHAN TRUMBULL, WASHINGTON HELD HERE HIS
FIRST CONFERENCE WITH THE FRENCH COMMANDER
COUNT ROCHAMBEAU AND ADMIRAL TERNAY

. . .

TO MARK THIS SITE ASSOCIATED WITH HIS NAME
THIS TABLET IS ERECTED BY THE
CONNECTICUT DAUGHTERS
OF THE AMERICAN REVOLUTION
IN ABIDING REVERENCE FOR
WASHINGTON
FEBRUARY 22, 1932
THE TWO HUNDREDTH ANNIVERSARY OF HIS BIRTH

I'm a Daughter of the American Revolution. It's true! One of my ancestors was an aide to Lafayette. He may have even visited Jeremiah Wadsworth's house. He may have walked on the ground beneath this building two hundred and fifteen years ago.

My family isn't a Mayflower family exactly. We left Scotland around 1747 after the chief of clan Fraser was executed on Tower Hill. The Frasers have been here for quite some time. Not as long as the Wadsworths, perhaps, but quite some time.[5]

She turns and moves through and past the group as she speaks. She begins walking back around the Wadsworth Building to the front of the Atheneum and beyond, walking past the Colt Memorial toward the Morgan Memorial.

Above the din and discord of our confused political, economic, and social life there may be heard the clear, pure note of those who sound their belief in the principles upon which our country was founded . . . those organizations with members qualifying for their part therein by ancestral lines tracing back and linking them to . . . the Colonial and Revolutionary worthies who, as fact and legend, have nurtured the roots of our patriotism and have sent through every branch of our ancestral trees the life-giving fluid of pride in country and family.[6]

Now, Daniel's father was a compatriot of Connecticut Governor Jonathan Trumbull—the only colonial governor to side with the colonists in the Revolutionary War. Daniel married Jonathan's daughter Faith, becoming the nephew of the

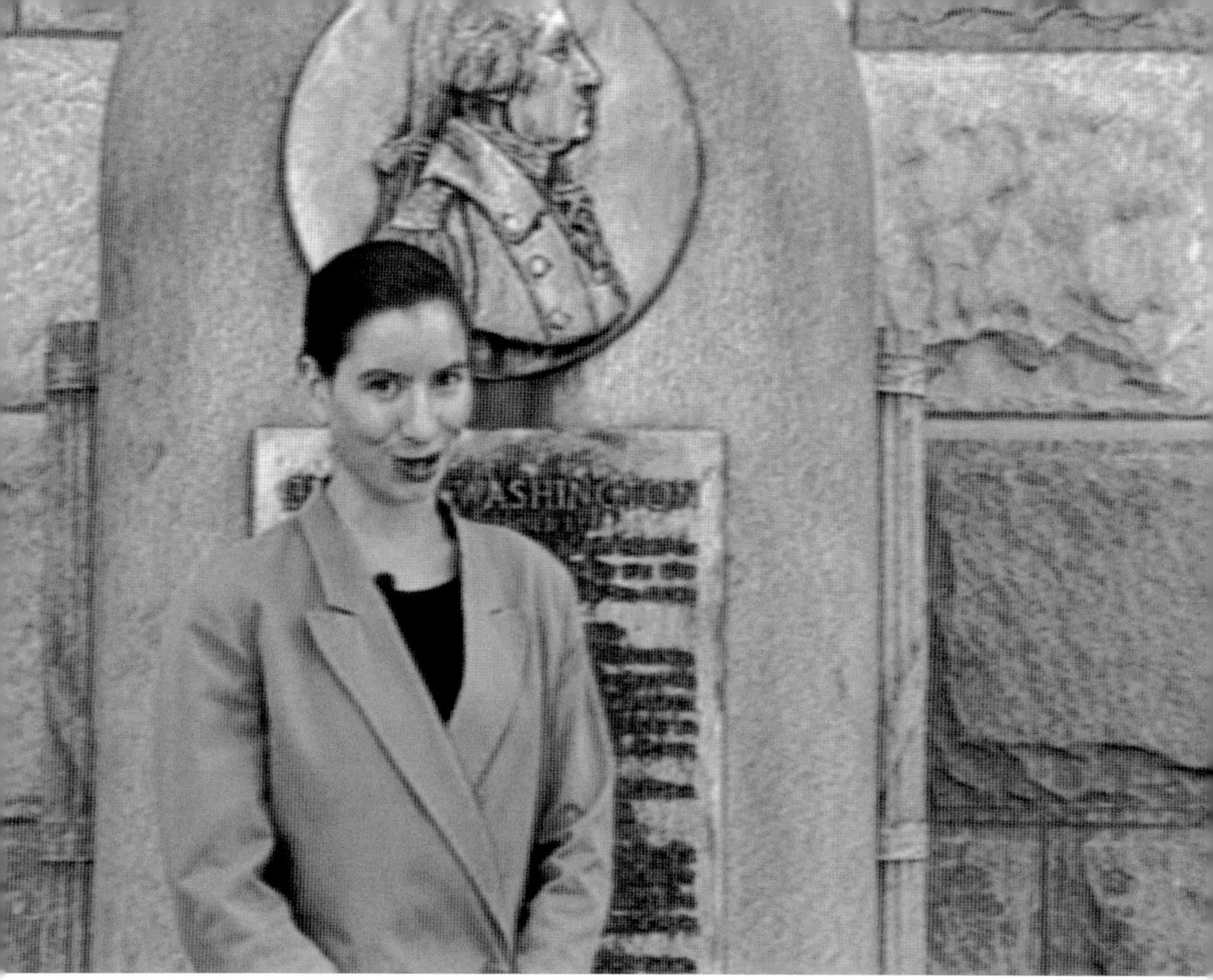

11.2 Andrea Fraser, still from *Welcome to the Wadsworth,* 1991. Videotape of live performance at the Wadsworth Atheneum, Hartford, Connecticut. Courtesy the artist.

painter Colonel John Trumbull, Jonathan's brother. Daniel's family connection to John certainly spurred his interest in art and played a great role in his inception of the Atheneum.[7]

The collection Daniel left to the Atheneum included a number of paintings of Revolutionary subjects by his uncle John.

Daniel also gave the Atheneum a beautiful "Marble Bust of himself," and "A full length portrait of General Washington," and "A Portrait" of his father-in-law Governor Trumbull, and "A Portrait of his mother," and "A Portrait of his Father and himself in the same picture," and "A Portrait of his sister," and "A Portrait of his Father alone," and "Another Portrait of himself," and a painting of his Avon farm Monte Video by Thomas Cole, a Hartford native.[8]

After Daniel's death, the Wadsworths didn't play much of a role in the Atheneum. I don't know what happened to them.

Well, not much went on at the Atheneum until the 1880s, when the Reverend Francis Goodwin became President of the Board. Now, the Goodwins were also descendants of Hartford settlers, and the Reverend Francis was an old-fashioned Puritan in his heritage: mild, unassuming, idealistic, and shrewd.[9]

The Reverend Francis, first thing, went to his uncle, Junius Spencer Morgan, for money to renovate and reorganize the Atheneum.

Now, Junius Spencer was only first-generation Hartford, but fifth in the New World. An old and distinguished New England family; he had since moved back to London. Junius Spencer, along with his father Joseph, was one of the original subscribers to the Atheneum, and Junius and his son John Pierpont kept up the family tradition.

They were always eager to do their best for their native city.

Well, the next year Junius Spencer died. John Pierpont immediately set about planning a memorial to his father next to the Atheneum. It was completed in 1910.

She stops in front of the Morgan Memorial and gestures toward the building.

This is the Morgan Memorial, here. It was built, along with the Colt Memorial that connects it to the Wadsworth Building, by architect Benjamin Wistar Morris—the Reverend Francis Goodwin's son-in-law. The Avery Memorial was built by Benjamin Wistar Morris's son-in-law, Robert O'Connor, along with A. Everett Austin Jr., the Atheneum's director at the time, who was married to Helen Goodwin, the niece of Francis Goodwin's son Charles Goodwin, who was then the president of the Atheneum's board.[10]

In the cornerstone of the Morgan Memorial is a tablet, deposited so that there may always be an imperishable record of the filial affection and public beneficence of John Pierpont Morgan.

And this beautiful building, dedicated to the name and record of Junius Spencer Morgan, will bear its own impressive and perpetual witness to that memory, which a son's constant and loving devotion has caused here to be so worthily enshrined.[11]

John Pierpont always had a passionate love for beautiful things . . . but he died without giving anything to fill the Morgan Memorial. During his final hours his mind wandered and he talked of boyhood days in Hartford. His body was brought back for burial in the family lot in Cedar Hill.

A faithful son carrying on the family tradition, John Pierpont Jr. gave the Atheneum over thirteen hundred objects from his father's collection to be arranged in a permanent display of his father's personal legacy.

She continues her walk around the Morgan Memorial, turning left into Ella Burr McManus Memorial Mall.

John Pierpont Jr. also gave the Atheneum the Wallace Nutting Collection of Pilgrim Furniture. His interest was entirely from the standpoint of history, although none of the objects had actually been owned by Morgans.

William Goodwin, the Reverend Francis Goodwin's son and the Atheneum's curator of decorative art at the time, wrote that "Pilgrim furniture exemplifies not only the sturdy character of our ancestors but their longing desire for the beautiful as well."[12]

Other Morgans continued to support the Atheneum. Caroline Morgan, the daughter of the senior Morgan's sister Sarah, gave the museum a beautiful bust of her father, Junius Spencer. And Mrs. Walter Goodwin gave the Atheneum a pair of portraits of Joseph and Sarah Morgan, the great-grandparents of both Walter Goodwin and J. Pierpont Jr.

Most recently, the Atheneum completed its renovation of the reception room of James and Lucy Morgan Goodwin's house.[13]

It's installed . . .

She moves quickly ahead of the group, gesturing.

It's installed right inside those windows, there.

Look . . . you can see the dark wood paneling of the shutters.

The Goodwin's reception room was designed to enhance the family's virtue and showcase its public spirit and faith. It was open and generous. . . . The needlework table cover is the handiwork of the daughter, Mary. She and her mother, Lucy, used to hold meetings of the Orphan Society and Hartford Hospital here, and they received a multitude of guests, from cousin John Pierpont to the minister of Christ Church. . . .[14]

Hartford in those days was bright and bustling; there was an aura of trust and friendship.

She gestures around Ella Burr McManus Memorial Mall.

Everyone felt confident of the future. Hartford would be larger and richer, but still the same pleasant place we loved, without any radical alteration in its character. It would always be a city founded on New England tradition and made up mainly of New Englanders who would observe Sunday and read the *Courant* every weekday morning. They would send their children to the public schools and their sons to Yale. They would have more leisure, larger houses, more servants, but life would all be cut from the same pattern, a pattern made for contentment and a sense of security among the prosperous.

In those days, Hartford was a town made up of a group a families wholly united by the ties of a common heritage and a common culture, and friendships fostered by the community life of a village.

She gestures in the direction of the Avery Memorial.

Daniel Wadsworth's old house behind the Atheneum had been converted into the Hartford Club.

I used to see the dignified high-hatted gentlemen go in and out by way of the lofty pillared verandah. They were gentlemen of the old school, well read, orderly, who keenly enjoyed doing the proper thing.

She walks in the direction of Prospect Street, gesturing to Hartford's Municipal Building, which sits opposite the Atheneum on Ella Burr McManus Mall.

My grandmother lived on a lot bought about 1842 from the Wadsworth estate, in a brick house my Grandfather built—a fine example of the opulent double-breasted style of those days.

My family lived in No. 38 Prospect Street, next to the north of the Wells house. Our house was one of the oldest; brick painted white with brown trimmings and a gambrel roof. My mother had become a widow at the age of twenty-five. She might have married again, but chose to devote herself exclusively to her love of beautiful furniture and works of art, and her two boys, my brother and myself.

But Hartford changed. The city closed in around us.[15]

The city closed in around the Atheneum, crowding it, cutting off its light.

Before John Pierpont bought this land here to build his memorial, it was all a terrible slum. It was big, filthy, crowded, poor, smelly, an unsightly slum, full of squatter shacks, pigsties, garbage dumps, and outhouses. It was a disgrace.[16]

John Pierpont cleared it. He cleared at all away.

But they kept coming, people from everywhere, in endless new waves.

They kept pouring into the city, crowding the river-front streets, filling up airless, dim-lit rooms in grimy, drab, losing ranks of moldy buildings.[17]

A derelict population living in squalor.[18]

Oh, *they* were quite satisfied. *They* were used to it.[19]

They could bear an infinite amount of crowding without interfering with their sense of decency.[20]

Mankind would have been better off if families had never left their farms.

She continues walking toward Prospect Street.

Wallace Nutting is correct when he says that intemperance, immorality, insanity, theft, cruelty, and most of the other horrors of the twentieth century should be attributed to bad homes.[21]

She gestures across Prospect Street to what is, in early April 1991, a pile of rubble left by the demolition of a large brick neocolonial building belonging to Travelers Insurance Company. By the end of April the site is a parking lot.

Now, this area over here is one of the worst slums in New England.

Look at it, filled with worn-out tenements, warehouses, and low-rent stores.

Old-world restaurants. A movie theater. A bowling alley.

Low-income housing, where women sit on their front steps and men congregate on the corner.[22]

She turns to address the group.

We have to reestablish our connection with seventeenth-century colonial values, rural values: egalitarianism, love of family and God, rugged individualism, self-reliance, and good taste.

Now in those days, the people of Hartford built better homes, had better furniture, were better clad, and spoke better English than at any time since.[23]

Art is not a luxury, to be afforded after necessities have been provided, but objects fashioned with care and enhanced with decoration which beautify a domestic environment.[24]

We have a moral obligation to have beautiful homes.[25]

Man is reflected in his home.[26]

She walks quickly to the Avery Memorial, gesturing. The building is undergoing renovation and its rear lawn is surrounded by a chain-link fence, through which piles of construction materials can be seen.

Now, over here, for example, over here . . .

A beautifully landscaped two-acre lot.

A modest, anonymous two-and-a-half-story frame colonial—no more than ten rooms—sitting at the end of a walk lined with coach lamps, beside a twenty-by-forty-foot flagstone terrace, with shutters painted gray, green, or chocolate brown.

Inside there's a cobbler's bench coffee table, a wing chair with a ruffled skirt, iron trivets on the wall, and a ship in a bottle on the mantel.

A station wagon. An atmosphere of simplicity.[27]

She continues walking around the Atheneum, turning left onto Atheneum Square North. At lunchtime the street is busy with people in business suits from the surrounding offices.

I want a quiet, small-town atmosphere, where the shops are neater and more attractive; where the streets are quieter, and they're faced by broader, greener lawns and more-elegant homes, tucked away among lightly rolling hills.

Green places where the shouts of children at play replace the city's din and bustle; places filled with duck ponds, swimming pools, rhododendron, and slender-steepled New England churches.[28]

Values and dreams: security, privacy, space, status, autonomy, land of one's own, good schools[29]—public schools, larger, cleaner and more generously conceived, flat, open, and well-tended, with lots of windows, grass, and trees.[30] More air, more space . . .

I deserve peace and tranquillity after a full day.[31]

I want a serene and simple, a secure and stable life. A better environment for the children.

The healthy and orderly life of a people with deeply rooted social and cultural traditions.[32]

I want a strong heritage to guide my values and help me to define my character. I want the traditions of a New England village to foster my sense of community.[33]

People who make a definite investment in the common enterprise. Reliable people, open-minded, humanistic, conservative yet dynamic, a balance between extremes.

Not an "ideal" democracy, not a "pure" democracy, but certainly a tough, practical self-government, nurtured by the talents of individual inhabitants and their ever expanding Utopian dream.

People committed to retaining the right to rule their own destinies.[34]

Home rule.

Homeowners should have the right to determine who lives in their neighborhoods and goes to their schools.[35]

People who share a personal willingness to work hard.[36]

I worked hard forty years so I could live in West Hartford and have my children educated here. No one bussed me in here.[37]

Everyone worked.[38]

A city is not intended to be some kind of reservation for dependent and unproductive people.[39]

A one-class community.

It disgusts me.[40]

I remember the regular Saturday afternoon trips, shopping, eating, walking around. But times have changed. There's not enough parking.[41]

Today, it's not a place I want to take my family.[42]

The city is dirty and crowded and full of crime, and I'm glad I'm isolated from it.[43]

People who share a common historical experience.[44]

And they keep pouring into the city, people from the South, from Puerto Rico, from the Caribbean, crowding the oldest, most blighted, most densely populated neighborhoods.[45]

People trained in the duties as well as privileges of citizenship.[46]

She gestures to the Avery Entrance of the Atheneum—the entrance used by the Travelers Insurance Company executives who, by special arrangement, eat at the Atheneum Cafe.

I was having lunch with Morrison Beach the other day at the Atheneum cafe, and Mr. Beach said to me, he said, "Andrea, for too long we have seen the futility of trying to build better neighborhoods with new bricks and mortar which soon turn to slums because of the joblessness and hopelessness of the people inside them."[47]

Community responsibility, personal commitment, common sense, and "steady habits."[48]

I'll be frank. Do you think that Hartford business looks forward to the day when a bunch of lower-class people, angry and embittered at a society they feel has done them in, have firm control of the city? The important thing is making Hartford a pleasant place to work. Business just can't attract talented young executives if the area is not pleasant.[49]

A little more successful, a little more sophisticated, a little more socially conscious.[50]

A new city is under construction in Hartford, and it promises to be a good-looking city: modern, shiny, and architecturally significant, with office buildings, and elevated pathways, elegant and generously conceived.[51]

A purified America.[52]

She stops at the small plaza next to the James Lippencott Goodwin Building and turns to address the group.

Mark Twain once said, "Of all the beautiful cities it has been my good fortune to see, this is the chief"—and we think he may have even sold us a bit short.

Hartford is more than just a beautiful city. Because the history of the greater Hartford area stretches to the earliest days of European settlement in New England, there is a decided richness to the attractions and cultural amenities it offers. These amenities not only enrich our lives, they also teach us common values and traditions.[53]

Over the last century and a half, the Wadsworth Atheneum, America's oldest public art museum, has amassed a collection that conveys the history of our nation. Its own history helped to shape our nation's culture. Its collection documents the rise of American consciousness from its European roots to the present day. It contains an intimate diary of American life: its heritage, its evolution, and its hope.[54]

Thank you.

Notes

1. *Tenth Anniversary Commemorative Booklet* (Hartford: Horace Bushnell Memorial Hall, 1940).

2. Gerald Silk, *Museums Discovered: The Wadsworth Atheneum* (Ft. Lauderdale: Penhurst Books, 1982), 5.

3. See Richard Saunders with Helen Raye, *Daniel Wadsworth, Patron of the Arts* (Hartford: Wadsworth Atheneum, 1981), 12, 62; and Marion Hepburn Grant, *In and about Hartford, Its People and Places* (Hartford: Connecticut Historical Society, 1989), 16–17.

4. *The Connecticut Historical Society and Associated Institutions* (Hartford: Connecticut Historical Society, 1989), 12.

5. While one of my paternal ancestors was in fact an aide to Lafayette, his name was not Fraser. The genealogy here is borrowed.

6. Foreword to *Colonial and Revolutionary Lineages of America* (New York: American Historical Company, 1968).

7. See Saunders and Raye, *Daniel Wadsworth,* 12, 62; Grant, *In and about Hartford,* 16–17.

8. See "The Will of Daniel Wadsworth," n.d., n.p., 2–3.

9. Ellsworth Strong and Marion Hepburn Grant, *The City of Hartford 1784–1984: An Illustrated History* (Hartford: Connecticut Historical Society with the support of the Society for Savings, 1986), 134.

10. Like his father, the Reverend Francis Goodwin—J. Pierpont Morgan Sr.'s first cousin—Charles Goodwin was president of the board of the Wadsworth Atheneum for nearly three decades. To his cousin and fellow trustee, J. Pierpont Morgan Jr., Charles Goodwin wrote, "We both of us have many other things to do but this is one thing that is hereditary." From a letter from Goodwin to Morgan (February 16, 1942, Charles Goodwin Records), quoted in Eugene Gaddis, "'The New Athens': Moments from an Era," in Gaddis, ed., *Avery Memorial Wadsworth Atheneum: The First Modern Art Museum* (Hartford: Wadsworth Atheneum, 1984), 65.

11. C. C. Cunningham, quoting the Morgan Memorial's cornerstone tablet and the Reverend Francis Goodwin, in *The Pierpont Morgan Treasures* (Hartford: Wadsworth Atheneum, 1960), 4–5.

12. Wallace Nutting, quoted in William B. Hosley Jr., *The Phillip H. Hammerslough Collection of American Silver, The Wallace Nutting Collection of Pilgrim Century Furniture at the Wadsworth Atheneum* (Hartford: Wadsworth Atheneum, 1984).

13. The Morgan/Goodwin family tree and their connection to the museum is elaborated in Gaddis, *Avery Memorial Wadsworth Atheneum;* Cunningham, *The Pierpont Morgan Treasures;* Albert Hastings Pitkin, *The Morgan Collection* (Hartford: Wadsworth Atheneum, 1918); and Gregory Hedberg, "The Morgans of Hartford," in Linda Horvitz Roth, ed., *J. Pierpont Morgan, Collector: European Decorative Arts from the Wadsworth Atheneum* (Hartford: Wadsworth Atheneum, 1987).

14. William Hosley, curator of American decorative arts, in a Wadsworth Atheneum gallery brochure on the Goodwin reception room. Reverend Francis Goodwin designed the Goodwin reception room, as well as the house in which it was situated.

15. Henry A. Perkins, *Prospect Street in the "Eighties"* (Hartford: n.p., 1939), 1–15.

16. John Alexopoulos, *The Nineteenth Century Parts of Hartford: A Legacy to the Nation* (Hartford: Hartford Architecture Conservancy, 1983), 14. My description of the turn-of-the-century "slum" next to the Atheneum is quoted from a description of the mid-nineteenth-century "slum" cleared for Bushnell

Park. Marion Hepburn Grant describes the acquisition of the land on which the Ella Burr McManus Mall now stands as follows: "J. Pierpont Morgan . . . was not pleased by the fact that the neighborhood just across the street from the lovely new museum was an ugly slum. So he bought up most of the property on this block, removed the slums, then presented the land to his native city with the proviso that the area be made a place of beauty" (*In and about Hartford*, 48).

17. Adapted from a poem by Albert Putnam, called *The New City . . . Hartford* (Hartford: Finlay Brothers, 1966), about a slum clearance project in the early 1960s that resulted in Hartford's Constitution Plaza.

18. "Hartford Opens 12-Acre Complex," *New York Times*, 10 May 1964, A1.

19. Putnam, *The New City*.

20. A description of Italian laborers from the 1875 annual report of the Connecticut Bureau of Labor Statistics, quoted in Bruce M. Stave, "Making Hartford Home: An Oral History of 20th Century Ethnic Development in Connecticut's Capital City," in Sondra Astor Stave, ed., *Hartford, the City and the Region: Past, Present, Future* (Hartford: University of Hartford, 1979), 41.

21. William N. Hosley Jr., *The Wallace Nutting Collection: A Gallery Guide* (Hartford: Wadsworth Atheneum, 1984).

22. This description is an aggregate of accounts of the neighborhood cleared for Constitution Plaza (from "Hartford Opens 12-Acre Complex" and Putnam, *The New City*); the area cleared for the Hartford Civic Center ("Hartford Civic Center as Catalyst for Downtown Revival: Natives Rap Pinstripes' Exit at Sunset," *Variety*, 8 July 1984); and the Park Street area (Jeffery Backstrand and Stephen L. Schensul, "Co-Education in Outlying Ethnic Communities: The Puerto Ricans of Hartford, Connecticut," *Urban Anthropology* 11, no. 1 [Spring 1982], 15).

23. Hosley, *The Wallace Nutting Collection*.

24. Philip Johnston, *Art in Seventeenth Century New England: Visitor's Guide to the Exhibition* (Hartford: Wadsworth Atheneum, 1977), 7–13.

25. Wallace Nutting, quoted in Hosley, *The Phillip H. Hammerslough Collection*.

26. Wallace Nutting, *Connecticut Beautiful* (New York: Garden Publishing Co., 1923), 182.

27. A description of West Hartford in Stephen Birmingham, *The Right People: A Portrait of the American Social Establishment* (Boston: Little, Brown, 1969), 212–213.

28. West Hartford Chamber of Commerce, "West Hartford, Connecticut Partners in Progress," n.p., n.d., n.pag.

29. Eugene Leach, "Response," in Stave, ed., *Hartford, the City and the Region*, 117.

30. Kirk Johnson, "The Schools, Separated by Poverty," *New York Times*, 29 April 1989.

31. Hartford Realty First, First Hartford Corporation [advertisement], *The Apartment Guide & Relocator Service of Connecticut,* October-January, 1991, 11–12.

32. West Hartford Chamber of Commerce, "West Hartford, Connecticut Partners in Progress."

33. The Greater Hartford Chamber of Commerce and Hartford Downtown Council, *Connecticut Magazine Celebrates Hartford,* a special supplement to *Connecticut Magazine,* September 1990, 75.

34. Grant, *In and about Hartford,* 13, 23–24.

35. Hartford resident Frank W. Russo, quoted in Everett Carll Ladd Jr., *Ideology in America: Change in Response in a City, a Suburb and a Small Town* (Ithaca: Cornell University Press, 1969), 158.

36. Grant, *In and about Hartford,* 24.

37. A West Hartford resident at a 1966 public hearing on a Connecticut Department of Education proposal to bus children to the suburbs from segregated city schools, quoted in Ladd, *Ideology in America,* 284.

38. Grant, *In and about Hartford,* 13.

39. Irving Kristol, quoted by Morrison H. Beach, in "The New Frontier: The Inner City," a paper delivered before the Annual Business Meeting of The Greater Hartford Chamber of Commerce on 24 May 1978; reprinted in Stave, ed., *Hartford, the City and the Region,* 71–72.

40. Alan P. Henry, "To These Kids, the City Is Poison," in Stave, ed., *Hartford, the City and the Region.*

41. Eric Lipton, "Viewpoints: How Area Residents See Hartford, Its Problems and Its Potential," *Hartford Courant,* 18 March 1991, A4.

42. Dennis Clemens of Wethersfield, interviewed by Paul Marks, *Hartford Courant,* 20 March 1991, A10.

43. Henry, "To These Kids, the City Is Poison."

44. Grant, *In and about Hartford,* 24.

45. As usual, most of Hartford's troubles are blamed on "minority" populations—now the city's majority—who, it is always implied, have come into the city in search of public services. In fact, however, the defense industry in the Hartford area began recruiting African-Americans from the South in the 1950s. With the help of a federal program, the tobacco industry was also recruiting up to 8,000 people a year from Puerto Rico until 1975 to provide cheap, seasonal labor for the Connecticut River valley plantations. See Diane Henry, "Hartford Inherits a Rash of Troubles," *New York Times,* 1 April 1979, IV6.

46. Grant, *In and about Hartford,* 23.

47. Beach, "The New Frontier."

48. Grant, *In and about Hartford,* 23.

49. A Hartford-area insurance executive, quoted in Ladd, *Ideology in America,* 162, 301.

50. Birmingham, *The Right People,* 214.

51. Sidney Sick, "The New City of Hartford," *New York Times,* 10 October 1982, CN 28.

52. Leach, "Response."

53. The Greater Hartford Chamber of Commerce, *Guide to Greater Hartford* (Hartford: Towery Publishing), 2.

54. Cultural Communications Consultants, *Wadsworth Atheneum: Of the World, for the City* (Hartford: Wadsworth Atheneum, 1990), 1–3.

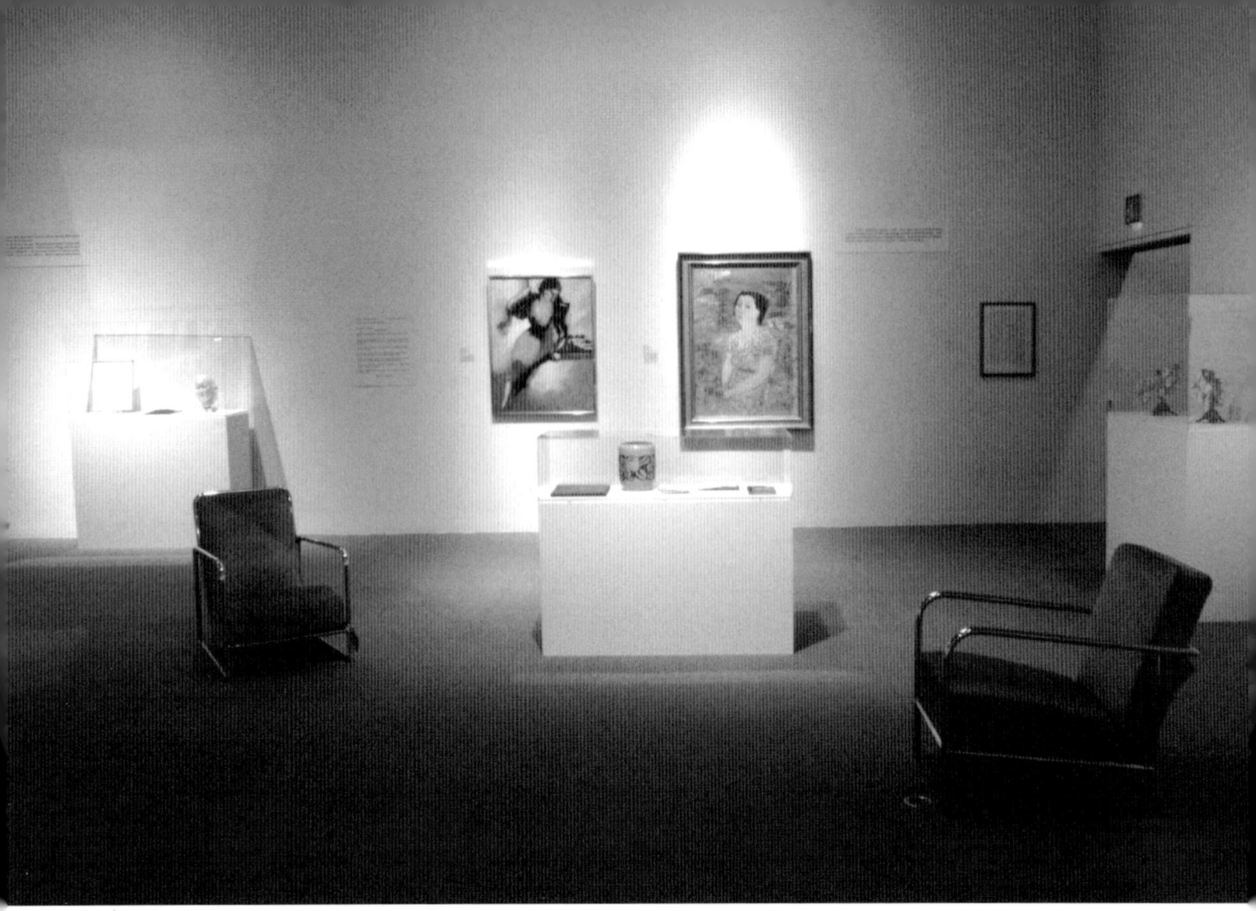

12.1 Andrea Fraser, *Aren't They Lovely?*, 1992. Installation at the University Art Museum, Berkeley, California. Courtesy the artist. Photo: Andrea Fraser.

12

AREN T THEY LOVELY? AN INTRODUCTION

In 1991, Lawrence Rinder invited me to create an installation with works from the collection of the University Art Museum at the University of California, Berkeley. The result was Aren't They Lovely?, *an exhibition of the bequest of Thérèse Bonney, Class of 1916, presented at the museum June 27–September 13, 1992. In addition to the hundreds of objects usually found in large museum exhibitions, the exhibition also included hundreds of wall texts and object labels featuring quotations from documents in the museum's archive. Most of these texts, along with the introduction reprinted below, were also published in the exhibition's brochure.*

Aren't They Lovely? began with an invitation by the University Art Museum to take up the function of a curator and create an installation with objects from the permanent collection. I decided to work with one particular bequest to the museum, the collection of University of California at Berkeley alumna (1916) Thérèse Bonney. Bonney died in 1978 and her collection arrived at the museum in 1984.

In one sense, *Aren't They Lovely?* is a narrative in which Thérèse Bonney is the central figure. It is the narrative of a woman whose life—an extraordinary life, perhaps—was reduced, at its end, to the value of the objects she owned by the institution to which she applied for final recognition. As such, it is a narrative which may or may not be "true"; its biographical accuracy would be merely accidental, as the documents with which I worked could not possibly tell so full a story. It is a narrative, in any case, that I produced in my choices of objects and text from the material I found.

As a narrative about Thérèse Bonney, *Aren't They Lovely?* may pose the question of what its protagonist wanted—in this case, from a museum. In the context of the exhibition, it is enough to say that what she wanted was the recognition that the University Art Museum granted her finally, if belatedly, and without much difficulty, six years after her death. She wanted to be seen, in the words of the article acknowledging her bequest with which *Aren't They Lovely?* begins, as a "graceful woman"; as a "remarkable woman" of accomplishments and passions who had received honors for her efforts, whose career had had an "impact"; as a woman whose "life 'could be an inspiration to the young,'" and whose "major bequest" "would be well cared for and appreciated."

She wanted, I would say, to be recognized for her achievement of all the aspirations that universities articulate for their students and museums for their public.

My intention, however, is not to tell the story of Thérèse Bonney, nor even to narrate the negotiation of her bequest. My intention, rather, is to produce a representation of the passage of objects from a private life to a public collection, and of the social struggles and subjective aspirations in which the definition of those objects—and their value—is a stake. My hope is that the closeness of those aspirations and the dearness of their stakes will be no less keenly felt for being articulated, not as the problem of an individual, but in the conflictual and ambivalent space between an individual and an institution.

The Thérèse Bonney bequest includes French paintings from between the wars, tapestries, art deco furniture, and one painting by Renoir. But in addition to the approximately fifty-five objects actually accessioned, over one hundred other objects that belonged to Bonney were received by the museum. These include coins and medals, souvenirs, eyeglasses, glassware, photographs of Bonney as well as of family and friends. While these objects are not officially a part of the museum's permanent collection, they have been permanently stored in the museum's basement. *Aren't They Lovely?* is an installation of all of these objects.

The presence of the nonaccessioned objects in the museum raises certain questions about what constitutes a collection—a museum's permanent collection, an individual's art collection—and, in a larger sense, what constitutes culture as a museum defines it. One of the primary operations of art museums is the transformation of what is essentially bourgeois domestic culture into legitimate public culture. That transformation is accomplished in the most basic way by the abstraction of art objects from their social location, first by their displacement from a home to a museum and second by the introduction of criteria of value and systems of classification whereby certain objects of determined interest are separated off from the other objects that constitute their total cultural context. In the case of Thérèse Bonney's collection, the nonaccessioned objects provide an opportunity to explore the mechanisms of this transformation and also work against them by reintroducing what is usually left behind.

My interest, however, is less in the relationships between objects in or outside of museums than in the social hierarchies that these relations objectify. My interest is less in a museum's definition of culture than in the subjective effects of the appropriation of that definition by a museum's public. The art-historically "objective" legitimacy that museums provide objects removed from their social context is one of the primary means through which museums seduce their public into aspiring toward the essentially class-defined competencies and dispositions—ways of knowing and being—demanded by the culture museums present.

The wall texts and object labels produced for the exhibition—some of which are included in this brochure—aim to represent the circuit whereby such aspirations are presented, internalized, and represented. In the case of *Aren't They Lovely?*, the first point in this circuit is Bonney's education at the University of California, a site where certain aspirations that she may have had in relation to culture might have been put into place and articulated for her. The second point is Bonney's collection, and the aspirations and also accomplishments she articulated through her relationship to cultural objects. The third is the reception of that collection at the University Art Museum, and the judgment the museum passed on its value and, with that, on her accomplishment of, or failure to achieve, the aspirations she invested in it. The fourth, which completes the circuit, is the purpose the University Art Museum articulates for itself in relationship to the university community and other publics, in particular, to contribute to a general cultural education and cultural atmosphere on campus, and the representation of alumni—like Thérèse Bonney—as models for the current student body.

The work that I hope the exhibition does is to introduce a break into this circuit, de-idealizing what museums publicize as legitimate culture by returning it to the context of the culture of everyday life—in this case, the domestic culture of which, for art collectors, legitimate culture is merely a part.

What museums institutionalize in a public sphere could be called symbolic struggles for legitimacy—struggles that are always taking place one way or

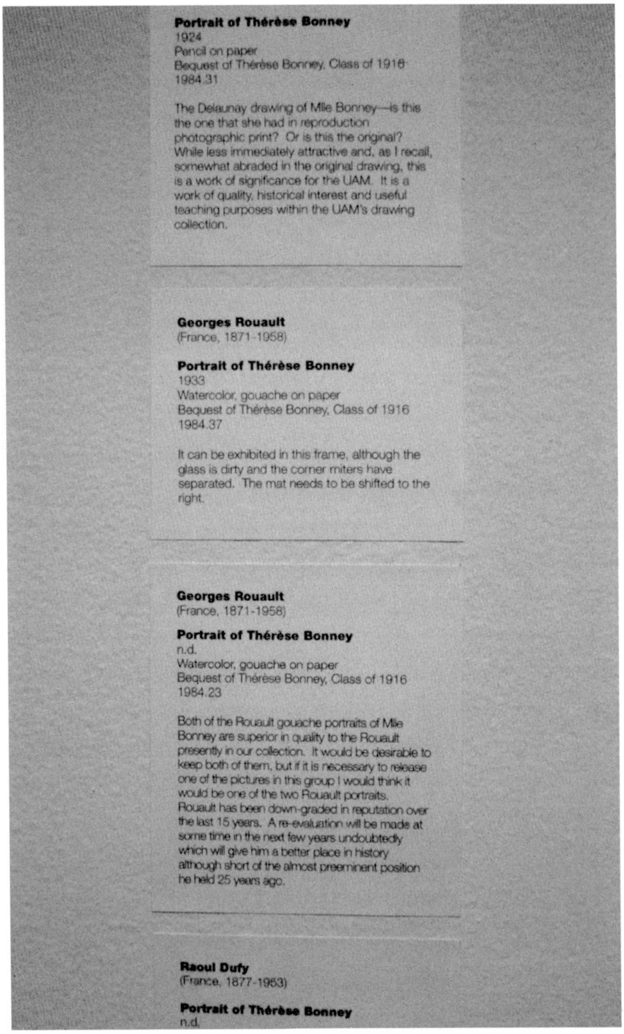

12.2 Andrea Fraser, *Aren't They Lovely?*, 1992. Installation view with object labels, University Art Museum, Berkeley, California. Courtesy the artist. Photo: Andrea Fraser.

another in thc field of culture between different classes and "class fractions." Symbolic struggles for legitimacy played out in the field of culture are themselves displacements of social and material struggles on the one hand, and subjective struggles on the other. Material needs and subjective wants are foreclosed in symbolic struggles; they are taken hold of and alienated by institutions as they seduce a public into aspirations which, because their accomplishment depends on other conditions, entail a necessary failure.

What is at stake in these struggles? Bound up with one's relationship to cultural objects is one's relationship to one's history, one's familial and domestic culture, one's environment, one's body, the ways that one identifies oneself socially, and the conditions under which one might see oneself as acceptable within one's community or the community toward which one aspires. In this sense the imposition by art museums of a class-defined legitimate culture in the public sphere constitutes a radical and quite intimate dispossession.

PROFESSIONAL

INTERESTS

13

A SPEECH ON DOCUMENTA

"A Speech on Documenta" was presented at a symposium organized by Texte zur Kunst *in Kassel in the summer of 1992 during the run of Documenta IX. None of the participants in the symposium was represented in Documenta IX.*

I am an artist.

I would have liked to have been invited to participate in Documenta IX. Whether it is a good exhibition or a bad exhibition has no bearing on the fact that I would have liked to have been in it; nor does whether it is a better or a worse exhibition than the last Documenta or the one before that—I would have liked to have been in those as well; nor does who the curator is; nor does its history or ideological function.

The fact that I would have liked to have been invited to participate in Documenta IX has nothing to do with the idea that I should have been in it, or that not being invited represented a significant or signifying exclusion of me, or of the kind of art making I engage in.

Nor does wanting to have been invited to participate in Documenta IX have anything to do with the idea that it would have provided me with the opportunity to produce a particularly effective work. Because I think of art making as a social practice through which I attempt to transform the relations organized by the institutions that authorize my activity, Documenta IX would have been as good a site as any other—no better, no worse. If anything, the relatively large, and necessarily heterogeneous, audience that Documenta attracts would have made it much more difficult than usual to understand the relation of that audience to the exhibition, and thus to formulate an effective intervention. But I don't believe that I would have found compensation for that additional difficulty in the greater number of people whose experience I might have affected, as I imagine few would even have been aware of my effort.

I would have liked to have been invited to participate in Documenta IX because the invitation would have constituted a moment of professional recognition that I would have found narcissistically gratifying, narcissistically stabilizing.

To say that being invited to participate in Documenta IX would have been narcissistically stabilizing is to say that it would have confirmed my identity with an image, established for me by Documenta VII in 1982 when I was student, of that which I should hope to become. The rather mild want of an invitation I speak of now is the shadow of a naive belief I harbored then that survey exhibitions like Documenta objectively represented the best, the noblest, the most beautiful, the most interesting, the most advanced, the most intelligent art of their time.

What I believed in was not Documenta as such. Until yesterday, I had never even visited a Documenta exhibition. What I believed in, rather, was the temporal logic of an order of professional succession. If I worked, and waited, I would be recognized. I would be received.

Art making is a profession of social fantasy. The instability of representations of one's social identity and legitimate aspirations means that professional consecration can be deferred endlessly into posterity. I would even say that overvaluing and overestimating possibilities, investing in futures that do not really exist, are occupational requirements. The representative function of art as a class culture, and its ideological function as a public culture, is partly based on the enormity of the aspirations fostered by producers—and the indeterminacy of the possibilities of their satisfaction. Those aspirations represent freedom from necessity for one dominant class fraction, individualism for another, entrepreneurial spirit for another, intellectual autonomy and integrity of conscience for another.

Transferred to a public sphere by exhibitions like Documenta, artistic aspiration is offered up as a mirror of the myth of social-mobility-as-the-redistribution-of-cultural-capital. Public exhibitions like Documenta offer us, as artists, the hundreds of thousands of people they draw as witness to our professional consecration—and these visitors bear little more than witness: our work, as a rule, is not addressed to them. Through such exhibitions artists, in turn, provide for the symbolic integration of these witnesses—people outside of the field of address of contemporary art—by offering up participation by proxy. In doing so, we also serve our own interests by extending the demand for and the rarity of our products.

Material integration should follow symbolic integration in a social order of succession which public art institutions establish as a legitimate aspiration. They are the guarantee. If their public works, and waits, they will be recognized. They will be received.

But if, as one might suppose, this symbolic integration sets off a competitive struggle for the cultural assets offered up for public appreciation, the result will be a devaluation of those assets, as the class by whose privilege their prestige is marked moves on to rarer and more exclusive things. The moment of integration will be deferred endlessly, into posterity.

The particular prestige of Documenta is a consequence more of its infrequency than its exclusivity. It banks on a scarcity of years rather than numbers, and a promise of continuity that, in contemporary art, is even rarer still.

The public life of artists is nasty, brutish, and short. Five years is two years longer than the usual life expectancy.

In five years, will I be a has-been?

If an invitation finally comes my way, I would like to respond to its promise of integration with Groucho Marx's line: I wouldn't want to be a part of any club that would have me as a member.

Still, that doesn't mean I wouldn't go in to use the facilities.

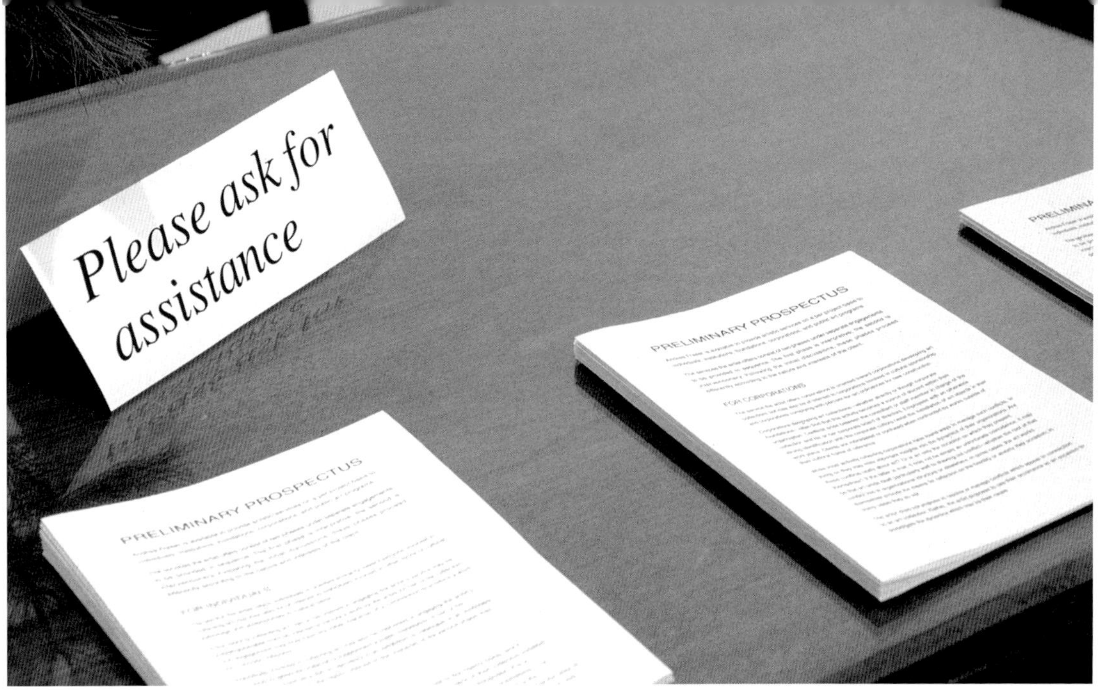

14.1 Andrea Fraser, *Please Ask for Assistance,* 1993. Installation view with *Preliminary Prospectuses,* American Fine Arts, Co., New York. Photo: Colin de Land.

The exhibition *Please Ask for Assistance* served as a stage set for the presentation of four *Preliminary Prospectuses: For Individuals, For Corporations, For Cultural Constituency Organizations,* and *For General Audience Public and Private Nonprofit Cultural Institutions.* Developed during the second half of 1993, these prospectuses attempted to formalize a model of artistic practice as service provision. Beginning with the *Project in Two Phases* undertaken with the EA-Generali Foundation, they served as the basis for most of my projects between 1994 and 1998. Each of the prospectuses shared the same basic two-phase structure, describing a first "investigatory" phrase and a second "interventionary" phase. The *Preliminary Prospectuses* were conceived both as practical documents and as performance scripts. Practically, they combined the functions of a contract and an advertisement with that of a generalized set of proposals. In doing so, they self-consciously appropriated aspects of the forms and language of consulting—particularly corporate consulting—to project an artistic performance as a kind of consultancy both within organizations and for individual "clients." In their content, however, the prospectuses aimed not only to advertise an "artistic service" but also to describe, in the clearest language possible, the critical orientation of that service. In this way, they sought to develop a model for a critical practice that might escape one of the fundamental contradictions of avant-garde traditions: that artistic ambitions to transgress or subvert are often aimed at the very institutions and individuals that artists turn to for support.

14

HOW TO PROVIDE AN ARTISTIC SERVICE: AN INTRODUCTION

"How to Provide an Artistic Service: An Introduction" was first delivered as an oral presentation in conjunction with the exhibition of the project Services *at the Depot, Vienna, in 1994.*

In our initial proposal for the "working-group exhibition" *Services*, Helmut Draxler and I offered the term "service" to describe what appeared to be a determining feature of what has come to be called "project work." We wrote:

> It appears to us that, related variously to institutional critique, productivist, activist, and political documentary traditions as well as post-studio, site-specific, and public art activities, the practices currently characterized as "project work" do not necessarily share a thematic, ideological, or procedural basis. What they do seem to share is the fact that they all involve the expense of an amount of labor that is either in excess of, or independent of, any specific material production and which cannot be transacted as or along with a product. This labor, which in economic terms would be called service provision (as opposed to goods production), may include:
>
> - the work of the interpretation or analysis of sites and situations in and outside of cultural institutions;
> - the work of presentation and installation . . . ;

- the work of public education in and outside of cultural institutions;
- advocacy and other community-based work, including organizing, education, documentary production, and the creation of alternative structures. . . .[1]

"Providing a service," in the sense described in our proposal, is neither an intention (such as benefiting society) attributed to particular artists nor a content (such as museum education or security) characterizing a group of works. Rather, we proposed "service provision" to describe the economic condition of project work as well as the nature of the social relations under which it is carried out. On the most basic level we could even claim that the prevalence of practices such as the payment of fees to artists by cultural institutions indicates that the emergence of art-as-service-provision is simply an economic fact.

We went on to write:

> there seems to be a growing consensus among both artists and curators that the new set of relations [emerging around project work] . . . needs clarification. While curators are increasingly interested in asking artists to produce work in response to specific existing or constructed situations, the labor necessary to respond to those demands is often not recognized or adequately compensated. Conversely, many curators committed to project development are frustrated by finding themselves in the role of producers for commercial galleries, or a "service department" for artists.[2]

The project *Services* was organized as an occasion to consider some of these practical and material problems, as well as the historical developments that may have contributed to the emergence of artistic service provision, and to provide a forum for discussion of the impact of this development on the relations among artists, curators, and institutions.

As an artist I have a particular interest in these questions. My motive for initiating *Services* came from the complications and conflicts I experienced as a result of entering into relations with curators and organizations for which there were no accepted standards of professional practice, as well as from the frustration of working full time and for very prestigious exhibitions yet still not being able to make a living. *Services*—and related activities I was involved in as I prepared the proposal—represented an effort by myself and other artists to represent and safeguard our practical and material interests by creating forums for the discussion of those interests; by collecting information from a range of artists about their preferred working arrangements in order to prepare a set of general guidelines and perhaps a basic contract; and by combining to form some sort of association.

What is implied in all of these activities is less a trade-union model of collective bargaining than a professional model of collective self-regulation. Like collective bargaining, this latter model could also, potentially, provide a certain leverage for artists in dealing with cultural institutions and other commissioning organizations, but achieving that would require a clarification of procedure and, perhaps, the development of a basic methodology in reference to which legitimate needs and demands could be collectively determined. For example, the fact that some artists collect a fee from an institution and then sell project results undermines the legitimacy of demands for fees. Should fees be opposed to sales? How should the integrity of project work be conceived? Do projects that require a high degree of participation by the institution give that institution some rights to alter the work or determine its disposition?

As Helmut Draxler and I wrote in our proposal, "resolutions on practical problems often represent political decisions which may impact not only the working conditions of artists but also the function and meaning of their activity."

I am speaking only for myself (and not for the project *Services*) when I say that my interest in all of these organizational activities derived as much from the possibility of artistic practice developing into something like a self-regulating profession as from the hope of gaining leverage in dealing with art institutions. Professional self-regulation is a matter of professional ethics as well as professional interests. In the artistic field, it is also a matter of the ethics of artistic practice. And, because of the reach of artistic practice from private homes to public buildings and streets, it is a matter of the ethics of the social and subjective relations manifest in and through artistic practices.

Proposing to talk about "How to Provide an Artistic Service" is part of an experiment I want to undertake to see if it's possible to develop a methodology that could function as a basis for something like a self-regulating profession of artistic service provision. This experiment could take the form of a book—called *How to Provide an Artistic Service*—the model for which would be handbooks of professional conduct and technique common in other fields, books like *The Psychiatric Interview* or *Organizational Diagnosis* or Freud's papers on technique, to mention three that I have found useful.[3]

What I'm presenting tonight would be something like the introduction to such a book, or an argument for why such a book might be necessary.

In addition to the material concerns motivating the project *Services*, a central question it sought to address was the potential loss of autonomy consequent to appropriating from other professional fields such models as contracts and fee structures as a means of resolving practical problems. Critical acceptance had created a demand for projects within cultural organizations that was clearly not only a demand for the works of individual artists. This demand provided for the possibility of acting collectively to determine and defend our interests—particularly economic interests—as well as to consider the history of that kind of action. But it was also clear that this demand, expressed in invitations to undertake projects in response to situations and under conditions explicitly defined by others, represented something of a threat to artistic autonomy. Designing contracts to safeguard our practical and material interests, or even simply demanding fees in compensation for our services, might further compromise our independence by turning us into functionaries of "client" organizations.

While many of us had taken up, in our work, the positions and activities of curators, gallerists, educators, public relations and employee-management relations consultants, security consultants, architects and exhibition designers, researchers, archivists, et cetera, we certainly did not do so to have our practices reduced to the *functions* of these professions. What would—should—differentiate our practices from the functions we appropriated is precisely our autonomy. That autonomy is represented, most importantly, in our relative freedom from the rationalization of our activity in the service of specific interests defined by the individuals or organizations with which we work. Included in this is freedom from the rationalization of the language and forms we use—a freedom that may or may not manifest itself in recognizably "aesthetic" forms. Also included is the freedom of speech and conscience—guaranteed by accepted professional practice as well as the First Amendment—which is supposed to safeguard our right to express critical opinions and engage in controversial activity.

We are demanding fees as compensation for work within organizations. Fees are, by definition, payment for services. If we are, then, accepting payment in exchange for our services, does that mean we are serving those who pay us? If not, who are we serving and on what basis are we demanding payment (and should we be demanding payment)? Or, if we are serving those who pay us, how are we serving them (and what are we serving)?

Such questions are not exclusive to project-based practice, whether or not such practice is defined as a service; project-based practice simply makes it necessary to pose them. I would say, rather, that we are all always already serving. Studio practice conceals this condition by separating production from the interests it meets and the demands it responds to at its point of material or symbolic consumption. Because a service can be defined, in economic terms, as a value that is consumed at the same time it is produced, the service element of project-based practice eliminates such separation.

An invitation to produce a specific work in response to a specific situation is a very direct demand, the motivating interests of which are often barely concealed and difficult to ignore. I know that if I accept that invitation I will be serving those interests—unless I work very hard to do otherwise.

The interests contained in any demand for art, whether or not it is expressed in an invitation to undertake a project, would make up a very large section of a book on "how to provide an artistic service." It would begin with a discussion of the objective character of the demand for art. This would be necessary to counter the subjective experience I believe most artists have of the purely individual nature of demand (addressed to themselves or others): the myth that there's no demand for art as such, but only for individual artists of particular genius, etc., as if, in the absence of such artists, the entire contemporary art apparatus would just disappear. Of course, this is not the case. Museums have been built and must be filled. Critics and curators are trained and have an interest in being employed, gallerists need new art to show and sell. Investments have been made and the field must reproduce itself.

This primary demand to supply the reproduction of the field is conditioned by a second level of demand: that invested with interests related to competitive struggles between and among artists, curators, critics, gallerists and so on. Struggles to maintain and improve one's professional status vis-à-vis one's peers and to impose the principle of status (that is, of legitimacy) and the criteria of value by which the position of others will be defined: such struggles are the dynamics through which the field reproduces itself. The demand for art addressed to artists is often also directly related to competition between institutions themselves: competition for funding, for press, for audiences, and all the other indices of influence over the popular and professional perception of legitimate culture and legitimate cultural discourse.

But cultural institutions are not unitary entities. They are composed of different sectors—for example, professional and voluntary—which are themselves in conflict. As a practitioner of what is often called institutional critique, I have often been asked, "Well, if you're so critical, why do they invite you?" It took me some time to realize that I was often invited by one sector of an institution to produce a critique of the other.

Pierre Bourdieu writes: "Products developed in the competitive struggles of which . . . [the field] is the site, and which are the source of the incessant changing of [its] products, meet, without having expressly to seek it, the demand which is shaped in the objectively or subjectively antagonistic relations between the different classes or class fractions over material or cultural consumer goods." This is why, he continues, "producers can be totally involved and absorbed in their struggles with other producers, convinced that only specific artistic interests are at stake and that they are otherwise totally disinvested while remaining unaware of the social functions they fulfill, in the long run, for a particular audience, and without ever ceasing to respond to the expectations of a particular class."[4]

The demand an artwork meets when consumed materially by an art collector, or symbolically by a museum visitor, may thus be conditioned by the struggles constitutive of the field of cultural production—where "supply," Bourdieu writes, "always exerts an effect of symbolic imposition." But as far as the interests, the needs, and the wants invested in that demand are concerned, the object is indifferent, as the demand itself is subject to perpetual displacement following the course of particular struggles within the field. I would even say that the demand generated by the competition among and between art collectors and museum visitors over the quantity and quality of cultural consumption is itself displaced from another locus and could just as easily attach itself to another field.

The cynical, debased version of this kind of analysis is that the artistic field is no different from any other market in luxury goods. They all serve social competition for status and prestige. But status is not only a matter of status symbols, and prestige is not just a luxury. The pursuit of prestige is only the dominant form of struggles for legitimacy of which culture is a primary site. The intimate character of the adequacy and competence at stake in these struggles is evident in the anxiety even the most socially dominant person may experience when confronted with an institutionally consecrated work of art. Nor does one enter into these struggles voluntarily, as if as a result of some form of vanity. Rather they are mandated, for example, by museums that, as public institutions, impose the competencies necessary to comprehend the culture they define as legitimate as a condition of adequacy within the cities or states that support them.

There are no artists I can think of who could credibly suggest that the functions their works serve have nothing to do with them or their artistic activity, as all artists are called upon to augment these functions for organizations and individuals at openings, dinner parties, press conferences, and so on. They would be right, in any case, to say that they serve no one, if—as Bourdieu writes—"they serve objectively only because, in all sincerity, they serve their own interests, specific, highly sublimated and euphemized interests."[5]

Am I really serving my own interests? According to the logic of artistic autonomy, we work only for ourselves; for our own satisfaction, for the satisfaction of our own criteria of judgment, subject only to the internal logic of our practice, the demands of our consciences or our drives. It has been my experience that the freedom gained in this form of autonomy is often no more than a basis for self-exploitation. Perhaps it is because the privilege of recognizing ourselves and being recognized in the products of our labor must be purchased (like the "freedom" to labor as such, according to Marx) at the price of surplus labor, generating surplus value, or profit, to be appropriated by another. In our case, it is primarily symbolic profit that we generate. And it is conditioned precisely on the freedom from economic necessity that we express in our self-exploitation.

Because we are working for our own satisfaction, our labor is supposed to be its own compensation. It often seems to me that our professional relations are organized as if the entire art apparatus—including cultural institutions and galleries—was established to generously provide us with the opportunity to fulfill our exhibitionistic desires in a public display. It isn't difficult to see what kind of labor market we provide with ideological justification by investing in such a representation.

The subjective freedom, autonomy of conscience, and empowerment of individual will that constitute artistic privilege are matched by economic and social disempowerment. This disempowerment is only partly a result of the atomization of the artistic field: the individualism and competition that consigns each producer to conducting her or his business in isolation, if not in a kind of secrecy. Attempts by artists to form associations—some of which are documented in the project *Services*—can only go a short way in alleviating such atomization and the dependence it produces. Its greater part lies not in material conditions of production but in the mechanisms of the system of belief which produce the value of works of art as well as the legitimacy of our activity. The divisions of labor within the field between production, distribution, and reception are effectively divisions of interest. The Kantian model is alive and well: these divisions of interest are necessary to create the appearance of disinterest essential to the production of belief in the judgment of artistic value. It is a system of belief that requires the judgment of others—people whose interests do not coincide with ours and do not include that of serving us with their evaluations. If curators and dealers appear to be working for artists, their judgment loses its "disinterested" character and thus its value—and they lose their powers to consecrate and sell. Similarly, whereas under the normal conditions of competition the judgment by artists of their peers has a high degree of credibility, if those same evaluations appear to be based, rather, on an identification of practical interests (for example, as with cooperative galleries), they become worthless.

The contradictory principle of our professional lives can thus be articulated as follows: dependence is the condition of our autonomy. We may work for ourselves, for our own satisfaction, responding only to internal demands, following only an internal logic, but in doing so we forfeit the capacity to regulate the social and economic conditions of our activity. And, in forfeiting the capacity to regulate our activity according to our professional interests, we may also forfeit the ability to determine the meaning and effects of our activity according to our interests as social subjects also subject to the effects of the symbolic system we produce and reproduce. As long as the system of belief on which the status of our activity depends is defined according to a principle of autonomy that bars us from pursuing the production of specific social use value, we are consigned to producing only prestige value.

If we are always already serving, artistic freedom can only consist in determining for ourselves—to the extent that we can—whom and how we serve. This is, I think, the only course to a less contradictory principle of autonomy.

Notes

1. Helmut Draxler and Andrea Fraser, "Services: A Proposal for an Exhibition and a Topic of Discussion," 1993, published in Beatrice von Bismarck, Diethelm Stoller, and Ulf Wuggenig, eds., *Games, Fights, Collaborations: Art and Cultural Studies in the Nineties* (Lüneburg: Kunstraum der Universität Lüneburg, 1996), 196–197.

2. Draxler and Fraser, "Services."

3. Harry Stack Sullivan, *The Psychiatric Interview* (New York: W. W. Norton, 1970); Harry Levinson, *Organizational Diagnosis* (Cambridge: Harvard University Press, 1972); Sigmund Freud, *Therapy and Technique*, ed. Philip Rieff (New York: Collier, 1963).

4. Pierre Bourdieu, *Distinction: A Social Critique of the Judgment of Taste*, trans. Richard Nice (Cambridge: Harvard University Press, 1984), 230, 234.

5. Ibid., 240.

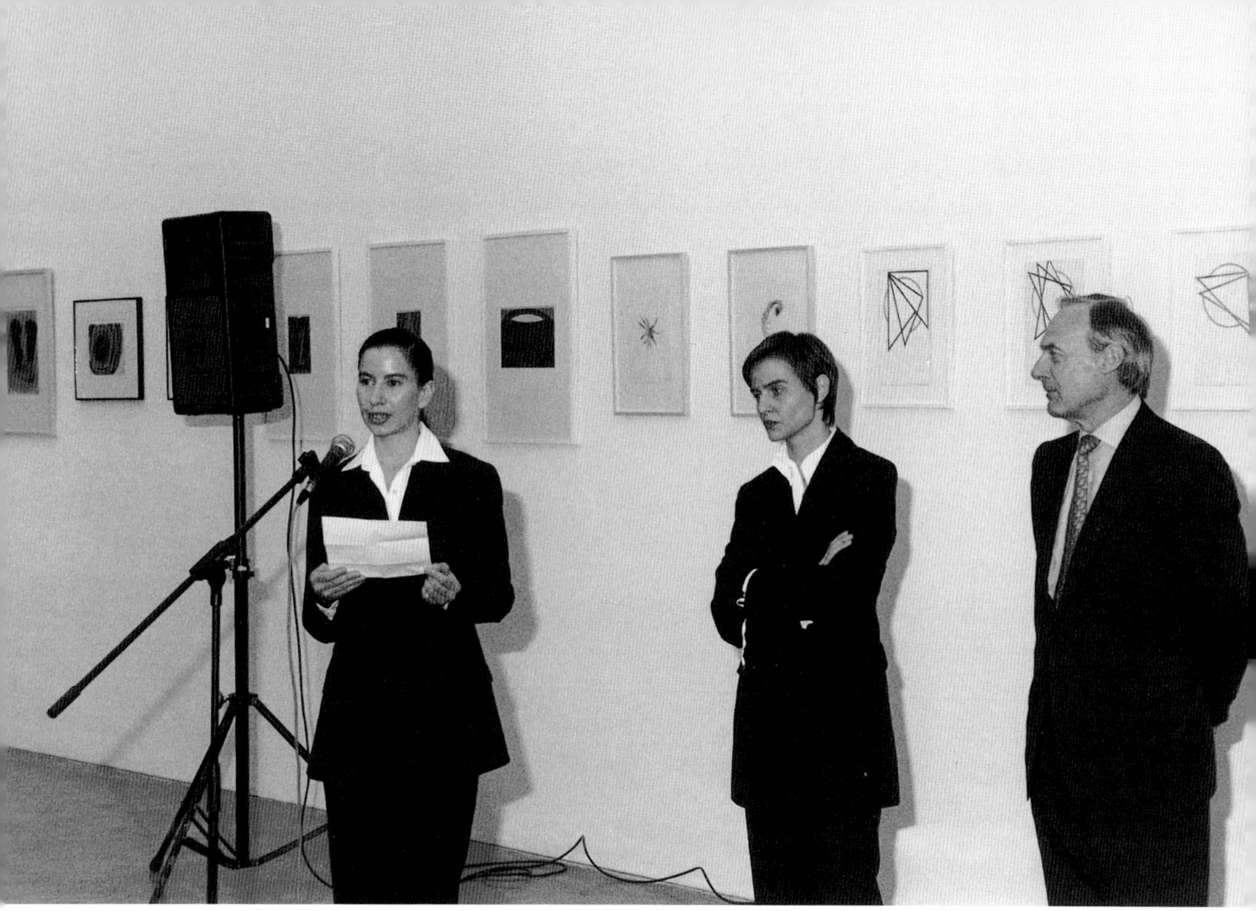

15.1 Andrea Fraser delivering "What Do I, as an Artist, Provide?" at the opening of *A Project in Two Phases* at the EA-Generali Foundation, May 13, 1995, pictured with Sabine Breitwieser and Dietrich Karner. Courtesy the Generali Foundation. Photo: Gerhard Koller.

15

WHAT DO I, AS AN ARTIST, PROVIDE? (A SPEECH AT THE EA-GENERALI FOUNDATION)

In April 1994, I was engaged to undertake a project with the EA*-Generali Foundation in Vienna, an art association established by companies belonging to the* EA*-Generali insurance group. In accordance with my* Prospectus for Corporations,[1] *the project was conceived as a service to be provided in two phases, the first defined as "interpretive" and the second as "interventionary." After a year of research at the corporation, the "interpretive" phase of the project concluded with a publication entitled* Report: The EA-Generali Foundation,[2] *which includes extensive quotations from interviews as well as interpretive text. The "interventionary" phase included a public exhibition of the art formerly installed in the corporate headquarters—which also produced, as an intended correlate, a "negative" installation of the corporate headquarters emptied of art.*

Because the Report *is still in circulation, I have decided not to excerpt it in the current volume. Instead, the project is represented here by the speech I delivered at the opening of the exhibition on May 13, 1995, which followed remarks by the director of the Foundation and the chairman of the corporate group.*

This evening represents the conclusion of what has been a long and, for me, extremely satisfying engagement with the EA-Generali Foundation. It is the appropriate moment to publicly thank the Foundation—and its artistic director, Dr. Breitwieser—as well as the EA-Generali Corporate Group—and its chairman, Dr. Karner—for their support of and participation in the project as it has unfolded over the course of the past year. My hope, however, is that such thanks are unnecessary. My hope is that this project has been equally satisfying for the

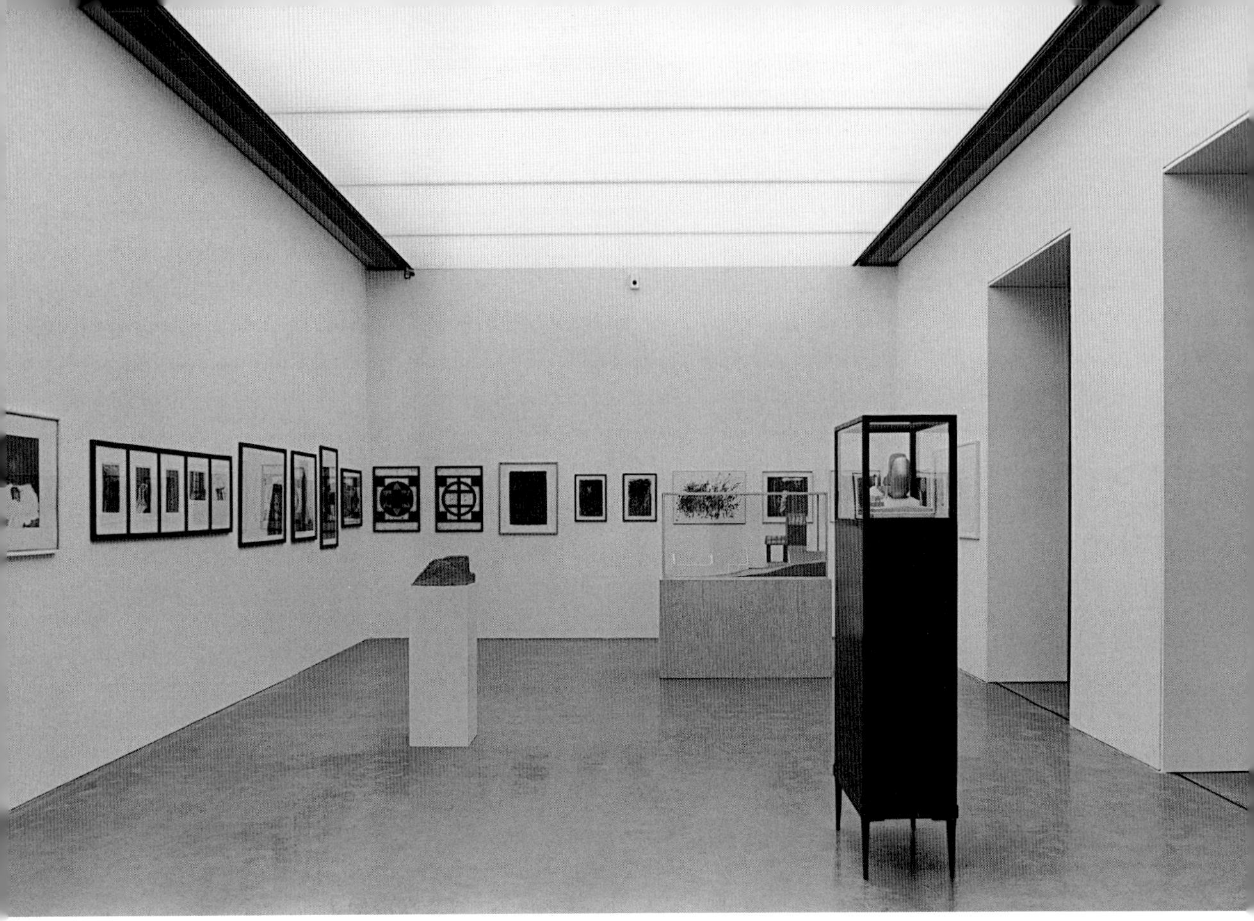

15.2 Andrea Fraser, *A Project in Two Phases*, 1995. Installation at the EA-Generali Foundation, Vienna, with art formerly installed in the corporate headquarters. Courtesy the Generali Foundation. Photo: Werner Kaligofsky.

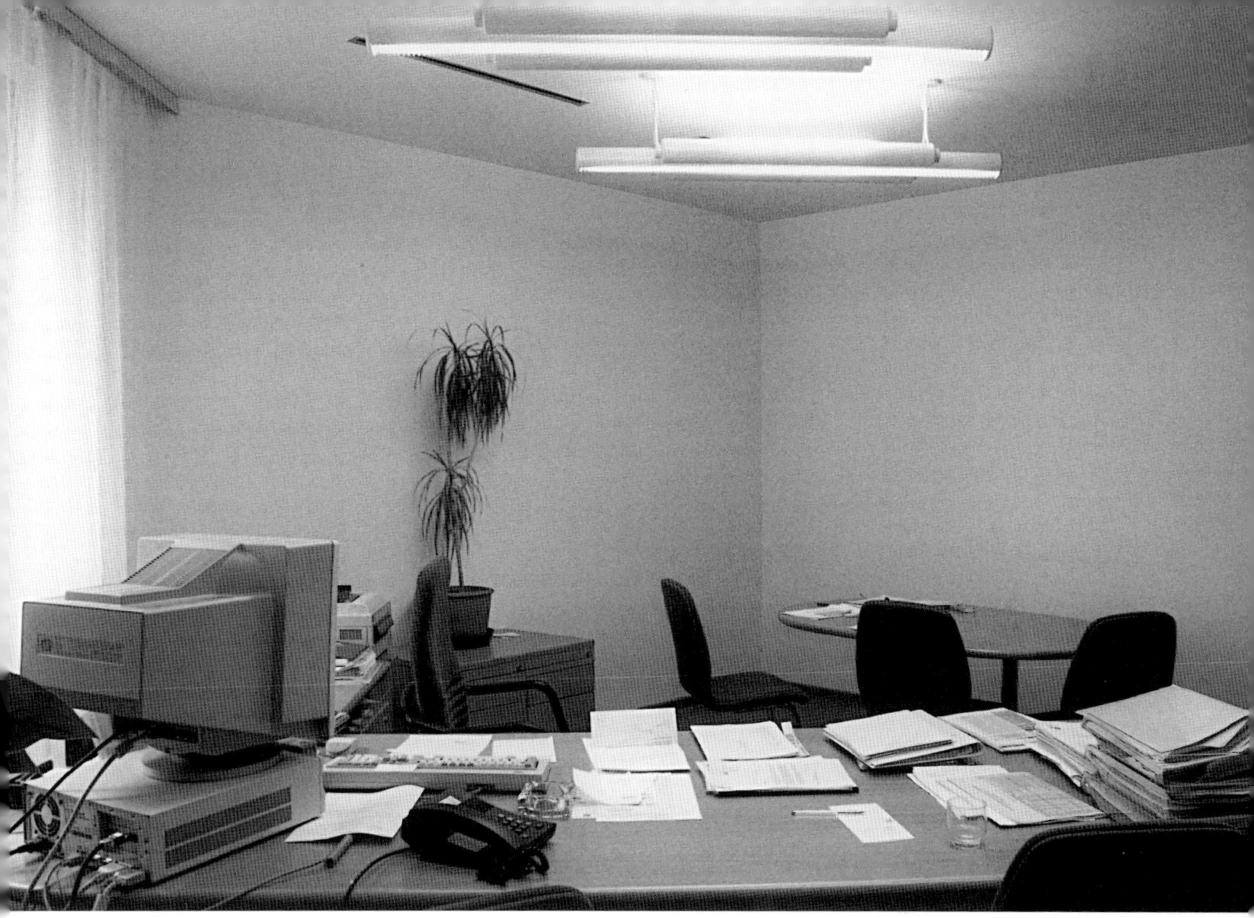

15.3 Andrea Fraser, *A Project in Two Phases*, 1995. Installation at the Generali corporate headquarters, Vienna (an office with art removed). Courtesy the Generali Foundation. Photo: Gerhard Koller.

Foundation and the corporate group. I was engaged by the Foundation to undertake a certain job, which I define as a service. My hope, simply, is that the Foundation has found that job well done.

What do I, as an artist, provide? What do I satisfy? The immediate answer to those questions may be found in the function of the Foundation for the EA-Generali Corporate Group. The Foundation, according to the marketing director, is not gratuitous or self-justifying. It has a function: to develop a particular profile for the EA-Generali Group, to satisfy a public expectation that a large and powerful corporation be engaged in meaningful social activities, and to address target groups with cultural interests. The extent to which I, as an artist, serve those functions does not depend on whether I define my artistic activity as a service. Those functions, rather, are generally fulfilled in the exchange that constitutes any kind of art sponsorship or patronage—public or private. They are fulfilled because the professional prestige that I, as an artist, augment in having my name publicized by a particular organization is identical with the public prestige that organization acquires by having its name associated with a particular kind of art. It's the same quantity of the same currency: the profit in moral legitimacy generated through the pursuit of activities not explicitly oriented toward material gain; the profit in social legitimacy generated by an association with exclusive tastes and practices; and the profit in professional legitimacy generated by the demonstration of competence in our respective spheres of activity.

However, in defining my artistic activity as a service, my aim is to fulfill a different kind of function: not to supply or satisfy given interests (my own or those of the Foundation), but to reflect on those interests and work toward their redefinition. I also hope that in doing so, it is possible to generate a different kind of value: not the symbolic value of legitimacy produced by artistic prestige, but a value generated in participation and expended in use; a value to be appraised, not according to the interest it produces within artistic or intellectual discourse, but according to its impact on social—and, in this case, organizational—relationships.

The Foundation, according to its function, is not self-justifying, but neither, I believe, can an artistic practice claim to be.

Notes

1. My *Preliminary Prospectus: For Corporations* is one of four "preliminary prospectuses" I produced toward the end of 1993. For further information, see the caption to figure 14.1 on page 152.

2. The *Report* is divided into two sections: "Public Image Transfer/Symbolic Profit" and "Corporate Culture/Symbolic Power." Each section is laid out in four columns running discontinuously, with the first column consisting of a descriptive text and the third column an analytical text. The second and fourth columns contain quotations from interviews conducted for the project, with quotations from the "corporate field" of management and employees in one column juxtaposed with quotations from the "artistic field" of Foundation staff and art advisors in the other. With this fractured, multicolumn layout, the *Report* aimed to produce a graphic mapping of the relations between these fields, representing both the contradictions between apparently consistent interests and the homologies that underlay apparent oppositions.

   Those contradictions and homologies are also analyzed in the text of the *Report*. The section on "Public Image Transfer/Symbolic Profit" considers the apparent opposition between artistic autonomy and corporate instrumentalization. Rather than functioning as a form of resistance to instrumentalization, the *Report* argues that such autonomy, in at least some of its aspects, is the very condition of the symbolic profit the corporation derives from art sponsorship. The value of the collection for the corporation depends on its legitimacy within the artistic field, which in turn depends on the freedom of its art advisors to pursue their independent, professional judgment in applying specifically artistic criteria. Thus, the Foundation's function for the corporation would decline in direct, inverse proportion to its instrumentalization, and vice versa.

   The second part of the *Report*, "Corporate Culture/Symbolic Power," looks at how that autonomy functioned within the corporation. One of the primary concerns of art professionals working with the Foundation was of being reduced to interior decorators and constrained by the taste of the corporate staff—employees and management alike. While the executives didn't like the art any more than their secretaries, they did see that the corporation had an interest in maintaining a polished, coherent, professionally put-together interior. The result was various workplace regulations that effectively excluded workers from certain decisions about their working environment—and also happened to protect Foundation staff from employee demands. As far as the corporate employees were concerned, the "autonomy" of the Foundation was just another management directive. The authority of the art advisors was perfectly homologous to the authority exercised by management but with one important difference: it appeared much more arbitrary. This was not only because any rationalization of the Foundation would contradict its public-relations function, but also because such resistance to rationalization is fundamental to the structure of artistic autonomy itself, to the definition of artistic competence and the valuation of artistic labor. At a moment when the corporation was taking its first steps toward introducing a neoliberal regime of performance-based compensation, putting ever more pressure on employees to produce profits, it was spending large sums of money on objects that it did not and could not account for in terms of the bottom line.

   See Andrea Fraser, *Report: The* EA*-Generali Foundation* (Vienna: EA-Generali Foundation, 1995).

16

SLASHING THE *AMERICAN CANVAS*, OR, WHY I WOULD RATHER HAVE A DAY JOB

"Slashing the American Canvas*" was written for a panel on "Support for Elite, Middlebrow, and Vernacular Cultures" at the conference "New Trends in Cultural Policy for the 21st Century" held at the New School University and New York University in the spring of 1998. A revised and expanded version appears below.*

I'd like to begin with the observation that, although I'm not the only artist participating in this conference, I do appear to be the only producer of "elite" culture without an institutional affiliation. I mention this not to complain about the conference—and I'd like to thank the organizers for inviting me to participate. I mention it, rather, because it's the most convenient example of the "trends in cultural policy" about which I would like to speak.

One of the major trends in cultural policy in the United States in the past decade has been the decline in direct support for unaffiliated producers of "elite" culture—otherwise known as individual artists. The National Endowment for the Arts' artists fellowship programs, after years of attack by the right, were finally eliminated in 1996. These attacks also had a chilling effect on state arts councils as well as on corporate and foundation support for individual artists. Of the few foundations that provide grants to individual artists, Art Matters Inc., one of the most active and progressive, was recently forced to discontinue its programs largely as a result of lack of support within the foundation community. In addition, what indirect support continues to exist, such as project funding that artists can pursue through the fiscal sponsorship of nonprofit organizations or through participation in institutional programs, is being narrowed by the growing emphasis, in the guidelines of public, foundation, and corporate sponsors, on public education, community development, and community-based engagement with what could be called, in the vocabulary of this panel, "vernacular" cultures.

My point here, however, is not to decry the drying up of funding for individual artists. When one's position on policy corresponds so neatly to one's professional interests, it's a good idea to take a second look at how those interests themselves are being defined.

A good place to start is *American Canvas,* the much discussed National Endowment for the Arts report authored by Gary O. Larson and released by the NEA in October 1997.[1] Based on a series of public forums held in six different U.S. cities, *American Canvas* takes up with a vengeance the notion of the arts serving social needs. It describes "using the arts to build strong communities" and to "promote civic responsibility and good citizenship"; it claims that art "stimulates the economy and attracts tourists, revitalizes neighborhoods and addresses social problems," and finally that art contributes to "a city's 'feel-good' element," making it "more attractive, both to the general public as well as to the business community" (Larson 4, 15, 81–82). The arts, we are told, are about "celebration rather than confrontation" (Larson 14). "No longer restricted solely to the sanctioned arenas of culture, the arts would be literally suffused throughout the civic structure, finding a home in a variety of community service and economic development activities" (Larson 127).

One need not dig deep, however, to find the dark side of the boosterism and uplift. Further into the document, arts professionals are advised to "target" HUD to subsidize what used to be called gentrification: "Artists' housing *can* . . . be used as a community revitalization tool" (Larson 129). And when it's stated that art should be built into "the fabric" of "basic public-sector functions," what's at the top of the list? Crime prevention! Yes, the criminal justice system is "among a number of . . . areas with which the arts community might profitably develop new relations" (Larson 128). We can decorate prisons! And so, the public sector's fastest-growing industry can rescue the one in the most precipitous decline.

This new emphasis on art's utilitarian value in serving social needs, developed to an extreme in *American Canvas,* might be traced back to two basic sources. First, for public and foundation funders, it may relate to the desperateness of those needs within an increasingly impoverished public sector. Second, for public and corporate funders, it may relate to what George Yúdice has called a shift in the strategies of legitimation of cultural sponsorship—and of the sponsors themselves—from one that depends on the symbolic value of culture in generating international or public prestige, to one that banks instead on art's supposed social use value.[2] For corporations, such a move may be an answer to the difficulty of rationalizing philanthropic activity as such in an era of mass layoffs and relentless pressure to cut wages and benefits. (This applies less to support for exhibitions, which usually comes out of advertising budgets, than to corporate collecting, which has declined, and to the programs of corporate foundations.) For public funders, and especially for the NEA, the new strategies of legitimation have been linked to the end of the Cold War and, most often, have been seen as a response to the right-wing attacks which charged that the art funded by the endowment is, among other sins, "elitist."

What interests me, however—and what makes these issues relevant to this panel—is less the political or economic conditions of this phenomenon, than its cultural logic. What one finds in *American Canvas* is that this totally instrumentalized vision of arts funding is propped on an equally instrumentalized and purely affirmative vision of "vernacular" culture, one that reduces the latter to the most generalized function of providing for the symbolic integration of communities. The resulting representation does justice to Pierre Bourdieu's characterization of "certain populist exaltations of 'popular culture'" as "the 'pastorals' of our epoch": "a sham inversion of dominant values" that functions to "produce the fiction of a unity of the social world."[3]

I quote *American Canvas:* "The legacy of the future may have a more common, if no less valued, profile. Included will be the art that is woven through the social fabric" (Larson 15).

The "dominant values" to be inverted in *American Canvas* are identified almost exclusively with "specialized, professional" cultural production, which art institutions are criticized for having stressed to the point that art has become "something that we watch other people do, usually highly skilled professionals, rather than something we do ourselves" (Larson 60). Now, the document argues, "the narrow, professional, institutional definition" of the past must be replaced with "a more expansive view," one that includes the "avocational and ethnic, participatory and popular" (Larson 162–63).

While it is strongly implied that such a redefinition justifies a shift of support away from "elite" cultural producers, support for the producers of this "vernacular" culture is never entertained. Why? Because, it can be supposed, their practices, being avocational and amateur, don't require economic support: they are defined, in fact, by their place outside of the relations of recognition and reward, subsidy and institutional sanction which define the places of professional artists within their professional fields. But if the function of cultural policy in relation to "vernacular" culture is not to support its production, what is it? According to the "expansive view" of culture articulated in *American Canvas,* art "is an essential part of the lives of most families. *The problem is that they just don't know it.*" What we must do is "help them recognize, nourish, and value the art they already possess" as well as "the artistic merit of their own creative efforts" (Larson 62, italics added). And why? To reverse the effects of domination imposed by cultural legitimacies? Guess again. Because a "larger, more committed audience for the arts" can "be developed out of a nation of avocational singers, dancers, painters, and musicians." And all this can be achieved without ever "losing sight of the standards of professional excellence that still have a role in providing benchmarks of achievement" (Larson 163).

And so at last we arrive at the ends of support for "vernacular" culture in the vision of cultural policy laid out in *American Canvas.* Its function is not to challenge cultural hierarchies or even the perimeters of "elite" art but, rather, to seduce a greater number into serving as "a larger, more inclusive base of support" for what is, in fact, the same old cultural pyramid. "Avocational and ethnic, participatory and popular" cultural practices are finally described only as raw material to be re-formed by art professionals or, even more insidiously, to be exploited.

Can "vernacular culture" exist within cultural policy as anything other than an object of the discourse and practices of arts professionals—whether administrators or "elite" artists themselves, who are increasingly taking up the roles of cultural mediators? Can it be more that an object of administration, appropriation, or even expropriation (as is suggested in *American Canvas* by the metaphor of taking "stock" of "pockets of creativity" in communities that might have been "overlooked in previous inventories" [Larson 163])?

I don't believe that the answer to this question depends on the definitions of "elite," "middlebrow," and "vernacular" applied to various cultural forms. It depends, rather, on how these terms—or better, the distributions of competence and credit, prestige and power they are often used to describe—relate to the networks through which various cultural forms are passed. What makes cultural institutions or policy "elite" is not the fact that they privilege "elite" culture, but that they privilege modes of appropriation of culture that require rarefied and socially valorized competencies. That these competencies are displaced, in *American*

Canvas, from producers and consumers of culture to administrators does nothing to mitigate their "elite" character: if anything, it represents a tendency to consolidate those competencies in administrative functions—functions made all the more important for the newly discovered "needs" they are supposed to satisfy.

American Canvas is not only a product of right-wing attacks on the NEA. It must also be read as a product of the professionalization of the cultural field which has taken place in the past few decades, a process that has coincided with the expansion and increasing rationalization of the intermediary functions of cultural management and administration. That process of professionalization was facilitated, if not made possible, by public sector intervention and subvention. Until the 1960s, a surprising number of the museums were still staffed by "gentlemen curators" or by art connoisseurs who began their careers providing personal consulting services to patrons and trustees. Most art dealers were also wealthy collectors. Foundations were run largely by the relatives and business associates of their founders.

With the establishment of the NEA and state arts councils in the mid-1960s, all this began to change. Public arts administrators and other cultural workers began to develop professional organizations in the space of relative freedom from specific private interests created by the public sector. The professionalization of foundation staff was spurred by the restrictions introduced in the Tax Reform Act of 1969 on the heels of a decade of governmental scrutiny of self-dealing and other abuses by foundations. Tax reform, together with the comparatively progressive social policy of the Johnson era, meant that the old patrons of "elite" culture didn't have as much money to give away—and, with new restrictions on charitable deductions, what they had was getting more expensive to give. Within museums, art professionals used the sudden weakness of private donors, and the increased dependence of museums on newly available public funds, as leverage in their efforts to establish a foothold of professional autonomy from trustees and patrons within their institutions. All of these forces combined to bring about an unprecedented professionalization in the field: beyond peer review panels, there were artists organizations and alternative spaces, unionization drives in cultural institutions, professional associations for arts administrators, arts lobbying groups, training and degree programs in curating and arts administration, art consultants for the expanding ranks of corporate collectors and sponsors, professional art dealers with investor backing, paid as well as voluntary presidents in cultural institutions and managing as well as artistic directors.

At the same time that arts administrators were expanding their autonomy as professionals, at least some of the so-called avant-garde segments of "elite" cultural producers were beginning to recognize the partial and ideological character of their autonomy as artists—of the freedom and independence which supposedly distinguished their activities from those of producers of "middlebrow" and "vernacular" culture. The realization that even the most formally autonomous art was used to serve social, political, and economic interests—often not in spite of but because of its aestheticism—led some artists to the realization that "elite" art is also, in a sense, the "vernacular" culture of a particular patron class, and led a few to see that it existed as the "vernacular" culture of its class of specialized producers as well. This critique of artistic autonomy from within the field of art joined together with struggles for cultural equality outside of it in an effort to redefine what is constituted as legitimate culture within the public sphere defined by nonprofit art institutions.

Within the visual art world, at least, I can say that a large part of the professional autonomy gained by cultural workers since the 1960s was won, not only with the aid of public sector support, but also in the name of the "public"—or publics—newly defined as composed of heterogeneous cultural constituencies: in the name, that is, of struggles for cultural democratization. I found only one reference in *American Canvas* to these struggles—struggles of which, in its call for an expanded view of culture, the document itself is the product. This reference is a quotation from Bernice Johnson Reagon of Sweet Honey in the Rock, and it goes far in explaining why this history would be omitted. "No sooner," she says, "had our efforts begun to result in funding for more complex cultural constituencies . . . than the mainstream institutions themselves began to maneuver to take over the very resources we had, through our lobbying efforts, created" (quoted in Larson 29). In the next sentence, the author of *American Canvas* interprets this phenomenon as a matter of "increased competition." In fact, it is just the opposite: the reassertion of the cultural monopolies of "elite" institutions.

My concern today is that those publics in whose names we pursued professionalization—even and perhaps especially as defined as complex constituencies of popular, participatory, ethnic, and avocational cultures—are being reduced once again to audiences, or even clients, of institutions and their administrators: a form of capital to be invested in the reproduction of what remains

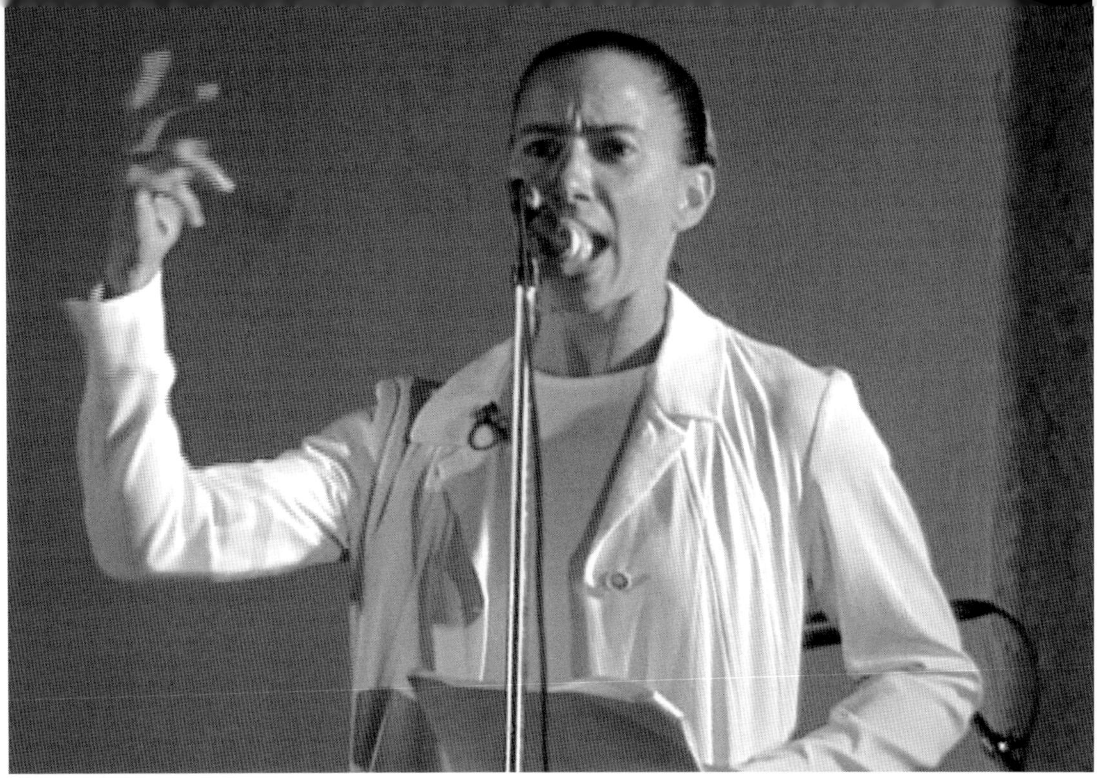

16.1 Andrea Fraser, still from *Inaugural Speech*, 1997. Videotape of live performance at inSITE97, San Diego. Courtesy the artist.

Inaugural Speech attempted to engage the politics of international exhibitions in the era of globalization. Following official speeches by politicians reading letters from U.S. and Mexican presidents Clinton and Zedillo, *Inaugural Speech* begins as an artist takes the podium to describe the show and thank the exhibition organizers. Rather than leaving the stage, however, she thanks the artist for the kind introduction and continues speaking, first as a curator, then as a trustee, then as a public official, and finally as a corporate sponsor. *Inaugural Speech* attempts both to map and to perform the pyramid of power in the field of art for which artists and art audiences form the base of support. In doing so, it tries to implode the rituals of mutual recognition and legitimation that cement the bonds between the apparently opposing interests at work in international art exhibitions—exhibitions that in turn often function as legitimizing cultural manifestations of the neoliberal agendas driving economic globalization.

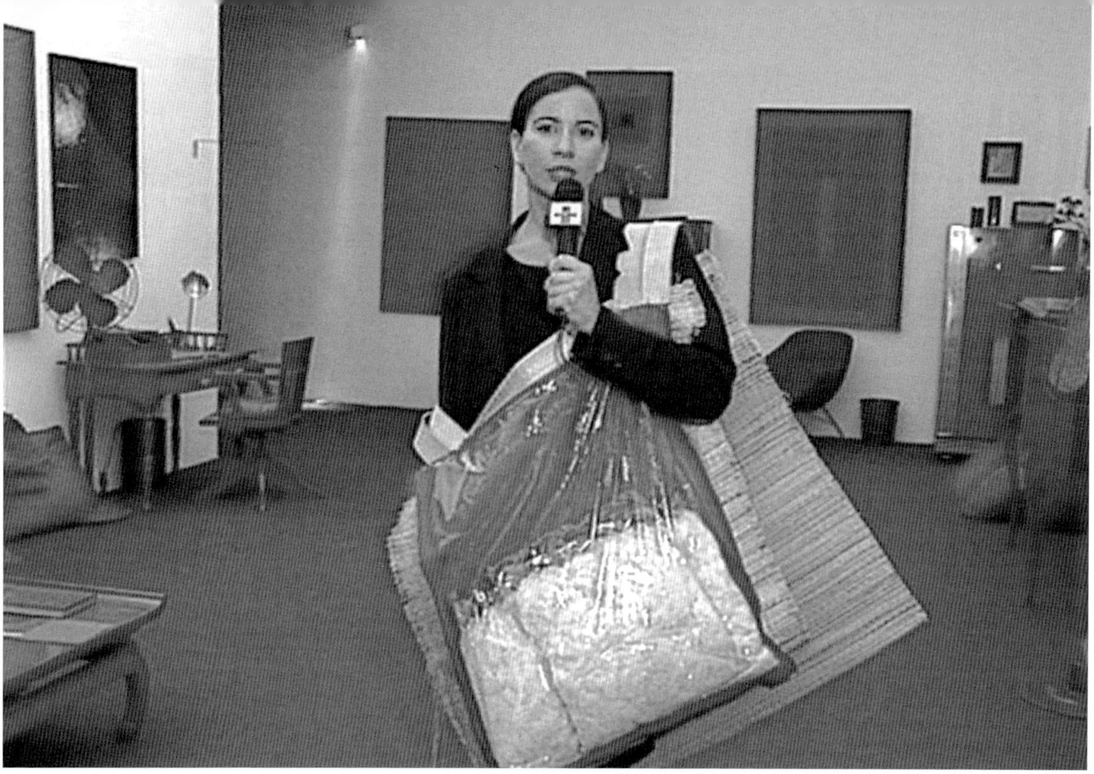

16.2 Andrea Fraser, still from *Reporting from São Paulo, I'm from the United States,* 1998 (with *Detour in Red* by Cildo Meireles and a *Parangolé* by Hélio Oiticica). Videotape. Courtesy the artist.

Produced for the North American section of the 24th Bienal de São Paulo, *Reporting from São Paulo, I'm from the United States* takes the form of five short television news reports about the exhibition. Working with a crew from TV Cultura, a nationally broadcast cultural station, the reports were to be broadcast in the context of a cultural magazine program, as well as exhibited in the exhibition itself. Owing to national presidential elections, local floods, a global economic crisis, and other events coinciding with the opening of the Bienal, the tapes were never broadcast. These events, however, provided an immediate context in which to examine the 24th Bienal's theme of "cannibalism" as well as the relationship between international biennial exhibitions and economic globalization.

a field of "elite" culture, albeit one now defined less by the rarefied and gratuitous forms of its products than by the conditions, at once specialized and professionalized, of their mediation and distribution.[4]

American Canvas is not about the democratization of cultural policy; it's about making public funding safe for arts administrators. The view I take of this is admittedly harsh. The professionalization of the cultural field did indeed provide arts administrators with a greater degree of autonomy: the freedom, for example, to identify constituencies other than a patron class. It also, however, created homologies of interest that can provide stronger motives for responding to the political and economic demands of sponsors than any relative weakness. Let's not forget that, as many commentators have suggested, the attacks on the NEA were successful largely because so many arts administrators capitulated—from the directors of the Corcoran and Artists Space to the chairman of the NEA—sacrificing artists to censorship in exchange for protecting their organizations. And now, adding to the political autonomy left behind in the triage of the "culture wars," *American Canvas* suggests that art's most fundamental form of freedom be forsaken: the freedom from rationalization with respect to specific functions. We are advised to jump to the service of "social needs," gentrifying neighborhoods, decorating prisons, enhancing cities for destination marketers. And why? Not because the demand exists: the function of cultural policy, according to *American Canvas,* is precisely to *produce* such demand. We should work to serve these "needs," rather, to generate, and justify, the funds necessary to maintain, or even expand, the organizations established during the nonprofit cultural boom years of the 1970s and '80s—and especially, of course, the most legitimate ones.

Is it really worth it? And, most importantly, for whom?

I, for one, would rather have a day job.

Notes

1. Gary O. Larson, *American Canvas* (Washington, D.C.: National Endowment for the Arts, 1997). For economy's sake, all future references to Larson will appear in parentheses in the text.

2. George Yúdice, "The Privatization of Culture," paper presented at the University of Kansas, Lawrence, November 6, 1997.

3. Pierre Bourdieu and Loïc Wacquant, *An Invitation to Reflexive Sociology* (Chicago: University of Chicago Press, 1992), 83.

4. Once again, I would turn to Bourdieu for a description of this process:

> The constitution of a socially recognized corps of experts . . . which is now coming about through the gradual professionalization of voluntary, philanthropic or political associations, is the paradigmatic form of the process whereby agents tend, with that deep conviction of disinterestedness which is the basis of all missionary zeal, to satisfy their group interests by deploying the legitimate culture with which they have been endowed by the education system to win the acquiescence of the classes excluded from legitimate culture, in producing the need for and the rarity of their class culture.

Pierre Bourdieu, *Distinction: A Social Critique of the Judgment of Taste,* trans. Richard Nice (Cambridge: Harvard University Press, 1984), 153.

17

A SENSATION CHRONICLE

Drafts of this essay were first presented as papers at the Privatization of Culture Project Seminar held at the New School University, and at the Center for Curatorial Studies at Bard College in November 1999. It was first published in Social Text *in Summer 2001.*

The controversy began on September 22, 1999, when New York City mayor Rudolph Giuliani attacked the Brooklyn Museum of Art for its plan to present "Sensation: Young British Artists from the Saatchi Collection," calling work in the show "sick stuff" that "desecrates religion." Giuliani's attacks were widely seen as politically motivated by his nascent campaign against Hillary Clinton for a U.S. Senate seat. When the Brooklyn Museum proceeded to present the exhibition as planned, Giuliani withheld the city funding that makes up almost one-third of the museum's budget. During the weeks that followed, the mayor's threats escalated to include evicting the museum from its city-owned building and taking over its board of trustees, and his attacks expanded to include charges that the museum violated its charter by presenting an exhibition which was more commercial than educational in nature and violated the public trust by securing funding from sources with financial interests in the show. The Brooklyn Museum responded to these attacks by filing a suit against the city for violating First Amendment protections for free expression. On November 1, less than six weeks later, a federal judge at the United States District Court in Brooklyn ruled that the mayor had indeed violated the First Amendment and ordered the city to restore its funding to the Brooklyn Museum.

Unlike the NEA crisis of 1989, the "Sensation" controversy was not exclusively about the border between art and the state, or the freedom of art from political interference. In addition to this border, two others—perhaps *the* two other borders by which the art field has long defined itself—have also been at stake: the border between art and economic interests and the border between so-called high and low, elite and popular culture. This conjunction of struggles at the three fundamental boundaries around the field of art make the "Sensation" controversy enormously instructive. It allows for a mapping of a broad range of positions within the artistic field as well as between fields and, through a comparison to the NEA crisis, of the trajectory they have taken over a decade of rapid transformation in the cultural world.

If the boundaries between art, political influence, economic interests, and popular culture make up the terrain of the "Sensation" controversy, the principles according to which these borders are defended have defined its dynamics. These principles, or logics of defense, can also be described as three dimensions of the autonomy traditionally claimed by the field of art. These include the artistic autonomy elaborated in aesthetic philosophy and institutionalized in public and nonprofit art museums as disinterestedness and distancing from specific functions—whether simple utility, communicative effect, emotional or sensual satisfaction, or the production of profit; the social autonomy of art as a specialized, professional field; and the political autonomy represented by constitutional guarantees of free expression.

If these three dimensions of autonomy in the field of art have been thoroughly interrelated, what the "Sensation" controversy reveals are fault lines of contradiction between them—fault lines that deepen as they play along the different borders between art and political influence, art and economic interests, and art and popular culture. This paper will argue that the crises called "the culture wars" may be products of a process of fragmentation along these fracture lines: a splitting of the social, aesthetic, and political autonomy according to which artistic freedoms have been defined and defended. If this is the case, the "Sensation" controversy may be no more than a phantom limb phenomenon, felt only in the systemic memory of a field whose freedom is already lost to the logic of its autonomy.

1. Between Art and Political Influence: Aesthetic Autonomy and the First Amendment

As a First Amendment case, the "Sensation" controversy was open and shut. While the Supreme Court's 1998 ruling in *National Endowment for the Arts v. Finley* was ambiguous with regard to decisions to award funding, it was clearer in finding that the NEA's "decency clause," if used to punish disfavored viewpoints, would violate the First Amendment. The prevalent interpretation, affirmed by Judge Gershon's November 1, 1999, ruling in favor of the Brooklyn Museum, was that while government agencies have no obligation to fund the arts, once the decision to fund has been made that funding cannot be withdrawn in a manner that would penalize protected speech.[1]

Once the Brooklyn Museum filed its suit against the city, few observers doubted that the museum would win. First Amendment rulings against Giuliani had become an almost weekly occurrence, with the mayor winning only two of over twenty-five cases brought against the city during his administration. While the city itself quickly dropped its initial charge that "Sensation" included "sick" and "blasphemous" art—art that would certainly be ruled protected speech—the museum's defenders kept the First Amendment at the center of the controversy. That strategy did not, however, prevent different representations of free expression from emerging.

"It's Like Herding Cats"

Giuliani's attack on the Brooklyn Museum was no surprise to most observers familiar with his record on First Amendment issues. Much more surprising was the remarkably slow and weak response from the city's cultural institutions. While civil libertarians were quick, loud, and clear in their condemnation of the mayor's actions, journalists were clearly incredulous as they reported "no comments" from New York City museum officials. It took the Cultural Institutions Group of organizations supported by the city five days to draft a feeble letter to the mayor. It began: "Dear Mr. Mayor: In view of how consistently enlightened and generous both you and the City Council have been in supporting the arts . . .". Most, but not all, of the group's thirty-three members finally signed. Alan J. Friedman, the group's chairman, said of his efforts, "It's like herding cats."[2]

The general explanation for this lack of support was fear of retribution from a mayor with a record of punishing organizations that disagreed with him. But is that explanation sufficient—particularly for such large and powerful institutions as Lincoln Center and the Metropolitan Museum of Art? The argument that these organizations had their own reservations about "Sensation" may be more convincing. However, it's also worth noting that few of New York City's cultural institutions raised their voices against Giuliani's many other violations of First Amendment rights as he attacked the city's gay culture, youth culture, street culture, and sex culture, closing clubs and bookstores and theaters and bars. When the mayor ordered the arrest of street artists protesting in front of the Metropolitan in 1998, the museum refused to take a side. An examination of the statements on the controversy by prominent art world figures, particularly museum directors and art critics, indicates that many were acting from the fairly limited space of their specific institutions and interests—a space in which disturbingly narrow conceptions of free expression appear to prevail.

"Making a Cause out of Bad Art"

The city's two most prominent museums, the Metropolitan Museum of Art and the Museum of Modern Art, initially responded to the crisis by simultaneously releasing identical nonstatements. Less than two weeks later Philippe de Montebello, the director of the Metropolitan, clarified his position in an editorial for the *New York Times* that provides stunning evidence of the dynamics underlying the passivity of New York museums. When, in one of the most remarkable moments in the controversy, we find the premier museum director in the United States and defender of the aesthetic faith in the new world lending his prestige to Giuliani's hardly aesthetic judgment, it's not enough to point to the museum's interest in receiving the many millions promised it by the city.

De Montebello begins his editorial, "Making a Cause out of Bad Art," by distinguishing the "crucial issue" of "art and its relative merits" from those of "politics, public financing and constitutional law." The latter, we are to understand, are less crucial. When de Montebello goes on to write, "I find no fault with the Mayor's aesthetic sensibilities, only with his efforts at censorship," the principles at fault are clearly not to be found in the Bill of Rights. Instead, he has recourse to Voltaire. However, when de Montebello paraphrases Voltaire's famous lines, it is not the right to speech that he volunteers to "defend to the death," but rather "the independent role of museums" and "their right" to mount exhibitions.[3]

De Montebello's editorial is written in the language of crusades against false prophets and the vanity of merely temporal powers. At the "risk of apostasy," he must reveal that "the emperor has no clothes," lest "too many unwary visitors come to pay obeisance to art they feel they should try to understand and, heaven forbid, even like." "Good art is not to be judged in the arena of politics or constitutional law," but has a "universal appeal that transcends space and time." He goes on to compare Kiki Smith's sculpture of "a figure defecating" with Lorenzo Lotto's painting of "a putto urinating": "one is simply disgusting . . . ; the other is of superior aesthetic quality."

Where did he cook up that comparison? The answer may be found in the pages of the *New York Post*. A week earlier, the *Post*'s "Metro Gnome," Gersh Kuntzman, concluded his tour of "offensive art" on view at city-subsidized museums with a visit to the Met, where, he begins, "I was so offended by the $10 'suggested contribution' that I almost didn't bother going inside to be offended by the art." But inside he went, and found Lotto's painting. "There it is for all to see: The God of Love, who looks like Deputy Mayor Randy Levine, taking a whiz all over the Goddess of Beauty as she fondles her breast." He notes that the accompanying text describes urination as "an augury of fertility."[4]

However, it's not only a contemporary American artist and an Italian Renaissance painter that de Montebello is comparing. He makes it clear that the former was on view at the Whitney Museum while the Metropolitan owns the latter. With that—and what looks like a scramble to escape the company of the Studio Museum in Harlem and El Museo del Barrio in the *Post* piece—we can now put the Met's "very limited" support for Brooklyn into perspective. What we find in de Montebello's defense of the mayor's "taste" is an example of the homologies that link dominant positions in the apparently opposed fields of art and politics. It's an alliance that turns, in Weberian terms, on the struggle between the traditional authority invested in age-old aesthetic values on the one hand and the Catholic Church (as defended by Giuliani) on the other, against the judicial authority of constitutional rights and the charismatic authority of young artistic and institutional challengers.

Glenn Lowry, the director of the Museum of Modern Art, took up this challenge a few days later in another *New York Times* editorial. Lowry takes aim at de Montebello by bemoaning the "hostility to contemporary art" that "Sensation" has elicited, and rises in (an implicit) defense of the Whitney. But when he goes on to write that the question of what makes "us intolerant of contemporary art" is as important as the First Amendment, his distinction between issues of art and democratic rights begins to sound familiar.[5] Like de Montebello's attack,

Lowry's defense of contemporary art is situated not, as he himself specifies, in the context of First Amendment protections. It is to be situated, rather, in the context of the competitive field of Manhattan museums and the Met's effort to reassert its class-by-itself authority within it. It's a field in which freedom of expression appears to be a less-than-universal principle.

"It's Those Antennas"

Whereas de Montebello's aesthetic essentialism leads him to place the "universal appeal" of "good art" above the universal claims of civil liberties, the Brooklyn Museum's own director, Arnold Lehman, appears to succumb to another kind of essentialism in his defense of the art and artists in "Sensation." In his first statements in response to the mayor, Lehman made it clear that he believes "it is part of a museum's job to support the right of artists to express themselves freely." A few days later he further elaborated his perspective on those rights, saying that artists "look at the world differently from you and me. . . . They either have better hearing or they have better eyes, or they have better vocal chords, or something, and that sensitivity is what's so important. It's those antennas, which may not be receiving the same things we receive, but they receive important messages. . . . They should be, I believe, the primary protected species of the human race."[6]

Lehman's identification of "the rights of artists" with supposedly unique and almost biologically preordained capacities becomes even more disturbing in connection to his statements about the work at the center of the controversy.

From the onset of his campaign against "Sensation," Giuliani singled out *The Holy Virgin Mary* by Chris Ofili, a collage consisting of a stylized painting of a black Madonna surrounded by cutouts from porn magazines and a ball of elephant dung attached as a left breast. Throughout the controversy, attacks on the work focused on the dung, with the cutouts at first mentioned not at all and then misidentified as "buttocks." Even when they were finally described as including genitalia, the cutouts failed to figure prominently. Could the association of the Holy Virgin with a neatly shellacked ball of elephant dung be so much more offensive than her association with crotch shots? Or, is the dung serving as a metaphor for the black face and African features that the representation shares with the artist, a fact never mentioned in the attacks?[7] Giuliani's initial assumption that Ofili is not Catholic was widely perceived as racial. However, it's from defenders of the painting that explicit racial identification comes. The Catholic,

Democratic City Council president Peter Vallone says he learned from the museum that Ofili was "trying to do something complimentary, because elephant dung in his particular society is almost sacred—it's a sign of growth."[8]

Since Ofili is a black Briton who first visited Africa as a young adult, traveling not to Nigeria, where his parents were from, but Zimbabwe, what is "his particular society"? By the opening of "Sensation," Lehman developed this essentializing racial representation of Ofili's work to the point of identifying it directly with African art in the museum's collection, saying that such work tells us "not a story of blasphemy, but a story of reverence. . . . But it is in a language foreign to many of us raised in the tradition of Western culture. Having these sacred objects in our museums teaches us lessons of tolerance, understanding and diversity."[9] Lehman, in effect, severs Ofili's work from avant-garde traditions and recasts it as an unmediated and affirmative expression of an undifferentiated black "society"—even to the point of describing it as a kind of African religious artifact.

"After All That Yelling, Time to Think"

While Lehman reinterprets Ofili's work in the ethnographic language of culture, another prominent representation—that of Michael Kimmelman—neutralizes its iconography in the aesthetic language of form. While Lehman implies that the painting's content should not be offensive to anyone, Kimmelman simply denies that it has content altogether.

From the beginning of the controversy, Kimmelman, the chief art critic of the *New York Times,* presented himself as a clear, balanced voice of reason who saw through the cynicism and self-interest on both sides of the debate. It is a position that finds explicit expression when Kimmelman finally considers the exhibition "itself," in a review entitled "After All That Yelling, Time to Think."[10] The opposition between "yelling" and "thinking," however, is anything but balanced, particularly when the writer himself is the one claiming to "think."

Kimmelman's first sentence judges "Sensation" "much less entertaining and far less significant than the political fight it kindles." The work, after all, is already "old news in the New York art world." However, "the failure to predict . . . that 'Sensation' might genuinely hurt people who are not art insiders . . . suggests the extent to which the art world is out of touch." On the other hand, controversy over artworks often "founders on the most basic level of interpretation": "Artists may intend certain things, but then their work gains unintended meaning as other people bring their own assumptions to it." "Unfortunately," when these assumptions take the form of angry public debate, they "overwhelm the artwork." The further these meanings stray from the artistic intentions of artists, the more "unfortunate" they become. When Kimmelman identifies artists as elitist for expecting viewers "to relate to their work on their terms," it's not a critique. Art is "an equal opportunity elitist: anyone who wants to can learn to speak the language."

This language is clearly his language. And when the chief art critic of the paper of record of the cultural capital of the world finally approaches the artwork around which the battle over content and iconography is raging, he brings all the authority of his position to his statement of the objective fact of the painting in question. "Mr. Ofili's art," he writes, is "basically abstract." His critical distance reveals itself as aesthetic distancing; his political neutrality realizes itself in the neutralization of content in formal analysis. He goes on to tell us that Damian Hirst is an interesting artist not because he cuts animals in half, but because he puts them in boxes that allude to minimalist sources. He tells us that Ofili's paintings are "throwbacks to '60s psychedelic art" and that Rachel Whiteread's sculptures, while "not exactly original," do "have a somber dignity."

This *is* the language of art, art's legitimate language: the language of formal description, historical allusion, the identification of artistic positions within a field of stylistic possibilities, and the positioning of that identification itself within a field of relative familiarity with what is more or less original, interesting, and new. It is a language anyone can learn—anyone who can "think" enough to overcome their investment in the content of representations and to join artists and critics in the aesthetic neutralization of all but artistic meanings.

To whom does this power of neutralization belong besides artists and critics? In what Kimmelman describes as a "lavishly installed" show that "sprawls luxuriously" across "grand galleries," "Sensation's" $500-per-head gala opening finds "New York's culturati" "nibbling shrimp and baby lobster tails."[11] Among the opening's guests, Peter Norton is described as being "quite taken" with Ofili's *Virgin*. "How pretty, how lyrical, how sympathetic it is. . . . If you get beyond the knee-jerk reaction, it's not offensive. It has the glowing quality of cloisonné or terrazzo." Michael Bloomberg is more direct: "I saw some pieces that I liked, some pieces I don't like. . . . I don't understand why there is a fuss."

Kimmelman concludes his review of "Sensation": "Under ordinary circumstances, bad art naturally gets sorted out and disappears. That is how history works when it is left alone to do its job. The paradox of the culture wars is that they have made celebrities out of some artists who would otherwise vanish. Censorship has become a growth industry. Maybe that's the best argument, in the end, for unfettered freedom of expression."[12] What we have here is the natural selection theory of art history: the genetic code of those antennaed mutants will prevail. But aesthetic Darwinism meets social Darwinism in Kimmelman's market metaphor: government interference in the world of art is bad because, as in the economic world, it distorts value that would otherwise find its natural level. Free speech is identified with free markets.

Moving the Discussion "to a Higher Level"

If Kimmelman sees content nowhere, Arthur Danto finds meaning everywhere. He begins his review of "Sensation" for the *Nation* by identifying a more direct, visceral response to the show with the honest and innocent enthusiasm of children.[13] Bring a child, borrow a child, or be your own child: "they are not cynics, nor are they 'taxpayers.'" But against the child's "wow!" or "yuck!" Danto poses the informed, philosophical reflections of adults—a status he identifies with his own perspective. While the child within and the child along with you may "keep you open to what you see," they "will not enable you to understand what anything means" because "we have not transformed thought into feeling as yet." For that ability, one must be "wise enough to respond to philosophical significance." Danto thus demonstrates his own contention that the artworks in "Sensation" are "more than toys for the rich." They serve equally well as playthings of philosopher-art critics who can use them to distinguish themselves not only from the toying rich, the childish masses, cynics, and taxpayers, but from the *hypocrites lecteurs* among art historians and critics as well. While the show gives Danto the opportunity to evoke Heidegger, Wittgenstein, *und* Kant, the latter have to settle with references to Chuck Close.

"Having ascended to this level of speculation, you can appreciate the foolishness of the museum's publicity." Instead of the vomiting promised by the Brooklyn Museum's notorious "Health Warning,"[14] Danto finds poetic allusion and metaphor and deep and serious topographies of the soul—the kinds of "reflections on art" in which a philosopher can always find "a philosophical dimension." There is the shark. There "is a lovely lamb . . . and a somewhat less successful pig."

There is one kind of meaning, however, that Danto does not find in "Sensation": religious meaning. He concludes his review with Ofili's *The Holy Virgin Mary:* "It is not a marvelous painting. . . . On the other hand, the Holy Virgin has never been especially choosy as to how she is portrayed. . . . The miraculous paintings of the Virgin rarely have much by way of aesthetic charm, but they are not prayed to for the rewards of aesthetic gratification." But paintings of the Virgin are rarely prayed to at all in secular art museums. In this, Danto echoes Judge Gershon's ruling. The First Amendment requires that "government remain neutral with regard to religious expression," whether it manifests a religious view, an antireligious view, or neither. While "the Museum's permanent collection contains many reverential depictions of the Madonna as well as other religious paintings and ritual objects . . . no objective observer could conclude that the Museum's . . . showing of religiously reverential works constitutes an endorsement by them of religion."[15]

Despite all the evocations of the First Amendment in defense of "Sensation," what one finds in the statements of many of its defenders are representations that render the First Amendment narrow if not unnecessary. "Freedom of expression" is reduced to a right of specific institutions—museums—or specific individuals—uniquely sensitive artists. And while civil libertarians emphasize that Ofili's work, no matter how controversial, blasphemous, offensive, or obscene, is protected under the First Amendment, in the discourse of the museum directors and art critics Ofili's *right* to produce an offensive or blasphemous work and our *right* to see it are almost nowhere defended. Instead we are told that the painting is not really controversial: the work is old news. Nor is it blasphemous: its iconography has its own sacred past—which has no religious function in a secular art museum anyway. Nor is it offensive: the artist does not intend to offend. Is it obscene? As we will see below, on this last point they would most readily agree: the work is not obscene, because it is art; it has artistic value and was produced with artistic intent.

The question raised by such representations is whether the aesthetic neutralization of art in art discourse and institutions performs its own kind of censorship, not only, as we have seen, of the iconography, intention, and artistic history a particular work may manifest, but of the many different meanings produced in the spaces of production and reception of culture. Sadly, far from defending freedom of expression as a universal principle to be applied to the whole range of meanings that emerge around a cultural form, the museum directors and art critics defending "Sensation" rush instead to reimpose, as exclusively legitimate, representations derived from their own artistic and intellectual traditions. Because the legitimacy of those traditions is at least partly based on claims of autonomy from politics and law—to say nothing of the functions politics and law would regulate—any attempt to deploy that legitimacy against political attack almost necessarily implies a marginalization of such constitutional principles as are found in the Bill of Rights.

In a sense, the battle over "Sensation" proceeded from the start on two separate fronts. Civil libertarians fought and quickly won the First Amendment battle. The art community, on the other hand, and particularly representatives of the museum world, fought a different battle over the autonomy of their field and the legitimacy of their judgments within it. With regard to aesthetic judgments we see a strategy of projecting that legitimacy "beyond" the temporal rule of law. But the aesthetic judgments of museum officials are also the expert judgments of organizational professionals. With the First Amendment battle lost almost from the start, it was against the legitimacy of this professional judgment that the Giuliani administration quickly turned.

2. Between Art and Political Influence: Professional Expertise

As I mentioned earlier, the sexual content of Ofili's work was never emphasized by its critics. Nor were its cutouts the only sexually explicit material in "Sensation." Why would a mayor who closed down the city's sex business with widespread approval ignore the sexual content in "Sensation"? One explanation relates to the logic of First Amendment protections with regard to obscenity. According to the test established by the Supreme Court in 1973 with *Miller v. California,* no matter how sexually explicit, prurient, etc., speech may be, if it's found to have "serious artistic, literary, political, or scientific value," it cannot be judged "obscene." According to the *Miller* test, even a Cincinnati jury packed with religious conservatives had to acquit the Contemporary Art Center on obscenity charges for showing Robert Mapplethorpe's photograph of interracial fisting. The jury concluded that if the art experts who testified claim artistic value for the photograph—the least legitimate of artistic media—then it must have artistic value. An obscenity charge against a painting wouldn't have a chance.

"If I Can Do It, It's Not Art"

In some sense, the culture war of 1989 was a war on artistic expertise as the basis for claims of artistic autonomy, from Senator Alfonse D'Amato's first attack on the NEA panel of "so-called art experts" to the trial in Cincinnati.[16] 1999 is not much different in this respect, except perhaps that Patrick Buchanan has now added "so-called exhibit" to the lexicon. As one *New York Times* columnist described it, against these "so-called art experts," Giuliani "appointed himself the city's chief art curator" and provided an "admirably succinct definition of art": "If I can do it, it's not art, because I'm not much of an artist."[17] But when the columnist goes on to call Barnett Newman a scam, it becomes clear that what's at stake aren't just the transgressions of "shock art" but the specialized artistic competence that the mayor affirms when he claims not to have it. If the modernist and avant-garde projects have been characterized by the repeated rejection of such competencies (which Newman, to follow the example, exchanged in part for a house-painter's craft), the irony of the culture wars is that the last line of defense has remained the artistic expertise that the avant-garde has tried so many times to dissolve.

The explanation for the Cincinnati jury's verdict is not to be found, where the right looks, in the "moral anesthesia" propagated by the "world of liberal opinion," but in the authority accorded experts of all kinds in a technocratic society. Within the framework of the instructions of a court, the testimony of art historians would be given the same consideration as that of psychiatrists, pathologists, and so on. The Cincinnati verdict shows the extent to which, at least according to the *Miller* test, First Amendment protections for artistic, literary, political, and scientific speech have become contingent on the professional judgment of experts.

The authority as well as autonomy accorded professionals in the exercise of expert judgment is generally thought to be based, first, on the recognition of their mastery of a presumably complex area of competence and, second, on the utility they provide society by exercising that expertise in the service of social needs.[18] Professional standards, institutionalized by professional organizations, function as guarantees of expert competence. As such, however, they also function as gatekeepers of professional monopolies, serving to exclude competing forms of training and practice. Against the threat to professional legitimacy posed by the potential abuse of professional power, professional ethics in turn exist as a limit placed on the exploitation of such monopolized competence. Professional ethics always imply that the provision of social benefit takes precedence over the pursuit of economic and symbolic profits—of individual or corporate benefit to professionals themselves.

"They Should Have Shown Better Judgment"

As with other professional fields, the autonomy of art as a professional field—its right to self-regulation free from external intervention—is justified on the basis of the integrity of its technical and ethical standards. Whether one considers those ethics as functioning principles or only elements of a legitimizing ideology, their power as representations is evident throughout the "Sensation" controversy. Just a few days after his first attacks, Giuliani shifted his focus away from particular works, claiming instead that the Brooklyn Museum forfeited its right to self-regulation by betraying its professional principles. The city escalated its threats, threatening to evict the museum and take over its board of trustees. According to the city's corporation counsel, Michael Hess, a board installed by the mayor "would have better judgment as to what is appropriate for this type of museum." In response to these new attacks, defenders adapted the First Amendment. Where we found defenders of "Sensation" identifying free speech with the rights of artists and museums, they now adapted the logic of *NEA v. Finley* to identify free speech with professional judgment: "once the financial support has been granted . . . institutions must be free to spend it according to their own professional standards."[19]

By the time Judge Gershon heard arguments, the city's charge that the museum's unethical actions had violated its nineteenth-century contracts with the city became Giuliani's last remaining rationale. Judge Gershon was not convinced. Questions relating to the professional judgment of the museum's officers, however, did not end with her ruling. Whereas the city initially focused on the museum's commitment to its public service mission, the *New York Times* and other defenders of artistic freedom were instead concerned with whether the museum itself may have compromised its professional integrity with sponsors—Charles Saatchi in particular. These accusations Giuliani quickly took up.

A front-page article by David Barstow running in the *New York Times* a month after Judge Gershon's ruling detailed the extent of Saatchi's involvement. According to Barstow, Lehman gave Saatchi "a central role in determining the artistic content" of the show down to "the smallest aesthetic details."[20] Lehman claimed that he "retained artistic control" but welcomed Saatchi's participation because of his "expertise in British contemporary art": "as an informed collector . . . Mr. Saatchi has a longstanding and intimate relationship with each object in the exhibition." Lehman wasn't the only art professional willing to cede expertise to Saatchi. According to Norman Rosenthal of the Royal Academy of Arts in London where "Sensation" originated, Saatchi "knows more about contemporary art in this country than any curator, including myself."

As Kimmelman reminded us in a previous article, most art museums in the United States were founded by wealthy patrons.[21] Until fairly recently these patrons often also served as curators. That Saatchi's influence was such a scandal only demonstrates the extent the field has professionalized. Such influence now represents a competing form of expertise, derived not from educational and professional capital, but from economic and social capital; not from the specific training and institutional experience, but from a patron's "intimate" contact with art and artists.

The professionalization of the field of art was not simply accomplished through the organizational boundaries erected between curators and trustees. It also was achieved through the reconceptualization of institutional mission around functions that art professionals are especially competent to fulfill. Paul DiMaggio has traced this process back to the 1920s, when museum professionals "sought radical changes in museum missions and policies that would tend to enhance their own positions relative to those of their trustees." These changes included a shift in the conception of museum education from one focused on connoisseurship and the "etiquette of appropriation" to one oriented toward broad public education in culture and design.[22] In terms developed by Bourdieu, while the former privileges the "domestic" relation to culture developed by patrons through the implicit learning of everyday contact, the latter requires the more "scholastic" relation acquired in the explicit learning of professional training.[23] From the standpoint of professional power, both Saatchi's influence and the "intimate" relation to culture it represents are clearly regressive. What would lead Lehman and Rosenthal to valorize his role—even at the expense of their own institutional authority?

"My 40 Years of Experience as an Investment Banker"

Saatchi is not the only patron of the Brooklyn Museum who intervened in the installation of "Sensation." Another example early in the controversy was the museum's chairman, Robert S. Rubin, who undertook unilateral and short-lived negotiations with the city on how "offensive" works in the show would be installed. His statement that the proposed concessions were his idea, based on "my forty years experience as an investment banker," does not inspire confidence in his artistic expertise. The *New York Times* reported that Rubin's authority at the museum is such "that he felt free to discuss concessions without informing the rest of the board or the director."[24]

The centralization of power on the board of the Brooklyn Museum is reportedly matched by Lehman's centralization of power within the museum's staff. A source working in the Brooklyn museum at the time reported that one of Lehman's first proposals was to eliminate the contemporary art staff altogether. Such a move may reflect a lack of interest in contemporary art, but it also represents the reportedly autocratic administrative style of a director moving to weaken the autonomy of curators and their departments. Whether or not Saatchi was the real curator of "Sensation," the Brooklyn Museum's curator of contemporary art, Charlotta Kotik, clearly had nothing to do with the show: to my knowledge, she never even made a statement to the press about the controversy.

What is transforming the professional autonomy of experts within museums are not belligerent politicians and meddling patrons so much as changes in the administration of museums themselves. Decisions on artistic programs and policy are increasingly handed down to curators from above. Those judgments come from paid presidents with no art backgrounds, as was long true at the Metropolitan; or from directors with no art backgrounds, as at the Los Angeles Country Museum of Art; or from directors with art backgrounds unrelated to their museum's focus, as at the Museum of Modern Art; or from directors whose judgment, as at the Guggenheim and the Museum of Fine Arts in Boston and in Brooklyn, has become so identified with administrative priorities that curatorial competence is becoming increasingly peripheral to artistic programs. As de Montebello conceded when he recently regained control over the Metropolitan from a paid president with no art background: "A museum is not a business. It is run in a business-like fashion."[25]

3. Between Art and Economic Interests

While the difference between museums and businesses may be diminishing in the area of administration, that difference, rooted in the nonprofit status of museums, nevertheless remains central to the autonomy claimed by museums and museum professionals. As DiMaggio notes, "the affinity between the legitimizing accounts of professionals and of nonprofit organizations—both based on claims to expertise, a service ethos, and disinterest in pecuniary gain—provides an ideological resource to professionals in the nonprofit sector."[26] It was at the third "ideological resource" listed by DiMaggio that Giuliani took aim when he launched his final attack on Brooklyn, accusing the museum of conspiring with Saatchi and the auction house Christie's, one of "Sensation's" sponsors, to inflate the value of Saatchi's collection. Giuliani turned the museum's claim to disinterestedness against its claim to autonomy.

But the charge of mercenary interests did not originate with Giuliani: according to the *New York Times,* the mayor was simply "picking up on criticism" in the art world. Nor does the charge relate primarily to the actions of a nonprofit institution; it also happens to be one of most common charges that art collectors hurl at each other in their struggles for prestige as collectors.[27] Even before Giuliani launched his attacks a *New York Times Magazine* profile noted that many of Saatchi's art world critics already viewed "Sensation" as only his "latest effort to inflate the value of his holdings, the sly move of a man for whom art is mainly a speculator's game." In their view, Saatchi is "not a bona fide collector but a glorified art dealer," "a commodities broker," even a "human Hoover."[28]

"Combining the City's Artistic Soul and Its Commercial Reality"

And so, on September 29, Deputy Mayors Joseph Lhota and Randy Levine accused the Brooklyn Museum of "hucksterism" and Christie's of "planning to profit from controversy surrounding the show." In an argument that would be suitable for a campaign against the city's Republican administration, Corporation Counsel Hess explained: "It's a scam and taxpayer's dollars should not be used to support that. . . . Taxpayer's dollars should be used for educating children, for building roads, for supporting the homeless."[29] Supporting the homeless?!

Why was the city's deputy mayor announcing the new charges against the museum? Who was minding the shop while the corporation counsel was making such patently un-Republican proposals? Where was the mayor? The mayor was in Las Vegas at a fundraising luncheon hosted by none other than Steve "Degas in Vegas" Wynn at the Bellagio Hotel. There, alongside boutiques such as Gucci, one finds the Bellagio Gallery, a for-profit presentation of Wynn's private art collection. Wynn recently pushed a bill through the Nevada legislature granting a property tax exemption to collectors who display their art publicly—even in for-profit settings like the Bellagio. If the bill, which is being challenged, becomes law, it could save Wynn over $15 million a year—in addition to the multimillion dollar fee he charges Mirage Resorts, of which he is the CEO, to lease the art.[30] According to the *New York Times,* Giuliani "was not at all uncomfortable raising money in a restaurant that was directly across from row upon row of slot machines." With "Mr. Wynn at his side, Mr. Giuliani said he was in favor of legalized gambling in New York City. . . . The Mayor has mentioned the federally owned Governors Island [soon to be turned over to the city] as the possible site of a future casino."[31]

Ronald O. Perelman—Revlon CEO, Giuliani supporter, and president of the Guggenheim Museum—arranged the event, a fundraiser for Giuliani's Senate campaign. Perelman is one of three cosmetics executives who currently rule New York's major twentieth-century art museums. While Leonard "I'm just a lipstick man" Lauder, the chairman of the Whitney Museum, generally shies from public positions, his brother Ronald, chairman of the Modern, is a familiar presence on the political scene. Alfonse D'Amato, who apparently found the time while bashing the NEA in Congress, sponsored his run for the Republican nomination for mayor against Giuliani in 1989. Lauder lost the nomination to Giuliani who in turn blamed Lauder for his own first loss to David Dinkins. But Giuliani and Lauder soon joined forces in a campaign to prevent the City Council from holding hearings on private companies taking over city services. Lauder was quoted as saying, "whoever is a friend of privatization is a friend of his."[32] Such views, however, have not prevented Lauder from pursuing city funds for the Modern. Last spring Giuliani announced a $65 million grant for its expansion plan. Long-time Giuliani supporter and MoMA vice-president Jerry Speyer was probably also instrumental in securing the unprecedentedly large public subsidy to a private institution. Last April, Speyer and Giuliani appeared together at Rockefeller Center to welcome none other than Christie's to its new multimillion dollar location—developed by Tishman Speyer. The mayor congratulated the real estate firm and the auction house for "combining the city's artistic soul and its commercial reality."[33]

The day before Giuliani's fundraiser in Las Vegas, the Guggenheim Museum announced its latest expansion proposal: a new Frank Gehry-designed "art and recreation" complex on city-owned East River piers.[34] The report mentioned that the Guggenheim had proposals for Governors Island as well. If Wynn's casino and Perelman's museum both make it to the island, one would have to call that fundraiser a smashing success.

One needn't belabor the point that Giuliani is no enemy of private interests nor friend of the public sphere. Nor is it adequate to charge museum patrons with influence-by-association, as the mayor has done. What the mayor's attacks on the Brooklyn Museum's "hucksterism" represent is an effort to discredit one of the few remaining public spheres that propose to resist the logic of economic and political power, another swoop in neoliberalism's end-of-the-millennium exercise of mopping up what's left of the public sector. Unfortunately, Giuliani's effort is greatly aided by the contradictions internal to the not-always-disinterested private nonprofit art world itself and the demands to which it increasingly responds.

"Experts in Museum Ethics Say . . ."

Another front-page article by David Barstow, run by the *New York Times* the day before Judge Gershon's ruling, detailed the extent of the museum's "unethical" fundraising practices "targeting individuals and companies who could directly profit" from it.[35] These donors finally included Saatchi himself, the auction house Christie's, the art dealer Larry Gagosian, and David Bowie, who donated his voice for the audiotour in addition to cash and was given the rights to present the show on his for-profit Web site. "At stake is nothing less than a museum's independence and integrity, experts in museum ethics say. Museums have a public trust to display art on the basis of merit . . . and are sure to suffer if they become viewed as instruments for private financial gain."[36]

Despite frequent references to supposed standards, however, exceptions quickly pile up. The Met concurrently had not one but two exhibitions of private collections. The show "The Work of Charles and Ray Eames" then at the Cooper-Hewitt was sponsored by Herman Miller Inc., which produces and sells Eames designs. The Guggenheim's 1998 "The Art of the Motorcycle" was sponsored by BMW, and Cartier sponsored the Met's 1997 show of Cartier jewelry. Even where policies restricting donations are in place, they generally serve only to mask the always-present play of interests between museums and the market. Finally even the *New York Times* was forced to admit that although the museum director's "code of ethics warns them to 'assiduously avoid' activities that compromise their institutions . . . on the subject of exhibition financing, their professional guidelines offer just two vague sentences."[37] Despite all the discussion of rules and codes of ethics, what becomes clear is that such standards hardly exist. They appear largely as legitimizing constructions of a professional ideology with little institutional authority.

"Impressions Are Important in These Affairs"

Once again, Kimmelman reveals more than he intends when he volunteers to cut through the rhetoric. Believing that Christie's and Saatchi were not thinking about the value of the collection is "simply naïve," he writes. The problem stems from "the notion that self-interest on the part of rich collectors necessarily pollutes the sanctity of the museum, as if American museums were not the result of rich collectors' donations." What's wrong with "Sensation" is that the museum turned "in an unseemly way" to those who may profit from the show: "Impressions are important in these affairs." The museum created a "very bad impression that Brooklyn is for sale," producing the public perception of conflict where, in fact, there is none.[38]

Kimmelman is correct that the conflict here is neither between money and art nor between donors and museums. The conflict is rather between donors and between museums, a conflict that is simply taken up by Giuliani in his competition against his own political opponents. If de Montebello's approval of the mayor's taste reveals a strategy of distinguishing the Met from the Whitney and so on, the Brooklyn, in its efforts to compete with Manhattan museums from a position of weakness in a poor outer borough, simply took their strategies one step further. The difference between the Brooklyn Museum's "Health Warning" and the Whitney Museum's ads for its recent Biennial exhibition—"Love it, hate it, see it"—is only a matter of degree: both appropriate artistic controversy for marketing purposes. And when it comes to comparing "Sensation" to "The Art of the Motorcycle," according to a traditional view of an art museum's mission, "Sensation" is much more justifiable.

But taking such a "one step further" threatens more than just the decorum that naturalizes previously established positions. It's the Brooklyn Museum's weakness that led it to risky alliances with Christie's and Saatchi. MoMA and the Met can place restrictions on loans because they have the power to dictate terms that less prestigious institutions don't have. Other New York museums broke ranks by not supporting Brooklyn, but Brooklyn widened the cracks in the walls protecting museums from demands made on them by patrons and donors.

4. Between Art and Popular Culture

A field's autonomy, according to Bourdieu, depends on its power to exclude competing norms dominant in other fields—the capacity of art museums, for example, to reject the demands of sponsors. Neither a particular set of norms nor the power to impose them is ever simply given. Rather, they are the object and product of continuous struggle both within fields and between them. Nor is the political value of such struggle ever simply given—as regressive or progressive, exclusive or democratizing. To the extent that such struggles are fundamentally competitive rather than specifically liberatory, their political value can be understood only on the basis of their effects.

The autonomy of the field of art has long been constituted according to the distance it maintains from economic influence and economic principles of hierarchization. This distance, as Kimmelman demonstrates, has been less a matter of the power of that influence than the degree to which the interests it represents are consistent with the interests of and in the field. Those economic interests that have appeared the most neutral within the field are those oriented toward its reproduction: ironically, the reproduction of its autonomy and freedom from external interests—particularly economic interests. These have included above all the interests of individual patrons who are best positioned to appropriate the norms of the field and the specific form of value it produces: the symbolic profit in legitimacy generated precisely by the field's claim to disinterestedness in the pursuit of aesthetic quality.

When we start to compare the interests evident in the influence of other museum patrons with that of Saatchi, it becomes obvious that what is at stake is not simply the economic basis of such influence, but the economic or, more generally, quantitative criterion that they are seen to impose. And what this quantitative criterion marks is the boundary not only between art and economic interests, but between art and popular culture as well.

"The Lowest Common Denominator"

The lines between art and popular culture were already drawn in the article that inaugurated the controversy. When the *New York Post* asks "Is this art?" Roger Kimball's response is to discredit both the museum and the artists by associating them with commercialism, calling "Sensation" "a rather pathetic attempt by the Brooklyn Museum, which has had difficulty drawing in visitors, to pander to the lowest common denominator. . . . These so-called artists are laughing all the way to the bank."[39] Giuliani picked up the theme a few days later when he accused the museum of "the worst kind of disgusting, commercial sensationalism": "I understand they want to make money. But this is what you do, like, on the 42nd street of about 20 years ago."[40]

Characterizations of "Sensation" as "a commercial enterprise" about "box office, not art" are the only point of agreement among almost all the commentators, from the *New York Post* to the *Village Voice*. Between these supposed economic interests and the field of popular culture there appears to be a very slippery slope. We begin with descriptions of a "publicity circus" created by a "Barnumesque" director overseeing "vulgar Barnum & Baily sensationalism" and end with various references to schlock and shock, kitsch, camp, and general commercial culture. The affair is tacky, vulgar, craven, crass, and cheapening. Even Jerry Saltz in the *Village Voice* agrees: "'Sensation' is not an exhibition . . . it's a franchise."[41]

Underlying these judgments is a familiar principle of cultural hierachization, of which Kimball's association of the "popular" with the "lowest common denominator" is only the most clichéd representation. According to this model, the larger the audience art "panders" to, the lower the specific competence possessed by that audience, and the lower culture slides on the scale of quality—from avant-garde to high-brow to middle-brow to vernacular. As Bourdieu has pointed out, this principle of hierarchization judges the entire cultural field according to the specific competencies defined by professional producers, constituting "an unprecedented affirmation of the most characteristic aspect of professionalism." In this sense, it is "the professional ideology of producers-for-producers and their spokespeople [that] establishes an opposition between creative liberty and the laws of the market, between works which create their public and works created by their public."[42]

"To Quote the Noted Art Critic Bart Simpson. . . ."

Thus one might see in the glee with which the tabloid press accused the Brooklyn Museum of sensationalism a populist stab at turning the tables on the principles of hierarchization imposed by cultural elites: "What's the show really like? Well, to quote the noted art critic Bart Simpson, 'I didn't think it was possible, but this both sucks and blows.'. . . The people at the Brooklyn Museum know it's bad. And if they don't know it's bad, then they're stupid. It's that simple. By far the lion's share of the work is ugly, technically incompetent and nihilistic. It's art that thumbs its nose at beauty and technique."[43]

But isn't it obvious that Bart Simpson would think "Sensation" was very cool? The tabloids are challenging not highbrow criteria so much as the authority of those who would impose them. Here again at the boundary between art and popular culture we find at stake, above all, the power of art professionals to define art as such. In this context, "popular culture" has no substantive characteristics: it figures only as "art's" foil. Against the exclusive expertise claimed by art professionals are posed not the popular competencies of everyday practices but the self-evident aesthetic truths of the most conservative highbrow tastes.

If one of the ironies of the culture wars is that the last line of defense has been the artistic expertise that the avant-garde has repeatedly sought to reject, that irony may itself be the manifestation of a duplicity in the avant-garde project. The rejection of specific competence and the negation of universal aesthetic criteria may indeed have struck a blow to the essentialism of cultural aristocracies. However, the institutional criteria that replaced it in the contemporary field only installed a competing principle of hierarchization that may be no less arbitrary in its exercise of cultural authority. Where universal aesthetic criteria held that artistic quality is immanent in a particular class of things, institutional criteria tell us that art is art because it is recognized and circulates within the field of art as art; because it exists for discourses and practices that articulate and appropriate it as art. Where judgments of aesthetic quality were justified by the sensitive *being* of esthetes, judgments of artistic status are now authorized by the *being there* of art insiders: there, in the institutions, in the field; there, in the networks of production and reception; there, at the moment of institutional inscription.

Such authority was evident throughout the "Sensation" controversy as art critic after art critic dismissed the controversy because the show was already "old news." The more contemporary the critic the more dismissive the rhetoric, as Jerry Saltz's review for the *Village Voice* demonstrates: "Until two weeks ago 'Sensation' seemed so over. The early reaction in the New York art world to the coming exhibition of Charles Saatchi's spunky but flabby collection of young British artists was blasé: 'Ten years late,' 'Juvenile and derivative,' 'It'll never play here.' Then Rudolph Giuliani, already looking more and more like Bela Lugosi, breathed a second life into 'Sensation.'"[44]

"A Present-Tense Kind of Guy"

The *being there* of contemporary art implies a principle of rarity as well as authority, one marked by a particular relationship to time. The rarity of the age-old aesthetic criteria of connoisseurs like de Montebello is defined by the scarcity of the historical objects it attaches to and by the time required to acquire subtle connoisseurship and elaborated technical mastery, stretched out by the distance its traditions push into the past (even, according to its myths, out of the time of history and the labor of learning). The rarity of tastes for the contemporary, on the other hand, is defined by the speed with which they take hold of the present and lay claim to the future.

In her *New York Times Magazine* profile of Saatchi, Deborah Solomon writes: "To collect, as Susan Sontag once observed, is to collect the past. Yet Saatchi is a present-tense kind of guy . . . he buys new art and, when certain pieces cease to hold his interests, he sells them off for newer art." Saatchi says, "I want to keep my collection fresh."[45] The rarity of contemporary taste defines itself less by the scarcity of its objects than by the limited time of their relevance, a time made ever shorter by the competition surrounding their reception: the less access to culture is restricted economically in social space, the more intense the competition to appropriate its products, the more rapid the transformation of tastes for them. Elite culture has long been defined by long-term cycles of production and reception (quality recognized first by a few and only later by many must be laid away like fine wine), which appear as distance from economic interests in immediate returns. Saatchi, on the other hand, operates according to the short-term cycle of production and reception usually associated with consumer culture.

"A Connoisseur of . . . Subculture"

As many critics noted, neither "Sensation" nor the group of young British artists it includes are linked by any specifically artistic criteria, leading hostile critics to claim it was curated according to economic criteria instead. The exhibition catalogue and more sympathetic critics suggest, however, that the artists are linked by social criteria: they don't share an art style, but bars, beds, and an alma mater (Goldsmiths College). In the words of Norman Rosenthal, they are artists "who not only show together but support each other in a thousand other ways too. Thus was established a new subculture."[46] A youth subculture, to be precise; a "gang" embodying a "generation's totally new and radical attitude"[47] with a "new youth oriented content," who make "art as they might have made any other lifestyle choice"[48]—and making Charles Saatchi "a connoisseur of Britain's art subculture."[49]

With his legitimacy as a collector threatened by his reputation as a "human Hoover," Saatchi's reinvention of himself as a connoisseur of subculture is a brilliant save: his taste is irreducible to the products of professional artists hoarded by ordinary collectors. Rather, it encompasses all the practices of the most distinctively transgressive cultural formations. Like the advertising genre he took part in inventing, Saatchi is a lifestyle collector who is presented not as buying art so much as subsidizing the community life of a subculture, the "patron" of its identity, its existence.

To the aesthetic language of form and the ethnographic language of culture we can now add the language of subculture. However, the appropriation of "subculture" within the field of art, doesn't only function to subvert the essentialism of traditional aesthetic taste. It also functions to defend the legitimacy of an equally rarefied contemporary taste by maintaining its distance from the "vulgar commercialism" of middle-brow culture and the economic criteria it supposedly reflects.

"We Wouldn't Want to Confuse That"

Exclusive tastes don't require rarefied objects. They can attach themselves to almost anything. Collectors, critics, curators, just like artists, have always invented distinctive ways of appropriating popular culture, just as publics have invented popular ways of appropriating high culture. But do the hundreds of thousands who line up for blockbuster shows indicate that unique artworks can become truly popular culture? In what sense can objects with price tags into the millions be "popular"?

The answer depends on the form of consumption one privileges. The mission of art museums has always been to popularize rarefied objects by withdrawing them from private consumption as commodities and offering them up for public view. Artworks presented in museums become split between material and symbolic value, material and symbolic modes of appropriation. Museum professionals tend to promote the latter mode with all the conviction of their own dispositions to purely intellectual possession. But as long as commercial markets exists for the class of objects publicized in museums, the conviction of those who pursue symbolic consumption will always serve the prestige of those who can consume them materially as well.

A system of rarity can always be introduced into a class of mass-produced objects, whether in competitive markets of subculture style, the popular connoisseurship of fandoms, or the gaze of highbrow aesthetes. Rarefied forms of symbolic appropriation tend to create material rarity as well, introducing distinctions that often reproduce the criteria of quality, authenticity, originality, provenance, etc. established in art markets. Unique and limited edition objects, on the other hand, can never be materially consumed en masse. The publicization of rarefied art objects in museums only serves to widen the gap between owning and merely appreciating them.

This gap, according to Bourdieu, is what makes works of art so distinguishing. As "symbolic objects with a material existence," they not only reduce "purely symbolic appropriation to the inferior status of a symbolic substitute," but also provide for the conversion of the economic capital into symbolic capital. The former is derided as vulgar, while the latter raises "the distinctive force of ownership to the second power."[50] The struggle between these two modes of appropriation is present throughout the "Sensation" controversy. Against the mere possession of hoarding, Hooveresque art speculators; against the mere appreciation seen in the pedantry of *hypocrites lecteurs* and the pageantry of blockbuster crowds, patrons are positioned in the doubly privileged space where economic and cultural capital combine.

Popularization per se doesn't threaten this privilege. Most observers have nothing but praise for Lehman's First Saturdays program, which now draws as many as 9,000 participants to films and popular music performances. By contrast, the first move during his tenure to attract dispute was an initiative aimed precisely at the space where the conjunction of economic and cultural capital is commemorated. While it usually "costs" millions to get your name on a museum wall, Lehman introduced an "Adopt a Masterpiece" program that would put your name on a wall label for just $500 a year. Anticipating the language of the "Sensation" controversy, critics claimed the program "lacks dignity and cheapens the museum atmosphere." As the Met's vice president of development explained: "we have many donors that have given the works or given money to purchase the works, and their names are on the labels. We wouldn't want to confuse that."[51]

Commercialization was not one of de Montebello's criticisms of the Brooklyn Museum. The Met, of course, pretty much invented the blockbuster show and museum mass merchandising. With kiosks located at the exit of all gallery groupings and thirty-nine satellite stores around the world, the Met's merchandising business generated revenues of $87.4 million in 1997. The difference between the two museums lies not in commercialization, merchandising receipts, or box office per se, but rather in the distance maintained from cultural forms associated with such quantitative criteria. What the Metropolitan is engaged in is not popularization, but the mass marketing of rarefied tastes. And, as a *New York Times* article noted, few museums "have the luxury of peddling class, not mass."[52] The Brooklyn Museum may not be one of them. The difference between the Met and the Brooklyn is finally the difference between stone sphinx doorstops and rubber shark key-chains, between chamber music and reggae concerts. It is the difference between a distance from the demands of profitability afforded by economic means and a freedom from the limits of marketability wrested, or not, from economic need.

"Down Came the Slightly Grimy Banner Proclaiming 'BROOKLYN MUSEUM OF ART FOR ALL'"

Does all this make Lehman a populist? As many commentators noted, the Brooklyn Museum is among the least elitist of New York's art museums, with a long history of serving an ethnically and socially diverse population. The museum's community programs, however, clearly represent a different kind of populism than "Sensation." A moment described by Michael Daly in the *Daily News* is telling: "Down came the slightly grimy banner proclaiming 'BROOKLYN MUSEUM OF ART FOR ALL.' Up went the spanking-new banner proclaiming 'SENSATION.'"[53]

As David Barstow's reporting revealed, the Brooklyn Museum made a trade-off between "Sensation" and the accessible public programming it has traditionally pursued.[54] Lehman's claim that the public was "well served" by Saatchi is everywhere contradicted, from the museum's initial willingness to restrict access of children, to the special admission fee, to halving the budget for visitor services and public education programs for the show. Most of the budget cuts were due to Saatchi's demands for a lavish installation. If Saatchi's budget priorities derived not from a populist impulse but from his interest in prestige among collectors, Brooklyn's willingness to accept those priorities relates not only to its competition with other museums, but to the growing attempts by museums to compete with other cultural sectors. As the Guggenheim's director of communication, Ben Hartley, has said, "we are in the entertainment business and competing against other forms of entertainment out there."[55]

Are art museums elitist? Are they undergoing widespread popularization? In a sense, the elitism and popularization of art museums are the institution's two most enduring myths—a structuring opposition that is not in fact a contradiction at all. It is the process of popularization of art through museums that gives what would otherwise be obscure if valorized cultural practices their properly symbolic power within institutionalized cultural hierarchies, hierarchies that are reproduced as museums create new forms of exclusive appropriation within an ever more popular space.

5. Conclusions: Between Freedom and Privilege

I began this essay by mapping out three borders at stake in the "Sensation" controversy—between art and political influence, art and economic interests, and art and popular culture—and the three logics of autonomy according to which these borders have been defined and defended. These logics include the social autonomy of art as a self-regulating specialized or professional field; the aesthetic autonomy manifest in aesthetic distancing; and finally the political autonomy guaranteed as freedom of speech by democratic constitutions. These three dimensions of autonomy in the field of art have been thoroughly interrelated in their genealogies as well as their structure. Neither guarantees for freedom of expression as applied to art nor the capacity to develop gratuitous forms of aesthetic practice would likely have developed without the emergence of art as a field of specialized production. Conversely, the field would not likely have secured its capacity to self-regulation without the legitimacy provided by the ideology of disinterestedness and without the civil liberties guaranteed in democratic constitutions.

The "Sensation" controversy reveals not just the contradictions between these three logics of autonomy, but their fragmentation as each develops to pursue its own logic more completely. As art becomes more professionalized as a cultural sector, valorization of the competencies held by art professionals increases and the contradiction between artistic and economic as well as social criteria is intensified. The logic of professionalization demands a rationalized cognitive base and the identification of social needs served by professional expertise. But, because professionalization has taken place largely within bureaucratic organizations, managerial competence becomes increasingly central, marginalizing the specifically artistic competence around which the field was formed.

These dimensions of professionalization put it on a divergent course from dominant modernist and avant-garde traditions. As these traditions pursue their logic in the continuous and increasingly rapid transformation of artistic competencies, those competencies themselves become less specific and more subject to economic and social criteria. Such criteria do even more to undermine the social service claims of art professionals than avant-garde resistance to instrumentalization. The duplicity of the avant-garde project thus becomes the contradictory condition of contemporary art as a professional field. It has emerged as a field dedicated to providing a social benefit continuously negated by its discourse and products; struggling with a cognitive base resistant to systematization; and founded on expertise based not on supposedly innate aesthetic sensitivity but on the equally inexplicable "sense" developed only through complete immersion in successive moments of the contemporary field.

Finally, as the principles underlying guarantees of free expression pursue their logic in greater cultural democratization, specific protections claimed on the basis of professional and aesthetic expertise become less and less defensible—particularly given the contradictions internal to that expertise itself.

The culture wars of the last decade are usually represented as struggles between cultural progressives within the field of art and social conservatives outside of it. The fragmentation described above implies, however, that it has largely been a civil war in which the low-intensity conflict that characterizes the field erupted into explicit battles—exploited, as is usually the case with civil wars, by external powers pursuing their own interests. In the "Sensation" controversy, this conflict—in the form of competitive struggles between museums, artists, collectors, critics, and so on—intensified by the fragmentation of the field, was simply taken up by politicians in their own struggles within the political field. That appropriation is neither arbitrary nor simply opportunistic, but is provided for by homologies in the hierarchies that structure apparently opposed fields according to parallel distributions of capital and competence.

It makes no difference whether we view the interests pursued in such competition as mercenary or disinterested, political or artistic. Such judgments are themselves the weapons through which such struggles reproduce themselves. The charges of cynicism that one finds, for example, in the pages of the *New York Times* reveal an interest in disinterestedness that is clearly tied to specific symbolic profits, evoking a mythological realm of intention pure and good, affect deep and true, that has the effect of depoliticizing the debate. The question to ask is not whether, but which interests are at work. Where are those interests located within prevalent hierarchies of value and power? What are the effects of the strategies employed to maintain or overturn those hierarchies? What principles of hierarchization are emerging in their place? What forms of value do those new hierarchies impose? And finally, in which social sites are those forms of value concentrated?

Similarly, what passes as reflexive self-critique among art professionals in discussions of the culture wars often displays its own disposition toward form by making cultural conflict sound like a public huff at a lapse in manners. We reflect that "we failed to engage the public," as if the problem was that we spoke out of turn; "we didn't do enough outreach"—next time, remember to call before you drop by. What the struggles around "Sensation" demonstrate is that such civilities do not elude but are often precluded by the interests produced and pursued within the field of art. The best-intentioned explanations will ring false so long as they misrecognize the ways in which the dynamics of struggle within the field articulate with the distributions of different forms of power, whether economic or cultural, political or professional.

Left unexamined, the competitive struggles within the field of art may form the limit to which cultural democratization can be pursued through public funding and freedom of expression. If, in the context of the culture wars, freedom of expression devolves from a right to a privilege, it should not be mistaken for expediency in defense. The function of such controversies, both for many defenders of artistic freedom inside the field and its attackers without, may be precisely to produce an identification of freedom with privilege. On the side of defenders, such an identification functions to increase their prestige; on the side of its attackers, it "exposes" elite privilege and thus reduces its legitimacy. Similarly, if what was at stake in the "Sensation" controversy was public subsidy for museums, both access to publicly funded institutions and their freedom from political influence were framed not in terms of democratic values and rights, but in terms of a very particular and privileged form of freedom: the freedom from economic rationality claimed for "disinterested" art.

Finally, however, if public arts funding is to function for cultural democracy, it must be disentangled from institutionalized forms of a disinterested aesthetic. If the defense of artistic freedom is to function for democratic rights, it must be disentangled from the protection of professional expertise and specific cultural competencies.

Notes

I would like to thank George Yúdice and Toby Miller at the Privitization of Culture Project Seminar and Norton Batkin and my students at the Center for Curatorial Studies for providing contexts in which to develop this essay. I would also like to thank Dietrich for the desk with the beautiful view where I finished it.

1. David Barstow, "Giuliani Ordered to Restore Funds for Art Museum," *New York Times,* 2 November 1999, A1.

2. David Barstow, "Brooklyn Museum Sues to Keep Mayor from Freezing Its Funds," *New York Times,* 29 September 1999, A1.

3. Philippe de Montebello, "Making a Cause out of Bad Art," *New York Times,* 5 October 1999, A25.

4. Gersh Kuntzman, "'Filth' to Rile Righteous Rudy," *New York Post,* 27 September 1999.

5. Glenn Lowry, "Art That Dares," *New York Times,* 13 October 1999, A20.

6. Dan Barry and Carol Vogel, "Giuliani Vows to Cut Subsidy Over 'Sick' Art," *New York Times,* 23 September 1999, A1; David Barstow, "Seeking Buzz, Museum Chief Hears a Roar Instead," *New York Times,* 25 September 1999, B1.

7. A similar interpretation was suggested by the Rev. Herbert Daughtry: "I wonder if the root of it all isn't the feces, but the black face of the Virgin Mary. I wonder if it isn't the porno, but the pigmentation." Quoted in Tom Topousis et al., "Galleries Jammed as Rudy Sounds Off," *New York Post,* 4 October 1999, 4.

   For a more complex discussion of the relation between Ofili's work and his background, see Mary Schmidt Campbell, "Collisions at a Museum," *Nation,* 22 November 1999, 5–6.

8. Dan Barry, "On Display at City Hall, 2 Catholics, 2 Views," *New York Times,* 25 September 1999, B1.

9. John Kifner, "Art Lovers Peruse Exhibit and Defy Giuliani," *New York Times,* 1 October 1999, B1.

10. Michael Kimmelman, "After All That Yelling, Time to Think," *New York Times,* 1 October 1999, E31.

11. Kifner, "Art Lovers."

12. Kimmelman, "After All That Yelling."

13. Arthur Danto, "'Sensation' in Brooklyn," *Nation,* 1 November 1999, 25.

14. Circulated first in print media and later as posters and shopping bags, the museum's ad read in black on yellow: "HEALTH WARNING The contents of this exhibition may cause shock, vomiting, euphoria, and anxiety. If you suffer from high blood pressure, a nervous disorder, or palpitations, you should consult your doctor before viewing this exhibition."

15. "Constitutional Law: Mayor's Decision to Stop Funding the Brooklyn Museum Is Held Unconstitutional," *New York Law Journal,* 3 November 1999, 25.

16. For excerpts from the *Congressional Record* and other documents relating to the NEA crisis, see Richard Bolton, ed., *Culture Wars: Documents from Recent Controversies in the Arts* (New York: New Press, 1992).

17. John Tierney, "At $35 Apiece, Everybody Is an Art Critic," *New York Times,* 27 September 1999, B1.

18. I am relying heavily here on Magali Sarfatti Larson, *The Rise of Professionalism: A Sociological Analysis* (Berkeley: University of California Press, 1979).

19. Abby Goodnough, "Mayor Threatens to Evict Museum over Exhibition," *New York Times,* 24 September 1999, B6. "The Battle of Brooklyn," *New York Times,* 2 October 1999, A14.

20. David Barstow, "Art, Money and Control: Elements of an Exhibition," *New York Times,* 6 December 1999, A1.

21. Michael Kimmelman, "In the End, the 'Sensation' Is Less the Art than the Money," *New York Times,* 3 November 1999, E1.

22. Paul DiMaggio and Walter Powell, Introduction, and Paul DiMaggio, "Constructing an Organization Field as a Professional Project: U.S. Art Museums, 1920–1940," in DiMaggio and Powell, eds., *The New Institutionalism in Organizational Analysis* (Chicago: University of Chicago Press, 1991), 31, 269–270.

23. Pierre Bourdieu, *Distinction: A Social Critique of the Judgment of Taste,* trans. Richard Nice (Cambridge: Harvard University Press, 1984), 54, 66.

24. David Barstow and David M. Herszenhorn, "Museum Chairman Broached Removal of Virgin Painting," *New York Times,* 28 September 1999, A1.

25. For further discussion of the corporatization of museums, see Andrea Fraser, "'A Museum Is Not a Business. It Is Run in a Business-like Fashion," in Melanie Townsend, ed., *Beyond the Box: Diverging Curatorial Practices* (Banff, Canada: Banff Centre Press, 2003), 109–122.

26. DiMaggio, "Constructing an Organization Field," 288.

27. Judith H. Dobrzynski, "Private Collections Routine at Museums," *New York Times,* 1 October 1999, B6.

28. Deborah Solomon, "The Collector," *New York Times Magazine,* 26 September 1999, 44.

29. David M. Herszenhorn, "Brooklyn Museum Accused of Trying to Spur Art Value," *New York Times,* 30 September 1999, A1. Within the month, Giuliani launched a particularly vicious and punitive campaign against New York City's homeless, including massive street sweeps and an attempt to force patrons of city-run shelters to work in exchange for services.

30. Jennifer Crowe, "Learning from Las Vegas: The Bellagio Gallery of Fine Art at the Bellagio Hotel and Resort," unpublished paper, 1999.

31. Elisabeth Bumiller, "Mayor's Good Day: $100,000 Raised, $29 at Craps," *New York Times,* 30 September 1999, B1.

32. Lauder spokesman Nelson Warfield quoted in Alison Mitchell, "Political Notes; Unlikely Ally: Lauder Lobbies for a Giuliani Cause," *New York Times,* 8 May 1994, A35.

33. Barbara Pollack, "Art and Commerce," *Village Voice,* 1 June 1999, 49.

34. Ralph Blumenthal with Carol Vogel, "The Guggenheim Proposes Gehry Museum for New York," *New York Times,* 28 September 1999, B5.

35. David Barstow, "Biggest Donors Stood to Gain from Brooklyn Museum Show," *New York Times,* 31 October 1999, A1.

36. "A Verdict on 'Sensation,'" *New York Times,* 2 November 1999, A26.

37. Barstow, "Art, Money and Control."

38. Kimmelman, "In the End."

39. Megan Turner, "Is This Art? Butchered Animals, A Dung-Smeared Virgin Mary and Giant Genitalia Spark Outrage at the Brooklyn Museum," *New York Post,* 21 September 1999, 57.

40. Betsy Scheinbart et al., "O'C Hits Art Exhibit: Says 'Sensation' Disrespects Catholicism," *Daily News,* 27 September 1999, 4.

41. Jerry Saltz, "The Revenge of the Real," *Village Voice,* 12 October 1999, 59.

42. Pierre Bourdieu, "The Market of Symbolic Goods," in *The Field of Cultural Production* (New York: Columbia University Press, 1993), 127–128.

43. "One Stink-ular 'Sensation,'" *New York Post,* 4 October 1999, 30.

44. Saltz, "Revenge of the Real."

45. Solomon, "The Collector," 47–48.

46. Norman Rosenthal, "The Blood Must Continue to Flow," in *Sensation: Young British Artists from the Saatchi Collection* (London: Thames and Hudson, 1997), 9.

47. Ibid., 10.

48. Martin Maloney, "Everyone a Winner! Selected British Art from the Saatchi Collection 1987–97," in *Sensation,* 26.

49. Solomon, "The Collector," 47.

50. Bourdieu, *Distinction,* 280.

51. Judith H. Dobrzynski, "'Adopting' Masterpieces: Touch of Class or Crass?," *New York Times,* 6 June 1999, A1.

52. Judith H. Dobrzynski, "Art(?) to Go: Museum Shops Broaden Wares, at a Profit," *New York Times,* 10 December 1997, A1.

53. Michael Daly, "Rudy's Making Real Sensation," *Daily News,* 26 September 1999, 6.

54. Barstow, "Art, Money and Control."

55. Quoted in Ralph Blumenthal, "Painting by Numbers: My Renoir Beats Your Vermeer," *New York Times,* 6 June 1999, IV6.

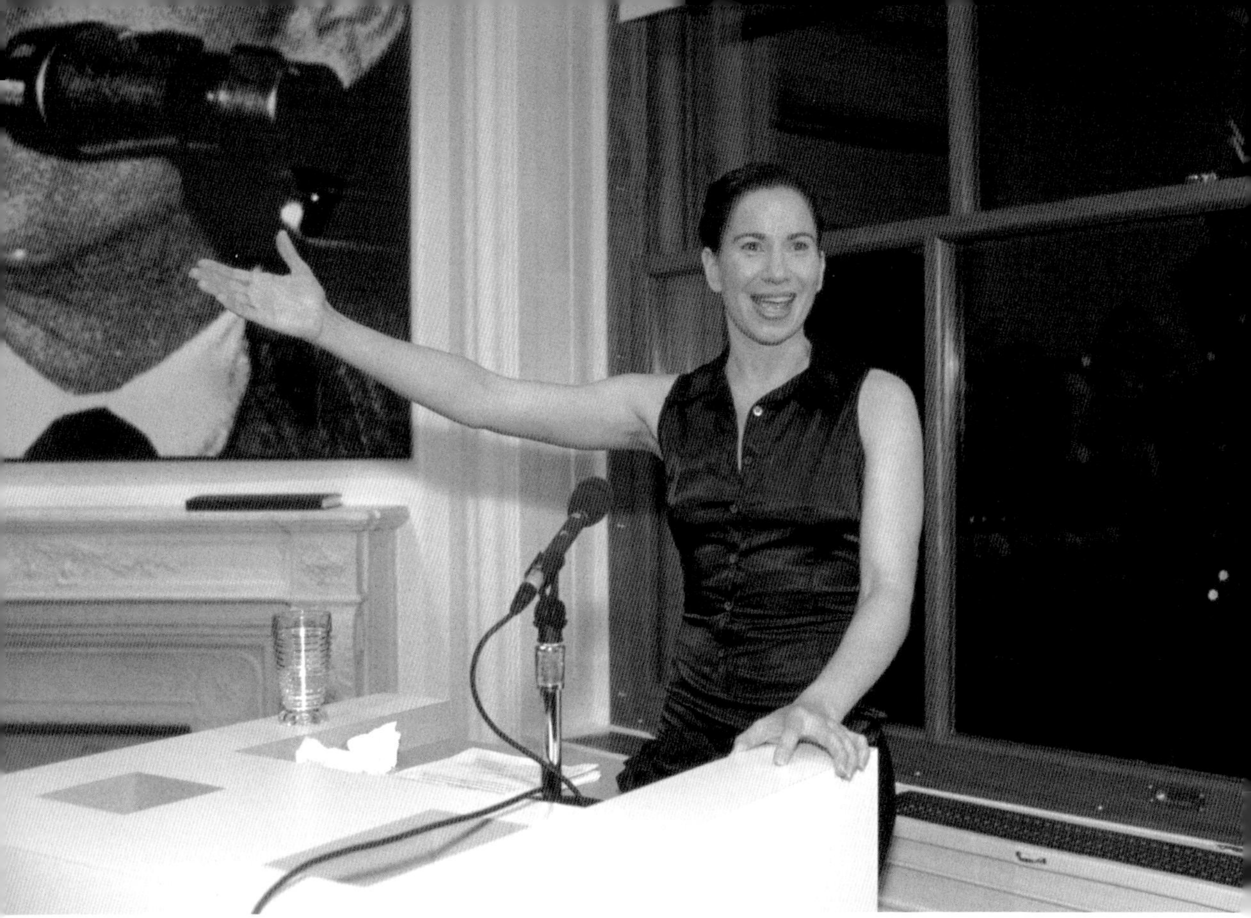

18.1 Andrea Fraser, *Official Welcome,* 2001. Live performance at The MICA Foundation, New York. Courtesy the artist and American Fine Arts, Co. Photo: Sarah Kunstler.

18

OFFICIAL WELCOME

Official Welcome *is a monologue that was commissioned by The* MICA *Foundation and first performed during a reception at the home of Barbara Morse, the president of the Foundation, and her husband, Howard Morse, on November 28, 2001, before an audience of invited guests. The script below was first published in the* MICA Foundation Newsletter *1, no. 2 (Fall 2001).*

Introduction

Good evening. Hello everyone.

I do know many of you, but I'll introduce myself anyway. I'm Andrea Fraser, and I'd like to thank you for coming to this presentation of my project for The MICA Foundation. It's called "Official Welcome" and, as most of you have probably guessed from the cameras and the lights, this is it. This is "Official Welcome."

So, I'm happy, I'm pleased, I'm honored, I'm privileged, I'm really thrilled, really, to welcome you, officially, to Barbara and Howard's living room. (This is, of course, a site-specific project.)

I'm going to have a tough time topping Colin de Land's remarks from last year, but I'll do my best.

I have to begin by saying that I've known Barbara and Howard for many years—more than a decade. For most of those years, Barbara and Howard were my only collectors. Even when I didn't want collectors, when I was against the whole idea that art was bought and sold, they were there, trying to buy.

But Barbara and Howard have always been supportive in other ways as well, and this commission is only the most recent example of that support. When I wrote up the first *Prospectuses* for my artistic services in '93, it was for a show they organized, and Howard helped out by lending his expertise in preparing corporate prospectuses. (Howard? Where is Howard? I just saw him a minute ago.) Later, I gave a talk about my first prospectus project, with the Generali Foundation, in this very room. Some of you may remember that event, when I started sobbing for no apparent reason and couldn't stop. It's true.

Points to someone in audience.

I know you remember that.

Well, I can't guarantee that it won't happen again this evening but . . . not now. I'm not choking up, really. I'm . . . just a little dry.

Takes a sip of water, then clears throat. Reading:

The mission of The MICA Foundation is to sponsor projects by artists that are positioned critically in relation to the production, exhibition, documentation, promotion, and distribution of art, and the conventional roles of artist, patron, and audience. It aims to provide crucial support for artists whose work has been rendered invisible because of political content, lack of marketability, or its challenging inquiry into the nature of art institutions.

The MICA Foundation's newest project is a perfect example of its commitment to critical and challenging art.

For its second commissioned project, MICA has selected an artist who is a leading practitioner of this genre. Her work is inventive, poignant, and brazen as well as humorous. She's an artist who takes no prisoners, even when she works in the belly of the beast. Her performative critiques are meticulously researched portraits of institutions, revealingly appropriated from original sources, yet they're often, they're often also tantalizingly ambiguous. And she's also successfully explored innovative models for artistic practice that would liberate artists from the strictures of traditional object production.

By engaging her to develop a text relevant to a private nonprofit foundation—and to deliver it here as well—The MICA Foundation is endorsing Andrea Fraser's role as an institutional critic.

And we're really very, *very* happy—we're privileged—to have been able to work with Andrea. We've followed her work for years. She's a phenomenal artist and it's just a, it's a terrific project. It's very smart and very funny.

Turns to right and gestures to come to the podium.

Andrea?

Artist

Turns to left, nods gravely, then reads:

This evening represents the conclusion of a very satisfying project. It is the appropriate moment to thank the Foundation for its support. My hope, however, is that such thanks are unnecessary. I was commissioned by the Foundation to do a certain job. My hope is that the Foundation has found that job well done.

What do I, as an artist, provide? What do I satisfy?

The immediate answer to those questions can be found in the function of the Foundation. But if I serve those functions, it's not because I have defined my activity as a service. Those functions are generally fulfilled in the exchange that constitutes any kind of patronage. They are fulfilled because the professional prestige I, as an artist, augment when my name is publicized by a patron is identical to the prestige they acquire by being associated with a particular kind of art. It's the same quantity of the same currency: a profit in moral legitimacy generated by activities with "higher" aims; a profit in social legitimacy generated by association with exclusive tastes and practices; and a profit in professional legitimacy generated by demonstrations of competence in our respective spheres of activity.

Takes deep breath to continue—

1.

Supporter

Thank you . . .

Turns to right.

. . . Andrea, for an exemplary presentation.

It *is* difficult to imagine what a critical art practice could be at the beginning of the new millennium. One factor in the demise of radical practice may be art's own collaboration with the forces of spectacle culture. If visibility has become art's primary horizon of aspiration, then for any radical aesthetic practice to be historically convincing it must now define itself in opposition to that culture.

Tonight we are considering an artist whose project meets this criterion, an artist whose interventions invite the viewer to recognize the fundamental conditions of art and its inability to resolve its contradictions. As a radical contestation of the hegemonic ordering of experience, his practice demonstrates that the desire to commemorate—which he inscribes as a grotesque echo of the fate of radical critique—is inextricably bound up with forms of culturally engineered adulation operating at the very center of artistic production and reception.

He thus inverts and counters all of the artistic fallacies that hindsight and history have made evident. Indeed, it would be difficult to conceive of any practice that could surpass his as a synthesis of the most complex and radical artistic projects of the recent past as well as the early twentieth century.

And it's a pleasure to introduce him this evening.

Looks to right.

Artist

Um . . .

Turns quickly to left.

. . . thank you. Um, I don't want to sound coquettish—this could easily come off the wrong way—but as an artist I'm always disappointed. Even though I say the end result isn't important, I'm never satisfied. But I guess that's why I keep trying. As an artist, I try to create an autonomous space in which a critical position can be made clear. People come to see my work, maybe they spend some time. I hope I can make people feel involved, but it's not about interactivity. I give something to people, but I don't expect communication. I hope I can make people think, but I don't want to be didactic—I don't want to make political art, I don't want to intimidate or exclude people. I want to implicate people in my work—I mean, in the world. That's my political statement. What's most important is not what people see in my work, but what they see when they confront reality again. I work in reality. So, why am I an artist? I guess it's because I take a critical position toward the world. It's not about hope. It's about showing my disgust with the dominant discourse.

2.

Supporter

Shaking head.

How much information can you receive from one artist in a few minutes?

Usually, when an artist explains his work, it lessens the allure. But that's hardly the case in this case. His friendly bombardment is an art experience in itself. The simultaneity of thoughts passing through the brain is never easy to capture, especially if the brain in question is brilliantly hyperactive. Well, he's in possession of just such a remarkable organ. No critic can possibly keep up with it. But I'll try.

Let me say that even while his words do offer a compelling explanation for the enduring impact of his work, they modestly underestimate its beauty, intrigue, pathos, and wit.

Simply put, his work is magical. And the best part is, you don't have to worry about the meaning of it all. Unlike so many artists, he doesn't preach.

If he is the most important artist of his generation—and I believe he is—it's because his imagination is so very big.

If masterpieces still can be made, he has managed to make them: full, exquisitely realized works of power, vision, and extraordinary beauty; works that rise to a level of humanistic allegory significant for all of us, even while we may not know exactly what they mean.

Looks to right.

I think we're all extraordinarily lucky to be able to honor him here this evening.

Artist

Looks to left.

Thank you, it's, uh, uh, thank you, uh.

Speaking in a painfully slow, almost stuttering voice.

If I, uh, if I, uh, if I, uh, deserve, uh, any of this, uh, I think that it can only be because, uh, because I have, uh, finally arrived, uh, at a point where, uh, my work has become, uh, has become, uh universal. It's about, uh, it's about, the desire, uh, of all human beings, uh, to be free and, uh, to achieve, uh, to achieve, uh, to achieve a kind of, um, self-realization; uh, to achieve, uh, to achieve, uh, to achieve . . . something. It's about achievement.

And, uh, all of my work, uh, investigates, uh, different possibilities, uh, of what it means, uh, to imagine yourself, uh, within the broadest possible parameters.

And, uh, um, that's why I, uh, I don't like to, uh, to talk about my work. I made it, and, uh, and, uh, I hope, I hope, uh, that's enough.

Supporter

Oh, it is enough. It is so much more than enough. It is so much more than I or any single person or the most devoted public can reckon with.

Arma virumque cano. Of arms and the man I sing.

Tonight we render homage to a man who fought and struggled for long years in solitude, years of tremendous ambition and investment, labor and attention, with no reinforcement or recognition, but with unshakable integrity and dedication to task, motivated, not by anything outside, but by an inner need, a compulsion, an obsession, by an intransigent artistic faith that transformed anew our vision not only of art, but of the world.

For opening doors on new realities and reawakening our dreams, it is my privilege to confer on you the very highest honor. As an artist, and as a friend of France—

3.

Artist

Oh stop it! Stop it! You're embarrassing me!

Supporter

That's what I love about the guy: his modesty!

You know, the last time I went to his studio, he'd been *working*. It was full of new work. But I was at a loss. It was so different, it was so new. So I asked him to give me a little guidance. Well, he paused for a minute and then he said, "I have to think because I don't want to give you the propaganda."

This is an artist who never says stupid things!

I remember him one night at the Odeon acting like a fly on the wall in swell company. Well, now you're all his good friends and here tonight. And that shows just how far he's come since those early days. Make no mistake: he was timid.

I've never seen anyone grow into his shoes so fully. I used to tell him, I used to say, you're going to have to learn how to be a *big* artist—and I don't just mean making *big art!*

Well he did it. He's big. He's very big. He's just, he's big opera. He's big art and a great big heart, and it's my great pleasure to introduce this modern master, my great friend—

Artist

After a long pause:

Wow, that does sound like a charmed life.

Well, at least he didn't say that I'm a great big FART. Really, that's what I thought you were going to say!

Look, if you're going to laud somebody, this kind of back-scratching won't do! You really gotta beatify 'em. "Modern master," my—

What do you mean, "I'd been *working*"?! Just because you read about me in the columns, you think all I do is go to parties? I'm working parties!

No, I'm not shy anymore. I learned a very simple social strategy. The trick is to say as little as possible to as few people as possible and to keep moving. That way, it looks like I'm circulating when I'm actually just walking away.

Breaks into a big smile, waves, and pretends to leave the podium.

No, seriously, I'm honored—really, I'm honored—to be, ehem, *honored* here this evening.

You know, "remember me" is what all artists whisper in their work. It's a mark you want to leave in the world. It's still you even when you're not you anymore. When you're gone. If my work really has brought me love, that's what it means. If not, it has failed me at the deepest level.

So, remember me.

4.

Supporter

Well, we do love you. We love you for all you've given us, for giving us your all.

You have reminded us that art is a joyful industry, neither difficult nor painful, but easy as breathing and redolent with pleasure. Yours is an art of courageous beauty. It is a fragrance, an essence that, in its finest and most artful moments, is like strolling through the most elegant beauty salon in the universe.

I want to make a confession: On the night of her opening, catching glimpses of her work through the glittering throng, I was smitten, just dazzled by the sexy modern flair of it all. It was so right, so now. I wanted to take it home.

We want various things of art—to reflect the world, to perfect the world—and of artists—to be one of us, to be better than us. Well, the fact is, she *is* better than us. She's more beautiful than we are, she's more successful, she's a much better artist with a much more interesting life.

She's our fantasy. She lives our fantasies for us.

Artist

Strips down to a Gucci thong, bra, and high-heel shoes.

I'm not a person today. I'm an object in an artwork. It's about emptiness.

Steps away from the podium and stands motionless for 15 seconds.

5.

Supporter

Moving back to the podium:

That's great! Isn't she great?! She's great! Exciting work.

It's fun to sell a big artwork, and it's profitable. In the end, a good artist is a rich artist and a rich artist is a good artist. But my relationships with artists are the most rewarding part of my profession. I'm responsible for their careers, their ranking in art history—and that's the bottom line for my artists. But for me, it's also about creating space for freewheeling people with the guts to invest in their dreams.

Well, he's just about the gutsiest artist around. He may be obsessed with death, but only because he has such an incredible passion for life. I love that kind of vision. I think we all do. The thrill, the fantasy, the sleek world where everything falls into place.

Well, he's done it again. He's back, and he's bigger and better than ever. He's staggeringly corporate, breathtakingly professional and eager to entertain. And I do hope he'll say a few words to us this evening.

Looks to right.

Artist

Yeah, I'll say a few words.

I used to think that I was changing the world.

Laughs.

No, I'd just like to say that, um, I think the only interesting people are the people who say, "Fuck off." Yeah, that's what I think.

I really like that piece Nauman did—you know that piece? Um, *The true artist helps the world by revealing mystic truths*. And you go, oh, yeah, great. And then you go, oh God, oh fuck, you know, what is this shit.

No, I love saying a few words at events like this.

Okay, here're a few more words. How about, "Kiss my fucking ass!" That's a great statement anywhere, right?

Right?!

Well, why don't you all kiss my fucking ass!

Steps away from podium and moons audience, then turns around and throws arms up.

I love you all.

Okay, how about, "Kiss my tits!"

Hey, I'm not being funny. You know that, don't you? Look, I'm just trying to do my fucking best.

Where's my cheque?

6.

Supporter

Back behind the podium.

Yes, yes and you always do do your, your fucking best.

You were our first major purchase when we started buying art, and we considered it an act of sheer courage. It was "difficult" work—it was totally grotesque! You cooked part of the piece on our barbecue and we had to get a microbiologist to make sure we weren't breeding anything lethal.

Most of the art we collect is about sex or excrement—we like to think of ourselves as connoisseurs of art subculture—and we always love her work, even when it makes us want to throw up.

Reading:

Reviled *and* acclaimed for her confrontational, confessional style, she was raped at 16, had abortions, drug problems and attempted suicide. She's an artist who knows what she's saying with her art. She lives it. And she lives with a raw intensity that most of us can't even dream of: the chemical highs and gut-wrenching lows, the passionate loves and tragic losses. She makes each and every one of us feel like we've shared profound intimacies. I for one worship her like a goddess and eat up even the most banal details.

It's really a special thrill to have her here tonight.

Artist

Yeah, well, you know I really do appreciate the support. It gets harder and harder to be an artist. Attention can be incredibly cruel, from critics, and even other artists, who think they're so superior.

I mean, if I'm such shit and my work is such shit, then why don't you just leave me alone?

Yeah, the art world likes "bad girls." But if you're really bad you tell the truth and people don't want to hear the truth. If you're honest about how stupid and fucked over life is, you end up in the tabloids. I don't go looking for. It just comes in a big stinking tidal wave.

Removing bra, then shoes and thong.

I'm used to it. It's boring.

I just want to say that my real achievement is getting up in the morning; staying alive and not giving up. Sure, I've had a few good moments workwise, but nothing I'd consider a masterpiece. Let's keep things in perspective. The level here is pretty minor. But at least I haven't fallen in with the system.

I should probably also say that my current project does not rely on public funds.

7.

Supporter

Steps out from behind the podium.

It takes a lot of courage to do what she does. She goes far beyond where most artists have the intelligence or audacity to operate. It's a place of commitment and depth and honesty at the very limits of our capacity to know ourselves.

Her work has the power to change lives. It changed mine.

Art with both emotional depth and real political belief is anathema to an art world as cynical as ours. If mainstream artists (and critics) often reproduce the values they claim to oppose, then perhaps only those artists who have been forced to remain on the margins can reveal the true nature of power.

She's an artist who has uncovered structures so pervasive and profound that no one is innocent in her work—not her characters, not her viewers, not even herself. She even performs her own artistic identity and her relationships with the people who seek to support her.

Some people think she's sacrificed her body for professional success. I personally see her success as a triumph, an instance where the art world has broken past its prejudices.

Artist

Back behind the podium.

Recognition is really weird.

I used to spend a lot of time hanging around people who had absolutely no respect for me as a human being. I don't know if that's really changed.

At first I thought it was just really ironic. I got a kind of giddy satisfaction out of knowing that someone had work of mine that was going to offend people. I mean, of course my work's going to go to rich, white collectors and they're going to be proud of owning me and I'm going to be, you know, corrupted by the man. And now they're trying to get rid of me. I think that's why they gave me that MacArthur! To shut me up! Because now I have nothing left to aspire to.

So, I just want to say, thank you for taking hold of these last years of my life and raising my hopes for the future.

8.

Supporter

Well, thank *you*. Thank you for your dedication, for your vision, for your life.

I think we all must dare, as artists do, to break free of the past and to create a *better* future, rooted in values that never change. That's the great lesson our artists teach us.

Putting dress and shoes back on:

I want to say again to our guests how very, very much we enjoy having all of you here for this celebration and tribute and recognition and absolute delight in an artist who represents not only the best of the arts, but truly the very best that comes from within the human spirit.

Artist

And, uh, I just want to say, I guess, I just want to say that, you know, I wanted to be an artist since I was, like, four, because my mother was an artist, a good one, who never got any recognition.

Starting to cry.

And I loved to make things. I lost that love, unfortunately.

But, I just want to say that despite all the ambivalence it helps, it just, um, it really helps, to know that there are people who are following what you're doing and who think it's important enough to try to understand and, um, to support.

Sobbing.

That's all really.

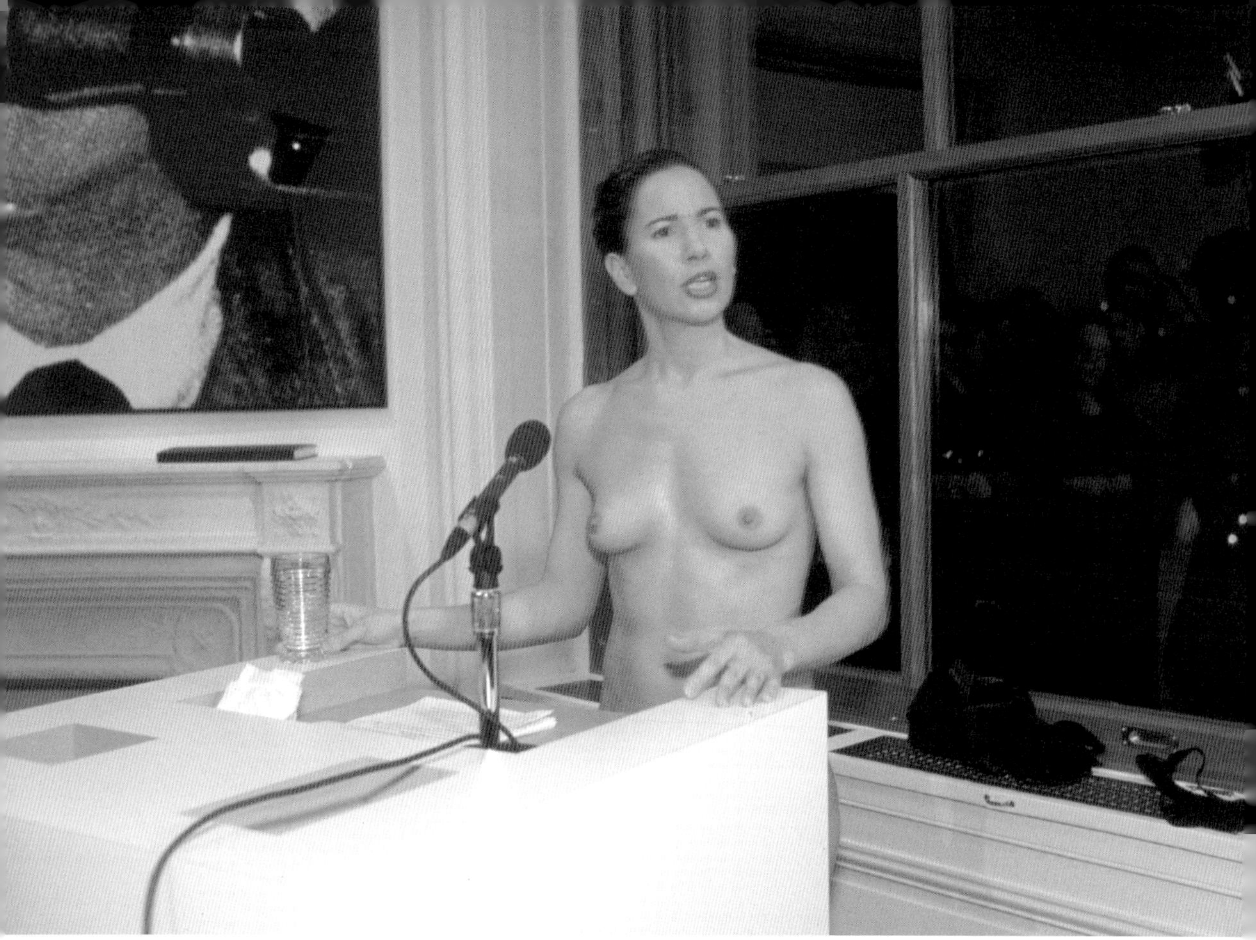

18.2 Andrea Fraser, *Official Welcome,* 2001. Live performance at The MICA Foundation, New York. Courtesy the artist and American Fine Arts, Co. Photo: Sarah Kunstler.

Supporter

Drying face with a tissue:

Thank you so very, very much. You were wonderful.

Can I ask everyone to give her a big hand? Isn't she terrific?

You were wonderful. Please come back.

And now, ladies and gentlemen, there's only one way that we can end this magical evening. I think we should end—I think Bob Hope should sing *Thanks for the Memories.* It's the only way we can end!

Thanks again to everyone and especially to our wonderful pianist.

Thank you, and good night.

Exit.

Sources

Introduction. Mel Brooks's acceptance speech for *The Producers* at the fifty-fifth Tony Awards ceremony, Radio City Music Hall, New York, 3 June 2001; *MICA Foundation Newsletter* 1, no. 1 (Spring/Summer 2000); Barbara and Howard Morse, letter written to Andrea Fraser at her request, unpublished manuscript, personal collection of Andrea Fraser; "What Do I, as an Artist, Provide?," speech presented at the opening of *A Project in Two Phases,* EA-Generali Foundation, Vienna, 13 May 1995, in this volume.

1. Benjamin Buchloh, response to Andrea Fraser's presentation at the panel discussion "Funding and Content," Basilico Fine Arts Gallery, New York, 3 April 1997; Benjamin Buchloh, "Cargo and Cult: The Displays of Thomas Hirschhorn," *Artforum International* (November 2001); Benjamin Buchloh, "Gabriel Orozco: The Sculpture of Everyday Life," in Benjamin Buchloh and Alma Ruiz, eds., *Gabriel Orozco* (Los Angeles: Museum of Contemporary Art, 2000); Benjamin Buchloh, "Process Sculpture and Film in the Work of Richard Serra," in Hal Foster and Gordon Hughes, eds., *Richard Serra* (Cambridge: MIT Press, 2000); Thomas Hirschhorn, quoted in Daniel Birnbaum, "A Thousand Words: Thomas Hirschhorn," *Artforum International* (March 2000); Gabriel Orozco, quoted in David Joselit, "Gabriel Orozco: Museum of Contemporary Art, Los Angeles," *Artforum International* (September 2000).

2. Daniel Birnbaum, "A Thousand Words: Thomas Hirschhorn"; "For Immediate Release: Gabriel Orozco, November 24, 1998–January 9, 1999," Marian

Goodman Gallery, New York, 1998; Jerry Saltz on Gabriel Orozco in "Here and Gone," *Village Voice,* 5 January 1999; Michael Kimmelman on Gabriel Orozco in "Art Review: When Meaning Emerges Slowly from Missing Parts," *New York Times,* 11 December 1998; Michael Kimmelman, "The Importance of Matthew Barney," *New York Times Magazine,* 10 October 1999; Arthur C. Danto, "Pas de Deux, en Masse: Shirin Neshat's Rapture," *Nation,* 28 June 1999; Shirin Neshat, quoted in Amei Wallach, "Art/Architecture: Striking a Balance between Western and Islamic Values," *New York Times,* Sunday, 21 November 1999; Ross Bleckner, home page (http://www.rbleckner.com), July 2001; Cy Twombly, quoted by Kirk Varnedoe in remarks at the opening dinner for "Cy Twombly: A Retrospective," Museum of Modern Art, New York, 21 September 1994 (transcribed from sound recording #94.34, Museum of Modern Art, New York, Museum Archives); Kirk Varnedoe on Cy Twombly, from remarks at the opening dinner for "Cy Twombly: A Retrospective"; Kirk Varnedoe on Jasper Johns, remarks at the opening dinner for "Jasper Johns: A Retrospective," Museum of Modern Art, New York, 15 October 1996 (transcribed from sound recording #96, Museum of Modern Art, New York, Museum Archives); speech given by the French cultural attaché on the occasion of the induction of Duane Michals as an *officier* of the French Order of Arts and Letters, New York, 10 March 2000.

3. Brad Gooch, "Ross Bleckner Revealed," *Harper's Bazaar,* May 1994; Harry Mathews on Francesco Clemente, in Lytle Shaw, "An Interview with Harry Mathews," *Chicago Review* 43, no. 2 (Spring 1997); Francesco Clemente, quoted in Jerry Saltz, "At the Guggenheim, an Artist in Partial Eclipse," *Village Voice,* 26 October 1999; Jerry Saltz on Francesco Clemente in "At the Guggenheim, an Artist in Partial Eclipse"; Dennis Hopper on Julian Schnabel, quoted in Philip Weiss, "Arteurs: Big," *New York Times Magazine,* 25 March 2001; Christopher Mason, "At Home With: Ross Bleckner," *New York Times,* 10 December 1998.

4. Dave Hickey, "Clemente: Solomon R. Guggenheim Museum, New York," *Artforum International* (January 2000); Jerry Saltz on Gary Hume, "Heat of the Moment," *Village Voice,* 3 April 2001; Katy Siegel on Matthew Barney, "Nurture Boy," *Artforum International* (Summer 1999); Judith Palmer, "Interview: Vanessa Beecroft—Empty Vessels," *Independent* [London], 27 October 1997; Roberta Smith on Vanessa Beecroft, "Critic's Notebook: Standing and Staring, yet Aiming for Empowerment," *New York Times,* 6 May 1998.

5. Larry Gagosian, quoted in Philip Delves Broughton, "Damien's One of the Good Guys," *Daily Telegraph* [London], 3 October 2000; Lewis Lapham, quoted in David D. Kirkpatrick, "'Oprah' Gaffe by Franzen Draws Ire and Sales," *New York Times,* 29 October 2001; Charles Saatchi, quoted in Deborah Solomon, "The Collector," *New York Times Magazine,* 26 September 1999; Jerry Saltz on Damien Hirst, "The Pursuit of Happiness," *Village Voice,* 17 October 2000; Sarah Borruso, "Artist's Statements, Excerpted from an Interview with Damien Hirst, June 11, 1996," *HotWired Pop Gallery* (http://hotwired.wired.com/gallery/96/27/statement.html); Damien Hirst, quoted in David Furnish, "Damien Hirst," *Interview,* September 1997; Chris Ofili accepting Turner Prize, quoted in Margaret O'Brien Steinfels, "Artists Have Rights, and So Do Taxpayers," *New York Times,* 25 September 1999.

6. Donald and Mira Rubell and Nora Stone, quoted in Nancy Hass, "Art: Living with Work that Needs Its Own Room," *New York Times,* Sunday, 9 August 1998; Charles Saatchi, quoted in Deborah Solomon, "The Collector"; Tracey Emin, quoted in "Emin Defends Her Art," *BBC News Online,* BBC, London, 13 August 2001 (http://news.bbc.co.uk/1/hi/entertainment/arts/1488713.stm); Bill Arning, "New York: Tracey Emin at Lehmann Maupin," *Art in America* (December 1999); Mia Fineman, "The Nan Goldin Story," Artnet.com, 12 December 1996 (http://www.artnet.com/magazine/features/fineman/fineman12-12-96.asp); Tracey Emin, "Tracey Emin Journal," *Modern Culture,* Modern Culture Gallery, New York (http://www.bway.net/~modcult/tej1299.html); Penny Arcade, quoted in "Janine Antoni," *Digital Consciousness Artist Database* (http://digitalconsciousness.com/artists/JanineAntoni); Andres Serrano, quoted in John Leland, "At Home With: Andres Serrano: Fitting Out a Triplex Cloister," *New York Times,* May 10, 2001.

7. C. Carr, "On Edge: A Persecuted Performance Artist Gets Past Her Suffering: The Karen Finley Makeover," *Village Voice,* 14 November 2000; Michael Kimmelman on Paul McCarthy, "Art Review," *New York Times,* 23 February 2001; Jerry Saltz on Kara Walker, "Making the Cut," *Village Voice,* 24 November 1998; Jerry Saltz on Nan Goldin, "On the Rocks," *Village Voice,* 13 February 2001; Lucy Lippard on Andres Serrano, "Andres Serrano: The Spirit and the Letter," *Art in America* (April 1990); Gwendolyn DuBois Shaw, "Final Cut," *Parkett* 59 (2000); Maurice Berger, quoted in Julia Szabo, "Kara Walker's Shock Art," *New York Times Magazine,* 23 March 1997; Kara Walker, interviewed by James Hannaham,

"Pea, Ball, Bounce," *Interview,* November 1998; Kara Walker, *Letter from a Black Girl* (1998), text on wall, dimensions variable.

8. Bill Clinton, "Remarks by the President in 'Toast at Arts and Humanities Dinner,'" State Dining Room, The White House, Washington, D.C., 5 October 1995, 8:31 pm; Hillary Rodham Clinton, "Remarks by the President and the First Lady at National Medal of Arts and Humanities Dinner," Pavilion, The White House, 20 December 2000, 9:15 pm.

IN

CONCLUSION?

ONWARD TO THE PAST, OR, ART AT THE FOREFRONT OF REGRESSION

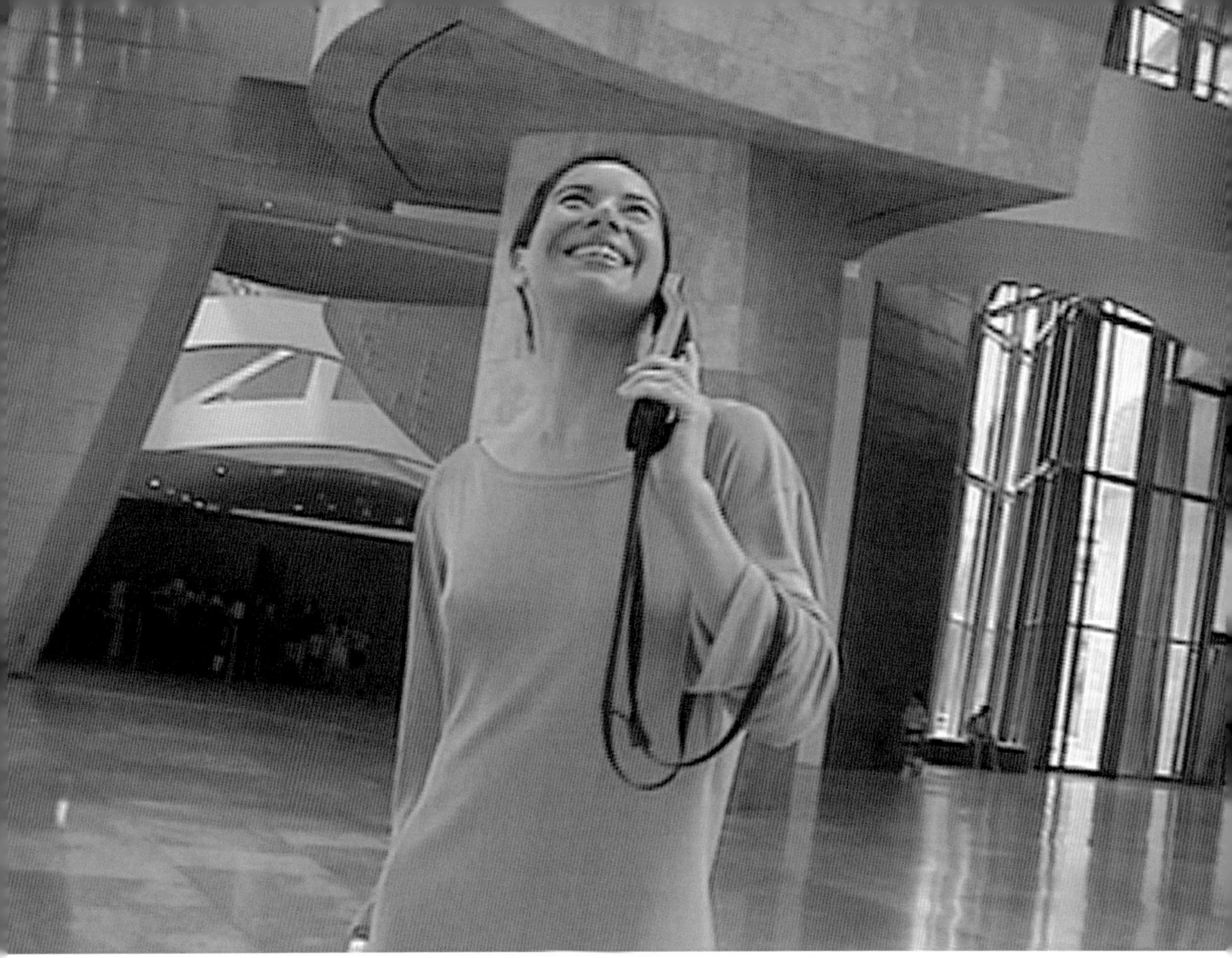

19.1 Andrea Fraser, still from *Little Frank and His Carp*, 2001. DVD. Courtesy the artist and Friedrich Petzel Gallery.

19

ISN T THIS A WONDERFUL PLACE?
(A TOUR OF A TOUR OF THE GUGGENHEIM BILBAO)

"Isn't This a Wonderful Place?" was written in the spring of 2003. It was originally planned as a contribution to the conference "Museums and Global Public Spheres," held at the Rockefeller Foundation's Bellagio Conference and Study Center in the summer of 2002. I was unable to attend the conference but was invited to complete the essay for inclusion in a collection of the conference papers. It was first presented publicly in April 2004 at the conference "Learning from the Guggenheim," organized by the Center for Basque Studies of the University of Nevada and held at the Nevada Museum of Art in Reno. Much of the research informing the essay was conducted in the context of the development of an artist project with the organization Consonni, Bilbao. The introductory audiotour of the Guggenheim Bilbao on which it is based also inspired a videotape entitled Little Frank and His Carp, *stills from which are reproduced with the essay.*

> If you haven't already done so, walk away from the desk where you picked up this guide and out into the great, high space of the atrium. Isn't this a wonderful place? It's uplifting. It's like a Gothic cathedral. You can feel your soul rise up with the building around you. This is the heart of the museum and it works like a heart, pumping the visitor around the different galleries. If you look up, you can see walkways, elevators, and stairways leading up and around the walls of the atrium between the galleries. These are the arteries. The separate galleries all lie off this central space and to go from one to another, you must come back here.

In the great museums of previous ages, rooms linked from one to another, and you must visit them all, one after another. Sometimes it can feel as if there's no escape. But here there is an escape: this space, to which you can return after every gallery, to refresh the spirit before your next encounter with the demands of contemporary art. This building recognizes that modern art is demanding, complicated, bewildering, and the museum tries to make you feel at home, so you can relax and absorb what you see more easily.

As you look around, you'll see that every surface in this space curves. Only the floor is straight. These curves are gentle, but in their huge scale powerfully sensual. You'll see people going up to the walls and stroking them. You might feel the desire to do so yourself. These curving surfaces have a direct appeal that has nothing to do with age or class or education. They give the building its warmth, its welcoming feel. And in this way the atrium tries to make you feel at home and prepares you for the purpose of the building: the art it contains.

Let's take a closer look at one of the stone-clad pillars in this space. If you stand with your back to the entrance, there's one to your right, holding up a large stone box that actually contains a tiny gallery. Go right up to it. This pillar is clad in panels of limestone. Run your hand over them. Squint along the surface. Feel how smooth it is.

Paradoxically, these sensual curves have been created by computer technology. Because of the way the surface of the pillar curves, each of these panels is slightly different. No two are quite the same. And this is true for all the curved walls of the building. If these panels had been produced by conventional means, this would still be a building site and the cost of the building would be astronomical. But these panels were cut and shaped by robots working to a computer program developed for aircraft design. To a computer, the mathematical problems involved in fitting together this vast jigsaw are simple. This process is very new, and it should have a revolutionary effect on the way architects work, because it will allow them to embody more freely the productions of their imaginations, as well as allowing them to build more cheaply, and to a better quality.

Now turn to your right and look at the glass tower that contains two of the elevators. The glass surface of this tower also curves, and again the curves are produced by panels fitted together. But here they overlap, like the scales of a fish. This is no idle metaphor. The architect who designed this building, Frank Gehry, has always found inspiration in fish. He dates this obsession from the days when he used to go with his grandmother to the market to buy a live carp, which he would then take home and keep in the bathtub until it was time to cook it. Here little Frank would play with the carp and here the magic of its sinuous, scaly form somehow entered his bloodstream.

If you look to your left now, beyond the pillar under the stone box that we looked at a moment ago, you'll see the entrance to a large space. This is the largest gallery in the museum and, believe it or not, it's known as the Fish Gallery, because the long curving shape of this part of the building is derived, once again, from the shape of the fish. Let's go in there now. Press your Pause button until you are in the gallery.

You are standing in a room of 3,200 square meters. It's 150 meters long and between 12 and 25 meters high. Contemporary art is big. In fact, some of it is enormous, and this gallery was designed to accommodate the huge pieces that artists have begun to create.
—Official audioguide, Guggenheim Bilbao Museoa

Yes, "in the great museums of previous ages, rooms linked from one to another, and you must visit them all, one after another. Sometimes it can feel as if there's no escape."

But, "here there is an escape." An escape from order: the order of one after another; the order of a rational, linear progression of rooms, objects, exhibits; the order of regulated movement; the order of looking; the order to look—to look at all and only look. Here, we are invited to feel. We are invited to touch.

Here, there's an escape from the rules of behavior that have always told us not to touch. We are made aware of our desire to touch, so direct, that we share with those around us, that transcends age and class and education.

Here, we can escape from our social selves, from social determination.

Here, we can escape from identity in a place of endless differentiation. We can escape from our place of origin. We can feel at home away from home.

Here, we can escape the boundaries of our discrete bodies. We become formless matter, fluid, pumped through the building's heart, its arteries, its corporeal passages; passages formed in masturbatory memories (what else are we to suppose little Frank was doing in the bathtub with that fish?); fantasies of sensual curves, sinuous forms, and powerful scales; fantasies of overcoming the weakness and smallness of little individualities with the magic of towering cybernetic members. Contemporary art is "big." "In fact, some of it is enormous."

Here, we can even escape the forces of gravity. We feel our souls rise up, limbs like airplane wings.

Here, like architects and artists, we can be free to embody the productions of our imaginations.

And that is the museum's revolutionary effect.

> *In the great museums of previous ages, rooms linked from one to another, and you must visit them all, one after another. Sometimes it can feel as if there's no escape.*

Douglas Crimp is often credited with introducing Foucauldian theory to the study of museums. In his 1980 essay, "On the Museum's Ruins," he famously writes: "Foucault has analyzed the modern institutions of confinement—the asylum, the clinic and the prison—and their respective discursive formations—madness, illness and criminality. There is another institution of confinement ripe for analysis in Foucault's terms—the museum—and another discipline—art history.[1]

Tony Bennett took up the challenge with his 1988 essay "The Exhibitionary Complex." Nevertheless, he opens the essay by misreading Crimp's proposal: "It seems to imply," he writes, "that works of art had previously wandered through the streets of Europe."[2] It's a wonderful image, but one that has little to do with Crimp's argument, which is concerned above all with the way technologies of reproduction may undermine the ordered discourse of the museum. A much more literal application of Foucault's work on carceral institutions can in fact be found in my *Museum Highlights: A Gallery Talk*.[3] A 1989 performance in the form of a museum tour, *Museum Highlights* juxtaposes the museum to another institution of confinement, the poorhouse, and develops the hypothesis that museums emerged in the context of the formation of urban public spheres as systems of goads and deterrences to particular forms of social behavior and cultural identification.

What Bennett is primarily concerned with, in any case, are not exhibits but the publics constituted by exhibitions—publics that one *could* say, according to Bennett's own arguments, had indeed wandered the streets as unruly crowds before being constituted as orderly audiences by and for orderly displays organized for their edification. Bennett goes on to distinguish carceral institutions from the nineteenth-century museums and exhibitions, panoramas and arcades that he calls "the exhibitionary complex." Following Foucault, Bennett is concerned with institutions above all as technologies of order and discipline, "instruments of the moral and cultural regulation of the working classes."[4] However, whereas institutions of confinement developed technologies of surveillance that rendered the populace visible to the forces of order, institutions of exhibition served rather "to render the forces and principles of order visible to the populace." As such they constituted "a set of cultural technologies concerned to organize a voluntarily self-regulating citizenry":

> Through the provision of object lessons in power—the power to command and arrange things and bodies for public display—they sought to allow the people, and *en masse* rather than individually, to know rather than be known, to become the subjects rather than the objects of knowledge. Yet, ideally, they sought also to allow the people to know and thence to regulate themselves; to become, in seeing themselves from the side of power, both the subjects and the objects of knowledge, knowing power and what power knows, and knowing themselves as (ideally) known by power, interiorizing its gaze as a principle of self-surveillance and, hence, self-regulation.[5]

I wonder if the anonymous author of the Guggenheim Bilbao's introductory audiotour ever read "On the Museum's Ruins" or "The Exhibitionary Complex." I suppose it's irrelevant. Reflections on the function and purpose, meaning and effects of museums and their architecture—which can now be found in the fields of art, art history, architecture, anthropology, sociology, history, and cultural studies and which have developed into their own discipline of museum studies—are also informing, directly and indirectly, developments within the field of museums themselves. In contemporary art museums in particular it's safe to assume that most of the educators preparing didactic materials, curators preparing exhibitions, directors setting policy and planning expansions, and architects developing new physical structures are at least aware of the existence of a critical discourse on museums. So it's not surprising to hear an echo of this critical discourse in the halls of new art museums themselves—even or especially within a set of negative representations: that is, as what new art museums do not want to be. Prisons. Carceral institutions. Institutions of confinement, discipline, surveillance, order, regulation. Factories of edification and of taste.

But here there is an escape . . .

Of course, the museum's audioguide isn't telling us anything that hasn't already been proclaimed in the reams of writing on Frank Gehry's Guggenheim Bilbao, a building that seems on its way to becoming one of the most written about structures in the history of architecture. "Exultant eruption, frozen explosion, stormy volumes, floral splendor, titanium tentacles, Tower of Babel, a Basque bomb, Lourdes for a crippled culture, the reincarnation of Marilyn Monroe" are among the metaphors compiled in one critic's survey of the literature.

The building has been described as a "world of sand castles and fairy tales," a euphoric world of "radical heterogeneity," and "a place of contested borders" like the Basque region itself. It finds beauty and meaning in "social fragmentation" and "diversity," proving that "many languages can not only coexist but also babble around within a broad and vibrant vista of the world."

It's a statement "on behalf of irregularity."

It "lives in the spirit of risk and experimentation."

It's "a sanctuary of free association. It's a bird, it's a plane, it's Superman. It's a ship, an artichoke, the miracle of the rose."

Its "free-flowing and undulating surfaces" are the very "'images' of architectural freedom" and a monument to art "understood as an excessive, impossible, even farcical dream of freedom."

"If there is an order to this architecture, it is not one that can be predicted from one or two visual slices of its precisely calculated free-form geometry. But the building's spirit of freedom is hard to miss."[6]

Yes, the spirit of freedom.

. . . this space, to which you can return after every gallery, to refresh the spirit before your next encounter with the demands of contemporary art. This

building recognizes that modern art is demanding, complicated, bewildering, and the museum tries to make you feel at home, so you can relax and absorb what you see more easily.

Have new museums like the Guggenheim Bilbao finally succeeded in replacing the pedantic discipline of a nineteenth-century ordering of things with the fluid freedoms of unprogrammed flows? Is the "Bilbao effect" indeed a realization of the "myth of the next reality" in heterotopic spaces of radical heterogeneity? Or is the "Bilbao extravaganza" just another symptom of the spectacularization of museums and their transformation from public educational institutions into corporate entertainment complexes—a process in which the Guggenheim has been counted as leading the avant-garde?

The audioguide reminds us explicitly that art museums are not all fun and games. Modern and contemporary art, at least, is still "demanding, complicated, bewildering." Art remains a challenge to be met; a bitter pill after which one needs to "refresh the spirit" with a draught of soaring space. The architecture recognizes this. The architecture knows. The architecture understands. It not only sees (and speaks) but also listens to its visitors. And in the wisdom of its understanding it works, not to reinforce art's impositions, but to provide a respite from art's disturbing effects. As in a dentist's chair, we're given a shot of Novocain before a root canal. Now, you just relax. I'll try to spare your pain. But the operation must be performed.

Another kind of discipline still seems to be at work here, but it's one that the "architecture," at least, would explicitly disown. It's not a discipline deployed *by* the institution of the museum, but *within* the museum, it seems, by the institution of art itself. Or, can we say, by the art museum as an institutionalized form of art?

A program of movement is in fact laid out for us. We can go from one gallery to another as we please, but we must always come back "here." No, it's not a linear movement through a succession of rooms; its more of a spiral up through space. The grand staircases of Beaux-Arts museums elevated us for civilization. To enter the Guggenheim Bilbao, however, we must first descend, pouring into the museum lobby through funnel-shaped front steps. It is only from there that we are to ascend. From the atrium to the galleries to the atrium to the galleries to the atrium we are to wind our way from uplift to bewilderment to sensual communion to confronting demand and on to magical release in a dialectic of aesthetic transformation that promises to sublate us into fluid and finally perhaps even into air.

Yes, here there is an escape.

> *As you look around, you'll see that every surface in this space curves. Only the floor is straight. These curves are gentle, but in their huge scale powerfully sensual. You'll see people going up to the walls and stroking them. You might feel the desire to do so yourself.*

One may be able to speak of technologies of discipline common to an entire range of "exhibitionary" institutions—from panoramas and dioramas to expos, fairs, and the ever-growing family of museums. However, to understand the functions, meanings, and effects of art museums as a particular class of "exhibitionary" institutions, one must consider the very particular form of discipline they impose.

This form of discipline may very well be what Crimp had in mind when he called for a Foucauldian analysis of the art museum. When he returns to Foucault in his essay, he refers not to Foucault's work on the prison or the asylum but to his reflection on the work of Manet, in which Foucault found an acknowledgement of "a new and substantial relationship of painting to itself, as a manifestation of the existence of museums and the particular reality and interdependence that paintings acquire in museums."[7]

What began to make modern art so "demanding" in the nineteenth-century may have been less the physical closure of museum spaces than the emergence of a kind of discursive closure which, in the words of Bourdieu, "*categorically* demands a purely aesthetic disposition which earlier art demanded only conditionally." And it is precisely this demand that was "objectified in the art museum; there the aesthetic disposition becomes an institution."[8] There, we can add, the aesthetic disposition also becomes a social discipline as the dialectic of aesthetic transformation is inserted into a specifically moral economy of freedom and renunciation, sacrifice and self-realization.

The aesthetic discipline institutionalized in the museum has been exemplified by the asceticism, silence, and stillness associated with art museums until so very recently. It is a discipline practiced in the renunciation of what so much aesthetic philosophy has described as the direct, immediate, obvious, easy gratification of the senses; a discipline performed in the bracketing off of corporeal wants and material needs, of economic interests and social prejudices; a discipline realized in the neutralization of ordinary urgencies and practical ends that has been considered the prerequisite of taste, of aesthetic pleasure, of contemplation and reflection, even of critical distance and reflexivity—the prerequisite, that is, of all there is to be gained from a trip to the museum for an encounter with works of art.

Art museums were built and their contents collected and ordered to accomplish this aesthetic neutralization. The social world, with its noise and movement, urgencies and ends, was banished by the silence and stillness of windowless rooms. The uses of objects and representations were neutralized by their withdrawal from everyday life and by the juxtaposition of forms "originally subordinated to quite different or even incompatible functions."[9] And above all, perhaps, the economic value of things as commodities was neutralized by their permanent withdrawal from private consumption and material exchange into the public collections of public institutions.

These curving surfaces have a direct appeal that has nothing to do with age or class or education.

In Bourdieu's analysis, however, the aesthetic neutralization institutionalized in the art museum is anything but neutral. Aesthetic principles exist, rather, as the "universalization of the dispositions associated with a particular social and economic condition."[10] The aesthetic disposition "is one dimension of a total relation to the world and to others, a life-style, in which the effects of particular conditions of existence are expressed in a 'misrecognizable' form." Like the philanthropic acts of donation through which so many objects find their way into museum collections and on which so many museums themselves depend, the aesthetic and its institutions are both the product and the manifestation of a distance from economic necessity: of economic power that is "first and foremost a power to keep economic necessity at arm's length." The world of artistic freedom institutionalized in the museum is a world "snatched, by economic power, from that necessity." As such, it is engendered as "the paradoxical product of a negative economic conditioning."

In other words, according to Bourdieu, the aesthetic and its institutions presuppose a "distance from the world . . . which is the basis of the bourgeois experience of the world."[11] It is an experience of the world, one might say (at the risk of suggesting too direct a correspondence), common to the patrons of art museums, the previous owners of much of their collections, and, in the American tradition, their founders and trustees.

The particular ideological power of the aesthetic lies in the almost complete circularity of its essentialism: another kind of institutional closure, perhaps; another kind of prison. As Bourdieu demonstrates over and over again in *Distinction,* a disposition to aesthetic experience is a clear product of social and economic conditions, such as "age and class and education." However, it exists as a manifestation of those conditions precisely to the extent that it denies and distances them in its affirmation of the "direct appeal" of surface, shape, color, form, etc. And it is this very distancing that defines the experience it produces. The aesthetic is thus the perfect manifestation of a determination that frees us precisely through a negation of the (negative) determinations of freedom (from necessity) of which it is the "paradoxical product."

Like all essentializing ideologies, the aesthetic accomplishes its seduction by way of a cruel ruse: the promise that the pleasures, satisfactions, advantages, capacities, and above all, freedoms provided for by particular social and economic conditions can be achieved by an individual effort of the mind and willful disciplining of the body. If museum visitors were to be "liberated from the 'struggle imposed by material needs,'" as a Philadelphia Museum of Art pamphlet promised in 1922, it was not by way of the satisfaction of those needs, but by way of their distancing and displacement, mastering and renunciation: a liberation to be achieved by way of submission, not to the omnipotence of a surveilling gaze of power so much as to the omnipotence of the neutralizing gaze of the aesthete institutionalized in the art museum.[12]

They give the building its warmth, its welcoming feel. And in this way the atrium tries to make you feel at home and prepares you for the purpose of the building: the art it contains.

But museums aren't like that anymore. They're neither ascetic nor silent nor still but warm and welcoming and open to the street and full of everyday life. And they're not only for the well-educated middle and upper classes but teeming with the most diverse people with the most diverse interests and reasons for being there. "The museum is really free space. People do what they want to do," from "sleeping there, to looking at art, to having a meal . . . to picking each other up."[13]

Aestheticism may still be represented in a modernist corner of the collection, but you'll also find pop art and maybe even pop culture—like fashion, movies, and motorcycles—as well as contemporary art in all *its* diversity: not only painting, but performance, photography, digital media, big slabs of rusty steel, and monumental puppies made of flowers.

And most important of all, museums no longer leave their visitors at the mercy of such demanding, complicated, and bewildering art. Having learned from such ground-breaking studies as *The Love of Art*,[14] museums now offer a wide range of educational programs and materials to help guide visitors without backgrounds in art through their experience at the museum.

Like this introductory audiotour.

Now . . .

> *Let's take a closer look at one of the stone-clad pillars in this space. If you stand with your back to the entrance, there's one to your right, holding up a large stone box that actually contains a tiny gallery. Go right up to it. This pillar is clad in panels of limestone. Run your hand over them. Squint along the surface. Feel how smooth it is.*

Like so many other visitors, I obediently run my hand over the limestone panels. Yes, I do feel how smooth it is. I press my body against the column. I lift up my dress and start to rub up against its "sensual curves." No one moves to stop me: not the security guards—men in uniforms with guns—patrolling from the walkway-arteries; nor the gallery attendants—women in gray skirts, elegant red jackets, and colorfully printed silk scarves carefully tied so that the word "security" is visible between lapels. After all, I'm only following the suggestion of the official audioguide. Then someone takes out a camera to snap a photo. The offending apparatus is immediately surrounded by a swarm of women in red.

Freedom, it seems, still has its limits.

The threat of ETA attacks explains the presence of an x-ray machine at the coat-check counter and guards with guns on the catwalks. The plaza in front of the museum is named after a policeman killed there by ETA militants whom he discovered planting a bomb in flowers destined for the opening ceremonies. The main job of the guards and gallery attendants, however, appears to be preventing people from videotaping and photographing the art and architecture. Visitors are encouraged to caress the walls, but they're strictly prohibited from photographing

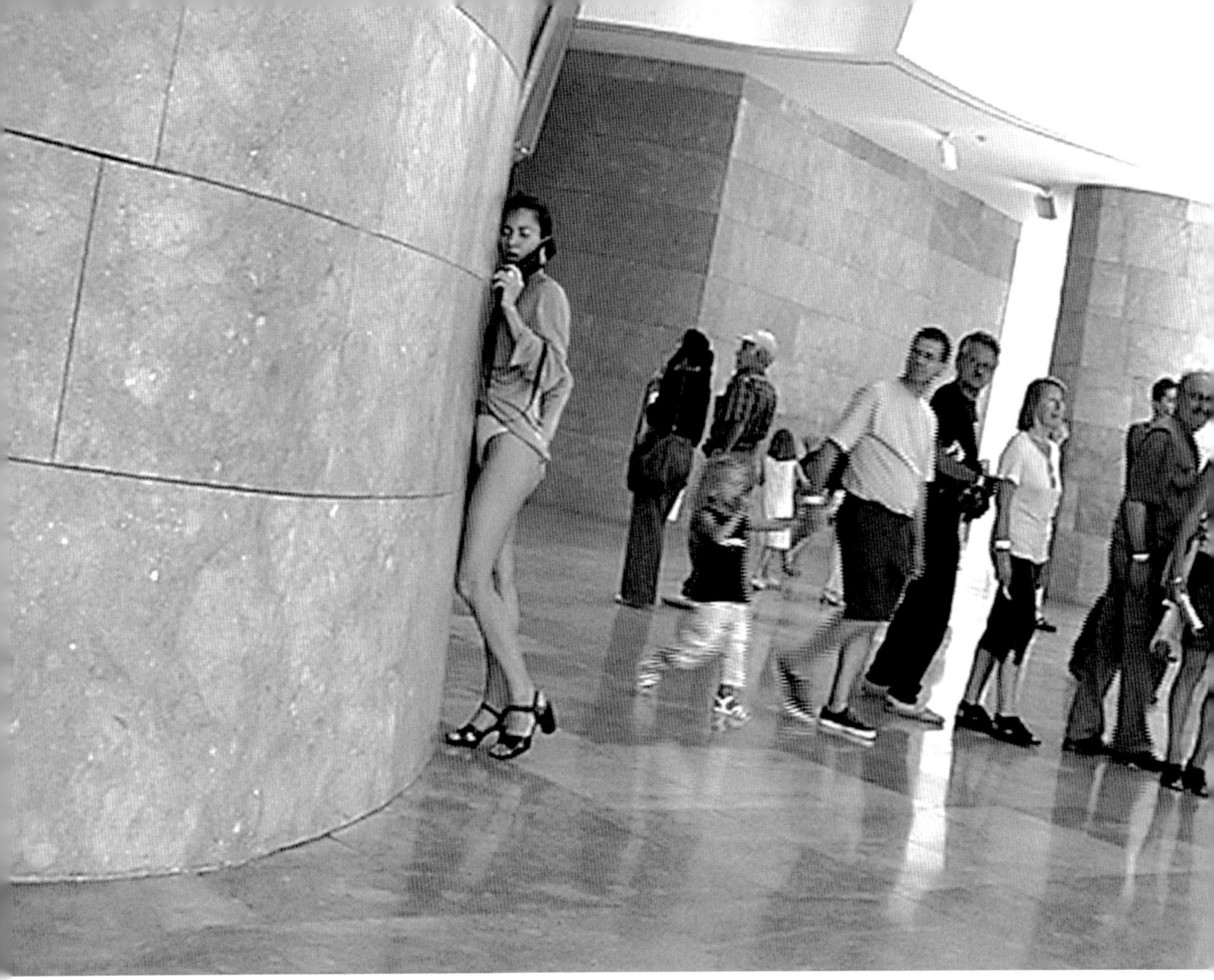

19.2 Andrea Fraser, still from *Little Frank and His Carp,* 2001. DVD. Courtesy the artist and Friedrich Petzel Gallery.

them. The museum is aggressive in enforcing its copyright to the image of the building and has threatened unauthorized reproductions with legal proceedings. When a local artist who runs a pasta shop started selling dry macaroni in the shape of Gehry's building, the response from museum lawyers was swift and unequivocal: cease production of the noodle or prepare to be sued.[15]

Such image control is evident in other ways in the museum's interior. Like the impeccably dressed gallery attendants and information staff, whose appearance and behavior are closely regulated by guidelines laid out in an employee handbook, the museum is spotless. The white walls are reportedly touched up daily. The glass always sparkles. The floor also looks clean enough to caress. Together, the security, corporate hospitality culture, and shine make the lobby feel like a cross between a business hotel and an airport—all that's lacking are trolleys with piles of luggage. It wouldn't be a surprising sight in a museum that prides itself on the fact that 85 to 90 percent of its visitors are from outside the region.

Paradoxically, these sensual curves have been created by computer technology.

If the discipline imposed by the art museum has always in some sense been an order of freedom, what the Guggenheim Bilbao represents may not be the transgression of the order and discipline of the art museum so much as the imposition of another kind of freedom: the "paradoxical product," perhaps, of a new set of social and economic conditions.

The Guggenheim Bilbao Museoa has now become the inevitable example of the success of museum-driven urban revitalization plans. Supported by the governing conservative Basque Nationalist Party, or PNV, and publicly financed to the tune of $150 million by various levels of government of the Autonomous Community of the Basque Country, the Guggenheim Bilbao is the product less of cultural policy than of economic policy.[16] As is well known, the social, economic, and environmental devastation of Bilbao had reached catastrophic proportions by the mid 1990s. With the collapse of mining, steel, and shipbuilding industries, the metropolitan area had lost 20 percent of its population and 47 percent of its industrial jobs in the two preceding decades. Its birthrate fell by almost half, to 7.4 per thousand. The area contained an estimated 465 hectares of industrial ruins, up to 50 percent of the total industrial land in some municipalities. Entire valleys were devastated by pollution, with hills dotted by toxic ponds of flooded open-pit mines and a river reduced to a bubbling ribbon of orange sludge. Last but not least, it was the metropolitan center of a region home to a militant separatist movement that had claimed over eight hundred lives since the 1960s.[17] The Guggenheim Bilbao Museoa became the centerpiece of a plan to turn Bilbao around: to rescue its image, revive its economy, and transform it, if not into a global city, at least into an internationally competitive city in areas of culture and advanced services.

The scope of the Basque government's ambitions is evident in the "Revitalization Plan for Metropolitan Bilbao" outlined by Bilbao Metropoli-30, a public-private partnership group created to promote redevelopment.[18] The Guggenheim Bilbao is listed alongside a series of other initiatives, such as the revitalization of the Stock Exchange, the redevelopment of the port, a new urban train system designed by Sir Norman Foster, a new airport by Santiago Calatrava, the new Euskalduna Palace Concert and Conference Hall by Federico Soriano and Dolores Palacios, the European Software Institute and the Technology Park of the Basque Country. Other projects include a new central train station by James Stirling and the redevelopment of a 30-hectare riverfront area next to the museum called Abandoibarra, designed by Cesar Pelli to include space for advanced services, high-income housing, shopping, leisure, and culture.[19]

"Cultural centrality" is one of the "eight critical issues" identified by the plan that "will allow Metropolitan Bilbao to compete successfully in the European system of cities." "Cultural centrality" means that Metropolitan Bilbao's "competitive advantage in the face of other cities in its sphere will be set by its new position as cultural center of international dimension"—that is, as "an obliged point of reference in cultural circuits and industries which are developing at an international scale."[20] "Cultural centrality" is linked to the expansion of tourism, the city's ability to attract congresses and fairs, and, perhaps above all, the creation of an environment favorable for the development of advanced services.

By the time the Guggenheim Bilbao Museoa opened on the banks of the Nervión River in 1997, Metropolitan Bilbao seemed on its way to accomplishing the economic restructuring envisioned by these strategic revitalization plans. According to a study of 1996 indicators by Rodríguez, Guenaga, and Martínez, service employment had already made up for many of the industrial jobs lost between 1975 and 1996, increasing its share of the economy from 41.7 percent to 65.2 percent while manufacturing dropped from 45.5 percent to 26.9 percent.[21]

However, service employment—in particular, advanced service employment—was strongly concentrated in Bilbao and in historically affluent communities on the right bank of the Nervión River. In the historically working-class communities and industrial zones of the left bank, unemployment and poverty rates continued to rise. Economic restructuring in Metropolitan Bilbao appeared not only to be reproducing and exacerbating "earlier patterns of differentiation between the left and the right bank areas of the river," but producing "new forms of social and spatial exclusion; demographic decline, rising unemployment and increasing poverty levels." According to the study's analysis, high unemployment rates "are only the most visible effect of a more profound dynamic associated with increasing deregulation and flexibilisation of the labour market" running parallel to the expansion of services: "the precarisation of employment conditions, evidenced by the proliferation of weakened forms of the labour relation (part-time, temporary and intermittent contracts, etc.), is of even greater importance."[22]

Because of the way the surface of the pillar curves, each of these panels is slightly different. No two are quite the same. And this is true for all the curved walls of the building.

"What is the impact of the ascendance of finance and producer services on the broader social and economic structure of major cities?" Saskia Sassen opens one of the final chapters of *Cities in a World Economy* with this question.[23] The tertiarization of the economy of Metropolitan Bilbao seems to show every sign of following the pattern of increased social polarization analyzed by urbanists such as Sassen. When manufacturing was the leading sector of urban economies, she explains, it facilitated unionization and other forms of worker empowerment.[24] It was based on household consumption, so that wage levels mattered. Now, "components of the work process that even 10 years ago took place on the shop floor . . . have been replaced by a combination of machine/service worker or worker/engineer," typically through computerization. Work that was once "standardized mass production is today increasingly characterized by customization, flexible specialization, networks of subcontractors, and informationalization." Economic regimes "centered on mass production and mass consumption" reduced "systematic tendencies toward inequality." So, Sassen adds, "did the cultural forms accompanying these processes."[25]

And the cultural forms accompanying the new production processes?

Art museums have long been considered institutions founded in opposition to the consumer culture of mass production. In the United States, cheap manufactured goods are among the emerging forms of urban popular culture (along with jazz, burlesque, and pulp fiction) named in the early documents of the Philadelphia Museum of Art. Against such cultural evils, philanthropists and reformers sought to impose, through museums, their own distinctive and exclusive cultural forms as exclusively legitimate public culture. Do current trends toward the popularization of art museums represent the collapse of this project? Many observers think so, and even offer some of the immensely well-attended exhibitions presented by the Guggenheim as examples—exhibitions like "The Art of the Motorcycle," "Armani," and a retrospective of the work of Norman Rockwell. What such exhibitions may represent, however, particularly in the context of museums like the Guggenheim that aggressively pursue mass-media publicity campaigns, is not the popularization of the museum but rather its opposite: a new subjection of cultural goods produced for mass distribution and consumption to the distinctive and exclusive modes of appropriation that are what finally distinguish high from low, elite from popular culture.

Within ever more popular art museums, cultural phenomena are subjected to a chiastic symbolic process. On the one hand, "popular" culture is articulated within the distinctive and socially and functionally neutralizing systems of perception, appreciation, and classification that define aesthetic appropriation. On the other hand (and at the same time), these exclusive and exclusionary modes of appropriation are inserted into popular cultural networks as the art museum itself becomes an ever more "popular" institution. And because the symbolic neutralization performed by art museums is inseparable from the economic neutralization that defines their publicity, this distinctive system is severed from the social conditions of its production and realization. The result is not the democratization of the museum, but the mass marketing of rarefied tastes that articulate an economic condition in a fundamentally misrecognized symbolic form.[26]

The unique, customized, and individualized objects and environment that the Guggenheim both architecturally represents and contains can be seen as the perfect products of the leading production processes of a new economic regime. At the same time, it may be that the mass marketing of unique, distinctive, and rarefied tastes by ever more popular museums contributes to consumer demand for ever more individualized products and services, demand which in turn may contribute to the expansion of the production processes—and labor relations—required to satisfy them.

> *If these panels had been produced by conventional means, this would still be a building site and the cost of the building would be astronomical. But these panels were cut and shaped by robots working to a computer program developed for aircraft design. To a computer, the mathematical problems involved in fitting together this vast jigsaw are simple.*

If, as Bennett writes of late nineteenth-century world fairs, museums always served "less as vehicles for the technical education of the working classes than as instruments for their stupification before the reified products of their own labour," the Guggenheim Bilbao may exist as a monument to the obsolescence of that labor.[27] It is represented as the product of computers and robots, obsession and magic, fantasy and imagination, facility and freedom; as the product of a world in which the human labor of production does not exist.

Construction of the Guggenheim Bilbao Museoa began in 1993 on the Nervión River a few kilometers upstream from where the Euskalduna shipyards once stood. The shipyards were closed in the late '80s amid violent protests that left one demonstrator dead. The Euskalduna Palace Conference Center and Concert Hall that now stands in its place was designed to look like a grounded ship. Between the Euskalduna Palace and the museum extends the 30-hectare Abandoibarra development area.

Widespread opposition to the museum in its planning stages seems to have given way to an acceptance of its positive effect on the image of the city and its contribution to urban regeneration. Although interpretations of the numbers differ, the museum reportedly generated economic activity that added .47 percent to the gross regional product in its first year of operation, contributing to the maintenance of 3,800 jobs, mostly through tourism. Even with these numbers declining, the public investment in the museum would have been repaid within three years by increased tax revenues. Bilbao and the Basque Country increasingly appear in the international media in connection with topics other than terrorism. While inflows of foreign capital don't seem to have increased significantly, the crucial role of the museum and related redevelopment projects in transforming Bilbao is not only a matter of direct investment. As suggested by Rodríguez et al., by bringing together culture, leisure, shopping, advanced services, and high-income housing in the very center of the city, the redevelopment "provides the basis for a new model of collective identification based on the lifestyles and aims of emerging power groups and urban elite."[28]

For most Bilbao residents, it's difficult to imagine that the museum's displays serve as object lessons in civic order, as Bennett suggests of nineteenth-century museums. Residents hardly go inside (only 10 to 15 percent of visitors are local). The museum itself, with its chaos of curves and surfaces, may rather serve as a lesson in the *disordering* of their lives by a new economic regime. The promises of that regime may remain for others to enjoy. The museum as a workplace itself provides evidence of the kind of jobs the new economy can be expected to bring. The information staff consists of sub-minimum-wage interns supplied by the degree program in tourism at the Deusto University across the Nervión River. Tours are given by freelancers, often also students. Gallery attendants and security guards are subcontracted. Art preparators are hired on a show-by-show basis, with no benefits or provisions for workplace accidents. These are hardly the kind of jobs that would provide residents with the material basis to pursue the new freedoms the museum represents. Instead, they impose other kinds of "freedoms": the freedom of freelancing, the freedom of temporary work and flexible hours, the "freedom" of insecurity. But they are precisely the kinds of flexible, part-time, and art-related jobs traditionally favored by artists who want time to "embody more freely the productions of their imaginations."

> *This process is very new, and it should have a revolutionary effect on the way architects work, because it will allow them to embody more freely the productions of their imaginations, as well as allowing them to build more cheaply, and to a better quality.*

Hal Foster concludes his 2001 essay "Master Builder" by asking of Gehry's architecture and then of himself: "So what is this vision of freedom and expression" proclaimed by so many Gehry fans? "Is it perverse of me to find it perverse, even oppressive?" He answers: "[It] is oppressive because, as Freud argued long ago, the artist is the only social figure allowed to be freely expressive in the first place, the only one exempted from many of the instinctual renunciations that the rest of us undergo as a matter of course. Hence his expression implied our unfree inhibition, which is also to say that his freedom is mostly a franchise."[29]

According to Freud, however, the instinctual satisfactions available to artists come at the price of turning away from reality,[30] making art what Bourdieu might have called a profession of social fantasy. The attractiveness to artists of flexible positions and individualized relations that are "vague and ill-defined, uncertainly located in social space" is that "they leave aspirations considerable room for manoeuvre."[31] And while the "privilege" of freedom—and instability—was once reserved for artists and intellectuals, it is now being extended to a whole range of service occupations, and beyond. So it is no longer only our own fantasies (and those of our patrons) that we artists project into our uncertain futures. Those fantasies already may have merged with what Bourdieu called neoliberalism's "utopia of unlimited exploitation": a system of structural instability not only of employment, but also in the "representation of social identity and its legitimate aspirations."[32] And through the increasingly popular publicity generated by institutions like the Guggenheim, artists (and some architects) have become the poster girls and boys for the joys of insecurity, flexibility, deferred economic rewards, social alienation, cultural uprooting, and geographical displacement, as if it's all just one big, sexy, lifestyle choice.

In the context of neoliberal economic regimes, the art museum is emerging as a privileged site for valorizing the increasing precariousness of work. Through representations of art and artists, architecture and architects, flexibility, spontaneity, customized products, individualized relations of production, and even insecurity itself are represented as positive values, sources of creativity, dynamism, and growth. The products of disempowerment are transformed into promises of freedom and previously unimagined pleasure.

Now turn to your right and look at the glass tower that contains two of the elevators. The glass surface of this tower also curves, and again the curves are produced by panels fitted together. But here they overlap, like the scales of a fish.

Why have modern and contemporary art museums become a favorite tool of urban regeneration and redevelopment schemes? How is it possible that cultural forms that even museums themselves admit are "difficult, demanding, bewildering," cultural forms widely identified with obscurantism, elitism, and exclusivity, cultural forms ridiculed in the media and periodically subjected to censorship, vandalism, and protest—how is it that such culture could possibly be placed at the center of multimillion-dollar development schemes whose logic depends on attracting massive numbers of visitors and worldwide media recognition?

The question has been taken up, but the answers offered only seem to beg it once again.[33] Is it just that a contemporary art museum offers a particular conjunction of attributes, like a product profile that suits a particular audience profile, sought-after market, or target economic sector?

One could rest the argument on a roster of substantive attributes that might tally up to a balance of the art museum's contradictions. Such a list may be informative. Taking another look at the text of our introductory audiotour, we can put "freedom" at the very top of the list. Then would come "open," like the space of the atrium and the plan of the museum, and "flexible" like the uses to which the building's materials have been put and the flow of our movement through it. That flow could be called "dynamic, moving, self-transforming." It allows us to experience the "future" of museums, of culture, of production in all its "novelty." It allows for "growth": the growth of the institution and its architecture to enormously powerful scales; our growth as "individuals"; the growth of "individualism" itself, perhaps, in the unique forms and objects and spaces of the museum in all its "diversity" and "democratic" populism.

> *This is no idle metaphor. The architect who designed this building, Frank Gehry, has always found inspiration in fish.*

My list is actually borrowed. All the terms in quotation marks are derived from an "ideological schema" of the rhetoric of neoliberalism set out by Bourdieu and Loïc Wacquant. Each appears in a series of opposed terms:

state	market
constraint	freedom
closed	open
rigid	flexible
immobile, fossilized	dynamic, moving, self-transforming
past, outdated	future, novelty
stasis	growth
group, lobby, holism, collectivism	individual, individualism
uniformity, artificiality	diversity, authenticity
autocratic ("totalitarian")	democratic[34]

The only term I left out was the first, "market," a term to which all the others in the right-hand column are directly or indirectly made to refer. I would add one final pair of terms to the set: local and global.

The fantasies of freedom packaged by the Guggenheim Bilbao can certainly be read as symbolic manifestations of the freedom from national, civic, and communitarian order, cultural tradition and social determination, political and economic regulation that are the foundation of neoliberal programs. They are freedoms increasingly realized by the global mobility of capital, production, and the transnational elites among whom cultural producers can be counted in growing numbers. And they are also freedoms increasingly sought and enjoyed, not only by artists and the individual and corporate patrons of museums but by the corporate entities many major museums themselves have become.

A more revealing exercise may be to consider the terms in the left-hand column as describing what museums have been considered—and no longer want—to be: instruments of the "state"; institutions of confinement and "constraint"; architecturally and discursively "closed" structures following "rigid" organizational and conceptual models that are as "immobile" and "fossilized" as their "outdated" displays of the "past," and so on.

No, we're not dealing with "idle metaphor" here but with extremely active homologies: homologies that accomplish their work of structuration by linking apparently distant or even opposed spheres through parallel sets of oppositions—oppositions which may themselves serve as the motor for the very "dynamism" they affirm.

> *He dates this obsession from the days when he used to go with his grandmother to market to buy a live carp, which he would then take home and keep in the bathtub until it was time to cook it. Here little Frank would play with the carp and here the magic of its sinuous, scaly form somehow entered his bloodstream.*

Like Frank Gehry, our "master builder" and "Greatest Living Artist" (as Foster facetiously calls him), contemporary art museums are transforming the old (culture, cities, economies) into the new—even as they transform themselves.

Folksy memories of grandma's quaint preindustrial consumption practices unfurl into towering cybernetic members. Obsessions, far from being pathologies, are celebrated on monumental scales. Idle metaphors spring into activity.

They are put to work like robots, like computers, performing their magic of production without need for human labor.

If the Guggenheim Bilbao represents an institutionalized form of art, it isn't because Gehry has been considered an artist and his building a sculpture. Nor is it in the sense, as Foster and others have suggested, that the museum has "trumped" contemporary art, corralling it and swallowing it whole, appropriating and incorporating its transgressions.[35] The Guggenheim Bilbao is neither more nor less an institutionalized form of art than the "great museums of previous ages." Rather, it's a different dimension of art that has become institution here—a different "class fraction," if you will, of the artistic field, whose products of imagination and freedom correspond to a different, ascendant, fraction within the field of power.

> *If you look to your left now, beyond the pillar under the stone box that we looked at a moment ago, you'll see the entrance to a large space. This is the largest gallery in the museum and, believe it or not, it's known as the Fish Gallery, because the long curving shape of this part of the building is derived, once again, from the shape of the fish. Let's go in there now. Press your Pause button until you are in the gallery.*

Peter Lewis, the president of the Solomon R. Guggenheim Foundation, the parent corporation of the Guggenheim Bilbao, has described its director Thomas Krens and himself as "change agents": "To accept the status quo is early death. Change is valuable for its own sake, whether or not it turns out to be an improvement."[36]

From an institutional aestheticism that reached its peak with modernism and museums of modern art, we have now moved on to what can be called institutional trangressivism: the museological manifestation of the avant-garde traditions whose legacies now dominate the field of contemporary art. Art for art's sake has been discredited in the field of art as in museums and, as Peter Lewis would have it, it has been replaced with change for the sake of change.

Interestingly, unlike most museum directors, Thomas Krens does not have a doctorate in art history. Rather, he has two master's degrees: one in studio art and one in business.[37] His appropriation of for-profit business models, aggressive globalizing through an international network of branch museums, ties to corporations, deals with foreign governments, and exhibitions featuring luxury consumer products have all inspired much critical writing. Under Krens's directorship, the Solomon R. Guggenheim Foundation has even been described as a rogue institution and compared to rogue corporations like Enron.[38] Despite often hostile appraisal, the Solomon R. Guggenheim Foundation has nevertheless become the leading model within the highly competitive market that the field of art museums has become. And the compelling force of that model has rested, above all, on the success of the Guggenheim Bilbao.[39]

> *You are standing in a room of 3,200 square meters. It's 150 meters long and between 12 and 25 meters high. Contemporary art is big. In fact, some of it is enormous, and this gallery was designed to accommodate the huge pieces that artists have begun to create.*

Thomas Krens has said "growth is almost a law. . . . Either you grow and you change or you die."[40]

As Foster has suggested, the gargantuan scales that one finds in contemporary art museums as well as in the contemporary art inside it are mechanisms of the spectacularization of art and its institutions.[41] They exist as two points in a self-justifying and self-perpetuating logic of expansion of which they serve, in turn, as symbolic manifestations. Big art demands big spaces. Big spaces demand big art. Big, spectacular art and architecture draw big audiences. Big, general audiences, with less specific taste for the specific traditions of modern and contemporary art and architecture, are drawn by big, spectacular art and architecture. Museums need big spaces to accommodate big art and big shows and the big audiences they draw. They need big shows and big art to draw big audiences to raise big money to build big spaces and organize big shows with big art to draw big audiences. . . .

The growth in the physical dimensions of museums like the Guggenheim Bilbao is only the most visible symptom of museum expansionism. It can also be seen as a manifestation of institutional ambitions and the strategies employed to realize them. It may be no accident that two of the most enormous museum spaces in Europe, the Guggenheim Bilbao's Fish Gallery and the Tate Modern's Turbine Hall, were developed by institutions pursuing expansion through the development of branch museums: the Tate within Britain and the Guggenheim globally.

The Guggenheim Bilbao is now only one of a growing number of Guggenheim branches in a family of franchise museums that spreads from St. Petersburg to Berlin, Las Vegas to Venice and soon to Rio de Janeiro. The Guggenheim

Foundation's growing international network of branches has also made it the leading model of globalization for museums, demonstrating that a global museum has potential for global sponsorship that single-location museums could never hope to secure.[42] That potential includes attracting sponsorship from public and private local interests in a wider range of localities as well as being more attractive to globalized corporate interests looking to reach more markets with their contributions.

As in so many other fields, one of the primary effects of globalization on the field of museums has been to transform it into a highly competitive market. Museums could once be relatively secure in local support, whether public or private, individual or corporate. Nations supported their patrimony. Cultural philanthropy, historically tied to urban reform movements, tended to be local, even among corporations, driven, at least symbolically, by civic pride. Certainly museums always played roles in the competitive struggles of nations and cities and their regional elites, and these struggles had economic and political as well as social and cultural stakes. Generally, however, the forms of competition that existed between museums themselves were of a highly sublimated kind: struggles defined by the criteria of the cultural fields to which the museums themselves belonged—such as conservation and research in art, history, ethnography, science, etc.

In the past decades, however, the spread of the American model of private support through Thatcherism in Britain and neoliberalism on the European continent and beyond has made museums increasingly dependent on private sponsorship. At the same time, these new private funders themselves, particularly corporations but also foundations and increasingly mobile elites, have undergone a process of globalization that makes them less interested in local institutions. Finally, enormous growth in the number of museums has created more competition at every level. The combination of these three factors may have effectively restructured the field of museums itself. Competition between museums may always have existed, but it now appears that the *survival* of many museums depends on their ability to compete, locally, nationally, and globally, for sponsorship and also for audiences.

Walk over to the left-hand side of the gallery and look up at the ceiling. You'll see a lighting gantry . . .

Oh, this tour is starting to seem interminable. Do we really need to know about the gantries? I turn off my headset and head back to the atrium. I want to give the walls another good grope.

Notes

Opening quotation: Guggenheim Bilbao, introductory audiotour, as transcribed by Andrea Fraser, June 2001. I would like to thank Franck Larcade, María Mur, and Aranxta Pérez of Consonni, Bilbao, for assistance with the research informing this essay. Additional research was assisted by Yasmine Nessah.

1. Douglas Crimp, "On the Museum's Ruins," in Hal Foster, ed., *The Anti-Aesthetic: Essays on Post-Modern Culture* (Port Townsend, Wash.: Bay Press, 1983), 45.

2. Tony Bennett, "The Exhibitionary Complex," in *The Birth of the Museum: History, Theory, Politics* (London: Routledge, 1995), 59.

3. Andrea Fraser, "Museum Highlights: A Gallery Talk," in this volume.

4. Bennett, "The Exhibitionary Complex," 73.

5. Ibid., 62–63.

6. The sources of these descriptions of Gehry's Guggenheim include Herbert Muschamp, "The Miracle in Bilbao," *New York Times Magazine*, 7 September 1997, 54–59; Joan Ockman, "Applause and Effect," *Artforum International* (Summer 2001), 140–149; Anthony Vidler, "Aformal Affinities," *Artforum International* (Summer 2001), 140–149.

7. Michel Foucault, quoted in Crimp, "On the Museum's Ruins," 47.

8. Pierre Bourdieu, *Distinction: A Social Critique of the Judgement of Taste*, trans. Richard Nice (Cambridge: Harvard University Press, 1984), 30.

9. Ibid.

10. Ibid., 493.

11. Ibid., 54–55.

12. Quoted in Fraser, "Museum Highlights," this volume, 107.

13. In the words of the Museum of Modern Art's Chief Curator of Architecture Terence Riley, in Hal Foster et al., "The MoMA Expansion: A Conversation with Terence Riley," *October* 84 (Spring 1998), 3–30.

14. Pierre Bourdieu and Alain Darbel, *The Love of Art: European Art Museums and Their Public* (Stanford: Stanford University Press, 1991).

15. Letter from Uría & Menéndez, Abogados, to Fausto Grossi, Bilbao, 4 July 2000, made available by the artist as part of his art project. That Fausto Grossi gets slapped for a noodle while I'm able to exhibit with impunity a video shot in the museum with hidden cameras—even at a conference organized by

the Guggenheim itself ("Museum as Medium," Mexico City, April 2002)—is a perfect example of how corporatized museums and a celebritized art world are colluding to bring about the particularization of universal principles such as freedom of expression, which increasingly appears rather as a form of privilege. For an extended discussion of this issue, see my "A 'Sensation' Chronicle," in this volume.

16. On the amount paid by the Basque government, see Kim Bradley, "The Deal of the Century," *Art in America* (July 1997), 48. That the Guggenheim Bilbao was the product of economic and not cultural policy is one answer to the riddle of why a nationalist party in power in one of the more nationalist regions of the world would spend $150 million on a museum more or less guaranteed to include no "national" culture. Another answer is that the museum can also be considered the product of a foreign policy. Through the museum project, the PNV pursued a kind of anti-Madrid globalism, bypassing the national cultural policy apparatus to establish a relationship with an international organization—the Solomon R. Guggenheim Foundation. It seems that the PNV understands the global public sphere quite well: it is defined not by nation-states, but by cosmopolitan financial and cultural centers for which national boundaries may be increasingly irrelevant, particularly in the context of a unified Europe. Considering the Guggenheim Bilbao as the product of a neoliberal nationalism on the part of the PNV would be an interesting topic for another paper.

17. See Mark Kurlansky, *The Basque History of the World* (New York: Walker Publishing Company, 1999); Joseba Zulaika, "'Miracle in Bilbao': Basques in the Casino of Globalism," in William A. Douglass et al., eds., *Basque Cultural Studies: Basque Studies Program Occasional Papers Series,* no. 5 (2000), 265–274; Arantxa Rodríguez, et al., "Bilbao: Case Study 2," *Urban Redevelopment and Social Polarisation in the City (URSPIC),* European Union in collaboration with the Department of Applied Economics of the Universidad del País Vasco-Euskal Herriko Unibertsitatea, Bilbao, Spain, <http://www.ifresi.univlille1.fr/PagesHTML/URSPIC/Cases2/Bilbao/BILBAO2.htm>.

18. Rodríguez et al., "Bilbao: Case Study 2"; Bilbao Metropoli-30, "Revitalization Plan for Metropolitan Bilbao," 1998a., <http://www.bm30.es/plan/pri_uk.htm>.

19. Bilbao Metropoli-30, "Revitalization Plan for Metropolitan Bilbao."

20. Ibid.

21. Rodríguez et al., "Bilbao: Case Study 2."

22. Ibid.

23. Saskia Sassen, *Cities in a World Economy,* 2nd ed. (Thousand Oaks, Calif: Pine Forge Press, 2000), 117.

24. Here it would be important to note that, in addition to its well-known history of militant nationalist separatism, the Basque Country (and Bilbao in particular) also has a long history of militant trade unionism and socialist politics. Bilbao was home to one of the earliest chapters of the First International, the first Socialist Party chapter in Spain, the first general strike on the Iberian peninsula, and "La Pasionaria," Dolores Ibarruri. In the first half of the 1970s, the Basque Country was also home to over 35 percent of all labor conflicts in Spain. While the old Basque financial and industrial capital behind the PNV might have mourned the passing of Bilbao's industrial might, it's unlikely that they shed

any tears for the collapse of its unions. However, to be fair to the PNV, it was the modern Socialist Party in Madrid that settled on a policy of "liberalizing" Bilbao's heavy industry, which had been subsidized for decades by the Franco regime. This policy played some role in expanding the ranks of radical left and nationalist political parties with disillusioned socialists—including many Franco-era immigrants from other parts of Spain and their descendants. See Cyrus Ernesto Zirakzadeh, *A Rebellious People: Basques, Protest, and Politics* (Reno: University of Nevada Press, 1991), 54–55, 65.

25. Sassen, *Cities in a World Economy,* 118–119.

26. For a more extensive discussion of these issues, see my "A 'Sensation' Chronicle," in this volume.

27. Bennett, "The Exhibitionary Complex," 81.

28. Rodríguez et al., "Bilbao: Case Study 2."

29. Hal Foster, "Master Builder," in *Design and Crime (and Other Diatribes)* (London: Verso Press, 2002), 40–41.

30. Sigmund Freud, "Formulations Regarding the Two Principles in Mental Functioning," in Freud, *General Psychological Theory,* ed. Philip Rieff (New York: Collier Books, 1963), 21–28.

31. Bourdieu, *Distinction,* 155.

32. Pierre Bourdieu, "Utopia of Endless Exploitation," *Le Monde Diplomatique,* March 1998, 3; Bourdieu, *Distinction,* 156. It may be in this sense that the vision of freedom that Gehry represents does indeed correspond to "'the cultural logic' of advanced capitalism," as Foster suggests in "Master Builder" (41).

33. For a discussion of perspectives on this question, see Evdoxia Baniotopoulou, "Art for Whose Sake? Modern Art Museums and Their Role in Transforming Societies: The Case of the Guggenheim Bilbao," *Journal of Conservation and Museum Studies* 7 (November 2001).

34. Pierre Bourdieu and Loïc Wacquant, "New Liberal Speak: Notes on the New Planetary Vulgate," *Radical Philosophy* 105 (January-February 2001), 2–5.

35. Foster et al., "The MoMA Expansion."

36. Quoted in Martin Filler, "The Museum Game," *New Yorker,* April 2000, 100.

37. See Filler, "The Museum Game."

38. Jerry Saltz, "Downward Spiral: The Guggenheim Museum Touches Bottom," *Village Voice,* 19 February 2002, 65. See also Michael Brenson, *The Guggenheim, Corporate Populism, and the Future of the Corporate Museum* (New York: New School/Vera List Center for Art and Politics, 2002).

39. It's now clear enough that the Guggenheim's expansion strategy is primarily a financial strategy. When it struck the deal with the Basque government, it was in dire financial straits. The Guggenheim's

primary assets were its collection and its image. But how does a museum generate income from collections, if entrance receipts are not enough? The Guggenheim had already tried deaccessioning some works, amid much controversy. But instead of selling works from its collection, the museum hit on the idea of renting them—to itself. Branch museums financed by foreign governments and corporations but directed entirely by management in New York would pay the Guggenheim for the privilege of presenting its exhibitions and collections. The museum could thus capitalize not only on its collections, but also on the value added by its expertise and the ever-increasing brand power of its global image. Thus, the Guggenheim's expansion strategy allowed it, like so many corporations of the '90s, to draw new investment that would cover debt from existing operations.

40. Filler, "The Museum Game," 104.

41. Foster, "Master Builder"; Foster et al., "The MoMA Expansion."

42. Guggenheim curator Lisa Dennison calls "the concept of global sponsorship" one of the "big secrets" of Krens's success. Corporations "want to support a museum that has many bases in as many places as possible. And ideally that means you're touching more markets." Quoted in Filler, "The Museum Game," 105.

BIBLIOGRAPHY

Writings by and Interviews with Andrea Fraser (Arranged Chronologically)

"Art at the Intersection of Social Fields." In John R. Hall, Blake Stimson, and Lisa Tamiris Becker, eds., *Visual Worlds*. London: Routledge, 2005.

"How to Provide an Artistic Service: An Introduction." In Zoya Kocur and Simon Leung, eds., *Theory in Contemporary Art since 1985*. Oxford: Blackwell, 2005.

Heiser, Jörg. "Andrea Fraser" (interview). In *Funky Lessons*. Frankfurt: Revolver, 2004.

Moll, Sebastian. "Vom Drang zum Wachstum bestimmt" (interview). *Die Tageszeitung*, 22 November 2004.

Praxis (Delia Bajo and Brainard Carey). "Andrea Fraser in Conversation with Praxis" (interview). *Brooklyn Rail* (October 2004).

"Displacement and Condensation: A Conversation on the Work of Louise Lawler" (with George Baker). In *Louise Lawler and Others*. Ostfildern-Ruit: Hatje Cantz Publishers, 2004.

"What Do We Want from Art, Anyway? A Conversation" (with Gregg Bordowitz). *Artwurl*, no. 6 (August 2004), <http://artwurl.org/aw_past_interviews.html>.

Hunt, Andrew. "Is This a Site Specific Interview?" (interview). *Untitled*, no. 32 (Summer 2004).

Sundell, Margaret. "Tale of the Tape" (interview). *Time Out New York*, 10–17 June 2004.

"What Do I, as an Artist, Provide? A Conversation between Andrea Fraser and Miwon Kwon" (interview). *Documents*, no. 24 (Winter 2004).

"Official Welcome." *Documents,* no. 24 (Winter 2004).
"What's Intangible, Transitory, Mediating, Participatory, and Rendered in the Public Sphere? Part II." In Melanie Gilligan and Marina Vishmidt, eds., *Immaterial Labor: Work, Research and Art.* London: Black Dog Publishing, 2004.
"Whatever Gets You through the Night: Andrea Fraser and Thyrza Nichols Goodeve Talk about *Exhibition.*" In *Exhibition: New Video Work by Andrea Fraser.* The Morris and Helen Belkin Art Gallery, University of British Columbia, Vancouver, 2004.
"Art Must Hang" (performance script based on a speech by Martin Kippenberger). In *Exhibition: New Video Work by Andrea Fraser.* The Morris and Helen Belkin Art Gallery, University of British Columbia, Vancouver, 2004.
"Polyphony of Voices, Bunkier Sztuki, October 2002: Remarks." *Critical Quarterly* 45, no. 4 (December 2003).
Dziewior, Yilmaz. "Interview with Andrea Fraser." In Yilmaz Dziewior, ed., *Andrea Fraser: Works 1983 to 2003.* Hamburg: Kunstverein; Cologne: DuMont Literatur und Kunst Verlag, 2003.
"Work Descriptions." In Yilmaz Dziewior, ed., *Andrea Fraser: Works 1983 to 2003.* Hamburg: Kunstverein; Cologne: DuMont Literatur und Kunst Verlag, 2003.
"Performance Scripts: 'Damaged Goods Gallery Talk Starts Here (Excerpt with Epilogue)'; 'Museum Highlights: A Gallery Talk'; 'Welcome to the Wadsworth'; 'May I Help You?'; 'Inaugural Speech'; 'Official Welcome.'" In Yilmaz Dziewior, ed., *Andrea Fraser, Works 1983 to 2003.* Hamburg: Kunstverein; Cologne: DuMont Literatur und Kunst Verlag, 2003.
"Feminism & Art: Nine Views." *Artforum International* (October 2003).
"Colin de Land." *Artforum International* (Summer 2003).
"Performance Anxiety." *Artforum International* (February 2003).
"A Museum Is Not a Business. It Is Run in a Business-like Fashion." In Melanie Townsend, ed., *Beyond the Box: Diverging Curatorial Practices.* Banff, Canada: Banff Centre Press, 2003.
Simpson, Bennett. "Fantasies of the Knowable Object" (interview). *Purple,* no. 12 (Summer 2002).
"'To Quote,' Say the Kabyles, 'Is to Bring Back to Life.'" *October* 101 (Summer 2002), and *Texte zur Kunst* 46 (2002).
"My Dear Mrs. Rockefeller." *De Witte Raaf* 98 (July-August 2002).
"Cultural Sociologist Pierre Bourdieu Dies at 71." *Art Papers,* May-June 2002.
Round Table, "The Present Conditions of Art Criticism." *October* 100 (Spring 2002).

"Meine liebe Mrs. Rockefeller." In Hans-Christian Dany and Astrid Wege, eds., *Ökonomien der Zeit*. Cologne: Museum Ludwig; Berlin: Akademie der Künste, 2002.

"Inaugural Speech." In Stephan Dillemuth, ed., *The Academy and the Corporate Public*. Cologne: Permanent Press Verlag, 2002.

"Questions for Andrea Fraser." In Beatrice von Bismarck et al., eds., *Interarchive: Archival Practices and Sites in the Contemporary Art Field*. Cologne: Verlag der Buchhandlung Walther König, 2002.

"Official Welcome." *MICA Foundation Newsletter* 1, no. 2 (2001).

"A 'Sensation' Chronicle." *Social Text* 67 (Summer 2001).

"Museum Highlights: A Gallery Talk." In Toby Miller, ed., *A Companion to Cultural Studies*. Oxford: Blackwell Publishers, 2001.

"Como prestar um serviço artístico: Uma introdução." In *O carteiro toca apenas duas vezes*. Lisbon: Museu das Comunicações, 2000.

"Talking to Art Matters." In Brian Wallis, Marianne Weems, and Philip Yenawine, eds., *Art Matters: How the Culture Wars Changed America*. New York: New York University Press, 2000.

"On the Post-Partum Document." In Mary Kelly, *Post-Partum Document*. Berkeley: University of California Press; Vienna: Generali Foundation, 1999.

"Andrea Fraser" (interview). In Jorge Ribalta, ed., *Servicio público. Conversaciones sobre financiación pública y arte contemporánea*. Salamanca: Universidad de Salamanca, 1998.

"Inaugural Speech." In Sally Yard, ed., *InSITE97: Private Time in Public Space*. San Diego/Tijuana, 1998.

"The writing of . . ." *Texte zur Kunst* 30 (June 1998).

"Andrea Fraser im Gespräch mit Christian Philipp Müller, Wien, Juni 1992." In Edelbert Köb, ed., *Künstlerinnen*. Cologne: Verlag der Buchhandlung Walther König; Bregenz: Kunsthaus Bregenz, 1997.

Student Show: Selections, Lists, Awards, Announcements. Moore College of Art and Design, Philadelphia, 1997.

"What's Intangible, Transitory, Mediating, Participatory, and Rendered in the Public Sphere?" *October* 80, Spring 1997.

"Services: A Working Group Exhibition" and "Services: A Proposal for an Exhibition and a Topic of Discussion" (with Helmut Draxler). In Beatrice von Bismarck, Diethelm Stoller, and Ulf Wuggenig, eds., *Games, Fights, Collaborations: Art and Culture Studies in the Nineties*. Lüneburg: Kunstraum der Universität, 1996.

"In and Out of Place." In Reesa Greenberg, Bruce W. Ferguson, and Sandy Nairne, eds., *Thinking about Exhibitions.* London: Routledge, 1996.
Report. EA-Generali Foundation, Vienna, 1995.
"It's Art When I Say It's Art, or . . ." *Texte zur Kunst* 20 (November 1995).
"Vorbemerkung/Prospectus préliminaire." *Hors Sol.* Geneva: Sous-sol Genève; Zurich: Shedhalle, 1995.
"Notes sobre la condició pública del museu/Notes on the Museum's Publicity" and "Prespecte Preliminar/Preliminary Prospectus." In *Els Límits del Museu.* Barcelona: Fundació Antoni Tàpies, 1995.
"Frankfurt, December 30, 1994." In Stephan Dillemuth, ed., *Akademie.* Munich: Kunstverein München, 1995.
"Daughters of the ReVolution" (by The V-Girls). *October* 71 (Winter 1994–1995).
Preliminary Prospectus: For Individuals; For Corporations; For General Audience Institutions; For Cultural Constituency Organizations. New York: Andrea Fraser, 1993.
"Damaged Goods Gallery Talk Starts Here." In Peter Weibel, ed., *Kontext Kunst.* Graz: Neue Galerie am Landesmuseum Joanneum, Steirischer Herbst, 1993.
"Two Audio Installations: Garden Program; Pavilion Program." In *Stellvertreter, Representatives, Rappresentanti: Andrea Fraser, Christian Philipp Müller, Gerwald Rockenschaub.* Vienna: Bundesministerium für Unterricht und Kunst, 1993.
Weskott, Hanne. "I Provide Services: Ein Gespräch mit Andrea Fraser" (interview). *Artis* (May 1993).
Eine Gesellschaft des Geschmacks/A Society of Taste. Munich: Kunstverein München, 1993.
"An Artist's Statement." In Ine Gevers, ed., *Place Position Presentation Public.* Maastricht: Jan van Eyck Akademie, 1993.
Aren't They Lovely? Berkeley: University of California, Berkley Art Museum and Pacific Film Archive, 1992.
"A Speech on Documenta." *Reden u.a. auf der Documenta IX.* Cologne: Texte zur Kunst, 1992.
"Museum Highlights: A Gallery Talk." In Moritz Kung, ed., *Denkraum Museum: Über die Rezeption von Architektur und Kunst.* Zurich: Architektur Forum, 1992.
"Another Kind of Pragmatism." *Forum International* (January-February 1992).
"Déplacé, à propos." *Faces: Journal d'architecture* 26 (Spring 1992).
Weiss, Brian, and Marcos Palermo. "The Desires of Museums" (interview). *Start: Interacting with Art* 5, no. 2 (Spring 1992).

"Museum Highlights: A Gallery Talk." *October* 57 (Summer 1991).
Decter, Joshua. "Interview with Andrea Fraser." *Flash Art International* (November/December 1990).
"Notes on the Museum's Publicity." *Lusitania* 1 (Fall 1990).
"Museum Highlights: Eine Führung." *Durch* 6/7 (1990).
"A Conversation with the V-Girls." *October* 51 (Winter 1989).
"Creativity = Capital." In *Allan McCollum*. Cologne: Verlag der Buchhandlung Walther König, 1988.
"Individual Works." *Faces: Journal d'architecture* 9 (1988).
"Damaged Goods Gallery Talk Starts Here." *Art Paper* (March 1988).
"Individual Works." *Individual Works*. New York: John Weber Gallery, 1988.
"Allan McCollum." *Investigations 18*. Philadelphia: Institute of Contemporary Art, 1986.
"On the Post-Partum Document: A Review." *Afterimage* 13, no. 6 (March 1986).
"In and Out of Place." *Art in America* (June 1985).
Woman 1/Madonna and Child 1506–1967. New York: Andrea Fraser, 1984.

INDEX

Page numbers in boldface indicate illustrations.